Albert Harkness

A Physical Introduction to Latin Composition

Salzwasser

Albert Harkness

A Physical Introduction to Latin Composition

1. Auflage | ISBN: 978-3-84605-306-5

Erscheinungsort: Frankfurt, Deutschland

Erscheinungsjahr: 2020

Salzwasser Verlag GmbH

Reprint of the original, first published in 1869.

A

PRACTICAL INTRODUCTION

TO

LATIN COMPOSITION.

FOR

SCHOOLS AND COLLEGES.

BY

ALBERT HARKNESS, Ph.D.,

PROFESSOR IN BROWN UNIVERSITY.

AUTHOR OF

"A LATIN GRAMMAR," "AN INTRODUCTORY LATIN BOOK," "A LATIN READER,"
"A FIRST GREEK BOOK," ETC.

NEW YORK:

D. APPLETON AND COMPANY,

90, 92, & 94 GRAND STREET.

LONDON: 16 LITTLE BRITAIN.

1869.

PREFACE.

THIS volume is intended to aid the classical student in acquiring a practical acquaintance with the difficult but important subject of Latin composition. It aims to be at once simple, progressive, and complete. Starting with the beginner as soon as he has learned a few grammatical forms, it conducts him step by step through a progressive series of lessons and exercises, until he is so far master both of the theory and of the practice of the subject, that he no longer needs the aid of a special text-book.

The work consists of three parts, of which the first is purely elementary, and is intended as a companion to the Reader. It aims to give the pupil familiarity with the power and use of grammatical inflections, and facility in the application of the great and controlling principles of the language.

Part Second will furnish the learner instruction and practice in Latin composition throughout the subsequent stages of his preparatory course for college. The exercises have special reference to the syntax of the language, and are, to a great extent, imitations of the ordinary constructions contained in the Commentaries of Caesar, and in the Orations of Cicero. In subject matter they also relate to topics contained in those works.

Part Third, intended for the earlier portion of a collegiate course of study, aims to introduce the student to a practical

acquaintance with the elements of Latin style. The Exercises
are, with slight changes, translations of sentences carefully
selected from the works of Cicero.

In making this selection, it has been the constant aim of the
author, not only to give the student clear and well-defined illustrations of Latin constructions and usages, but also thoughts
and sentiments of intrinsic interest and worth.

To explain more fully the plan of the work, the author begs
leave to call attention to the following points : —

I. For all grammatical rules and principles, the student is
referred directly to the grammar. The advantages of this
arrangement are obvious. It not only saves room, and thus
makes it possible to bring an extended course in Latin composition within the compass of a convenient manual, but also saves
the time of the pupil, by relieving him from the worse than useless task of learning new rules, instead of applying those with
which he is already familiar.

II. A series of Models, selected from the writings of Cicero,
the great master of Latin style, extends through the entire work.
English sentences are given to be translated into Ciceronian
Latin. Opposite each of these stands Cicero's own expression
for the same thought. Then follow Remarks, explaining the
process by which we pass from the English expression to the
Latin, and commenting upon such peculiarities as seem to require attention. Such a series of Models, properly explained,
will, it is thought, be the best possible guide for the learner in
the actual work of writing Latin.

III. Special attention has been given to the important subject of Synonymes and Idioms. But care has been taken not to
make peculiarities of construction too prominent. The learner
needs to become acquainted with the regular and ordinary

usages, before he is prepared to appreciate those which are exceptional and peculiar.

In this connection, the author is happy to say that Mr. Charles B. Goff has kindly aided him in the preparation of some of the Exercises of Part Second, and Mr. Edward H. Cutler in the preparation of the Vocabularies and in the reading of the proofs.

In conclusion, the author cannot forbear to express his grateful acknowledgments to the classical instructors of the country, who, by their fidelity and skill in the use of his books, have given them a success so far beyond his most sanguine expectations. To their hands this volume is gratefully and respectfully committed.

BROWN UNIVERSITY, *August*, 1868.

CONTENTS.

PART FIRST.

GRAMMATICAL FORMS AND RULES.

PART SECOND.

LATIN SYNTAX.

PART THIRD.

ELEMENTS OF LATIN STYLE.

CHAPTER I.

CHOICE OF WORDS AND CONSTRUCTIONS.

CHAPTER II.

ARRANGEMENT OF WORDS AND CLAUSES.

CHAPTER III.

STRUCTURE OF LATIN SENTENCES.

EXPLANATION OF REFERENCES AND ABBREVIATIONS.

ALL reference numerals in the "Lessons from the Grammar," and those marked "G" in other parts of the work, refer to the author's Latin Grammar. The other references are to articles in this work.

The following abbreviations occur : —

abl. . . . . . . ablative.
abl. abs. . . . ablative absolute.
acc. . . . . . . accusative.
act. . . . . . . active.
adj. . . . . . . adjective.
adv. . . . . . . adverb.
comp. . . . . comparative.
conj. . . . . . conjunction.
Conj. . . . . . conjugation.
dat. . . . . . . dative.
dep. . . . . . . deponent.
distrib. num. distributive numeral.
f. . . . . feminine.
gen. . . . . . . genitive.
ger. . . . . . . gerund.
impers. . . . . impersonal.

indec. . . . . indeclinable.
lit. . . . . . . literally.
m. . . . . . . masculine.
n. . . . . neuter.
part. . . . . participle.
pass. . . . . passive.
plur., or pl. . plural.
pred. . . . . predicate.
prep. . . . . preposition.
pron. . . . . pronoun.
relat. . . . . relative.
sing. . . . . singular.
subj. . . . . subjunctive.
subs. . . . . substantive.
superl. . . . superlative.
trans. . . . . transitive.

PART FIRST.

GRAMMATICAL FORMS AND RULES.

Lesson I.

DECLENSION OF NOUNS.
[1–6.] [1]

1. Lesson from the Grammar. [2]

I. First Declension. 42.

II. Second Declension. 45.

III. Third Declension. 48–51.

IV. Fourth Declension. 116.

V. Fifth Declension. 119.

VI. Agreement of Appositives. Rule II. 363.

VII. Genitive with Nouns. Rule XVI. 395.

VIII. Cases with Prepositions. Rule XXXII. 432–435.

---

[1] In Part First the enclosed numerals standing at the beginning of each lesson refer to the sections in the Reader which the lesson is intended to follow. Thus [1–6] shows that this lesson is to be learned after the pupil has read the first six sections in the Reader.

[2] The lessons from the Grammar contain the grammatical points involved in the Exercises, and should be carefully learned, or reviewed, in the Grammar itself. The references are all to the author's Latin Grammar.

2. MODELS.

I. Tigranes the king.	I. *Tigrānes rex.*
II. The love of glory.	II. *Amor gloriae.*
III. Before light.	III. *Ante lucem.*

3. REMARKS.

I. Tigranes the king.

1. TIGRANES. Looking in the vocabulary for the corresponding Latin, we find *Tigrānes*, the same as in English.

2. THE. The English article, *a, an, the,* has no Latin equivalent. It must therefore be omitted in translating into Latin. See Gram. 42, 4.

3. KING. The corresponding Latin is *rex,* which must be in the Nominative, in apposition with *Tigrānes,* according to Rule II.

4. The Appositive generally follows its subject, as in English. Hence
Tigrānes rex.

II. The love of glory.

1. THE LOVE, *amor ;* THE — not translated.

2. OF, sign of the Genitive.

3. GLORY, *gloria.* Of glory, *gloriae ;* Gen. Sing.

4. The Genitive may either precede or follow its noun, but seems more frequently to follow when not emphatic. See Gram. 598. Hence we have
Amor gloriae.

III. Before light.

1. BEFORE, *ante.* No Latin case expresses the relation *before.* Hence a preposition must be used.

2. LIGHT, *lux.* But the preposition *ante* is used only with the Accusative. Hence *lucem,* and not *lux,* must be used. See Gram. 433. Hence
Ante lucem.

4. VOCABULARY.

Art, *ars, artis,* f.	Boy, *puer, puĕri,* m.
Bird, *avis, avis,* f.	Chariot, *currus, us,* m.
Book, *liber, libri,* m.	Cicero, *Cicĕro, ōnis,* m.

Concerning, *de*, prep. with abl.
Eagle, *aquila, ae*, f.
Friend, *amicus, i*, m.
Friendship, *amicitia, ae*, f.
Hope, *spes, spei*, f.

Orator, *orātor, ōris*, m.
Prize, *praemium, ii*, n.
War, *bellum, i*, n.
Wisdom, *sapientia, ae*, f.

5. EXERCISE.

1. The eagle, the eagles. 2. Of an eagle, of the eagles. 3. For an eagle, for eagles. 4. Of friendship, of wisdom. 5. For friendship, for wisdom. 6. With friendship, with wisdom. 7. The friend, the friends. 8. Of the friend, of the friends. 9. For the friend, for the friends. 10. The books, the prizes. 11. The boy's book.

12. Of the bird, of the birds. 13. For the bird, for the birds. 14. The art of war. 15. The arts of war. 16. With the arts of war. 17. The chariot, of the chariots. 18. Of hope, with hope. 19. Cicero the orator. 20. Concerning Cicero the orator.

LESSON II.

ADJECTIVES AND PRONOUNS.
[7–10.]

6. LESSON FROM THE GRAMMAR.

I. Declension of Adjectives. 148; 150–153.
II. Comparison of Adjectives. 160–162.
III. Agreement of Adjectives. Rule XXXIII. 438.
IV. Declension of Pronouns. 182–191.
V. Agreement of Pronouns. Rule XXXIV. 445; 445, 1.

7. Models.

I. The Roman people.
II. *True* [1] friendships.
III. An animal which.
IV. This state.

I. *Popŭlus Romānus.*
II. *Verae amicitiae.*
III. *Anĭmal quod.*
IV. *Haec civĭtas.*

8. Remarks.

I. The Roman people.

1. In translating a noun and its adjective into Latin, we must begin with the noun, because the gender and case of the noun will determine the ending of the adjective, which must agree with it.

2. The people, *popŭlus* ; the — not translated.

3. Roman, *Romānus, a, um.* But as *popŭlus* is in the Nom. Sing. Masc., the adjective must be in the same case, gender, etc., according to Rule XXXIII. Hence *Romānus.*

4. The adjective may either precede or follow its noun, but seems more frequently to follow when not emphatic. See Gram. 598. Hence
Popŭlus Romānus.

II. True friendships.

1. Friendships. *Friendship* (for which you must look, not *friendships*) is *amicitia ;* friendships is *amicitiae,* the plural of *amicitia.*

2. True, *verus, a, um.* But as *amicitiae* is in the Nom. Plur. Fem., the adjective must be in the same case, etc.; hence *verae.*

3. In *true* friendships, as opposed to *false* friendships, *true* is emphatic. Hence *verae* must precede its noun. See Gram. 598, 2.
Verae amicitiae.

III. An animal which.

1. An animal, *anĭmal ;* an — not translated.

2. Which, *qui, quae, quod.* But as *anĭmal* is in the Neut. Sing., the relative must be in the same gender and number, according to Rule XXXIV.; hence *quod.*
Anĭmal quod.

IV. This state.

1. State, *civĭtas.*

2. This, *hic, haec, hoc.* But as *civĭtas* is in the Nom. Sing. Fem., the

---

[1] In the Models and Exercises, *italicized* English words are emphatic.

demonstrative which agrees with it as an adjective must be in the same case, etc. See Gram. 445, 1; hence *haec*.

Haec civitas.

9. VOCABULARY.

Acceptable, *gratus, a, um.*

Beautiful, *pulcher, chra, chrum.*

Certain, a certain, *quidam, quaedam, quoddam* and *quiddam.*

Crown, *corōna, ae,* f.

Diligent, *diligens, entis.*

High, *altus, a, um.*

Himself, herself, itself, *sui.*

I, *ego, mei.*

Kind, *benignus, a, um.*

Law, *lex, legis,* f.

Mountain, *mons, montis,* m.

My, *meus, a, um.* G. 185.

Present, *donum, i,* n.

Pupil, *discipŭlus, i,* m.

This, *hic, haec, hoc.*

Thou, you, *tu, tui.*

True, *verus, a, um.*

Useful, *utĭlis, e.*

Who, which, what, interrog., *qui, quae, quod,* adj.; *quis, quae, quid,* subs.

Your, *tuus, a, um ; vester, tra, trum.* G. 185.

10. EXERCISE.

1. A *kind* friend, of a *kind* friend. 2. Kind friends, of kind friends. 3. *True* friendship, of *true* friendships. 4. An acceptable present, with acceptable presents. 5. The beautiful books, the beautiful crowns, the beautiful presents. 6. Useful laws, of the useful laws.

7. A high mountain, a higher mountain, the highest mountain. 8. The most diligent pupils. 9. Of me, of you,¹ of himself, of whom? 10. With my books, with your ¹ books. 11. This mountain, this crown, this present. 12. A certain book.

---

¹ In the Exercises the pronoun *you* may be treated as singular, unless it is marked (pl.), or is shown by the sense to be plural. In like manner, *your* may be treated as referring to one person, unless the sense shows that two or more persons are addressed.

LESSON III.

VERBS. — SUM. FIRST AND SECOND CONJUGATIONS.
[11–13.]

11. LESSON FROM THE GRAMMAR.

I. Verb Sum. 204.

II. First Conjugation. 205, 206.

III. Second Conjugation. 207, 208.

IV. Subject Nominative. Rule III. 367.

V. Agreement of Verb with Subject. Rule XXXV. 460.

VI. Predicate Nouns. Rule I. 362.

VII. Direct Object. Rule V. 371.

12. MODELS.

I. God made the world.	I. *Deus mundum aedificāvit.*
II. Cincinnatus was dictator.	II. *Cincinnātus dictātor fuit.*

13. REMARKS.

I. God made the world.

1. GOD, *Deus.* As subject it must be in the Nominative, according to Rule III.

2. MADE. Look for the present *make*, not for *made* ; MAKE, BUILD, *aedifĭco* (I make) ; I MADE, *aedificāvi.* But as *Deus*, the subject, is in the Third Pers. Sing., the verb must be in the same person and number, according to Rule XXXV. ; hence *aedificāvit.*

3. WORLD, *mundus.* But as direct object of *aedificāvit*, it must be in the Accus. ; hence *mundum.*

4. The order is — Subject, Object, Verb. See Gram. 593.

Deus mundum aedificāvit.

II. Cincinnatus was dictator.

1. CINCINNATUS, *Cincinnātus*, the same as in English. As subject it must be in the Nominative.

2. WAS. The verb *to be* is *sum*, I am. I WAS, *fui*; but according to Rule XXXV., the verb must agree with its subject, *Cincinnātus*; hence *fuit*.

8. DICTATOR, *dictātor*, the same as in English. As predicate noun, it must agree in case with *Cincinnātus*, according to Rule I., hence in the Nom.

4. The Predicate Noun may either precede or follow the verb. Placing it before the verb, we have

Cincinnātus dictātor fuit.

14. VOCABULARY.

Accuse, *accūso, āre, āvi, ātum*.	Grieve, *doleo, ēre, ui, ĭtum*.
Advise, *moneo, ēre, ui, ĭtum*.	Happy, *beātus, a, um*.
Be, *sum, esse, fui*.	Praise, *laudo, āre, āvi, ātum*.
Blame, *vitupĕro, āre, āvi, ātum*.	That, *ille, a, ud*.

15. EXERCISE.

1. This law is useful. 2. That law was useful. 3. These laws will be useful. 4. We may be happy. 5. You (pl.)[1] might have been happy. 6. I praise, we praise. 7. He was blaming, they were blaming. 8. I shall praise, we shall praise. 9. He accuses, he is accused. 10. He will accuse, he will be accused.

11. They praised Cicero. 12. We will praise Cicero. 13. Cicero has been praised. 14. I grieve, we grieve. 15. He was grieving, they were grieving. 16. I shall grieve, we shall grieve. 17. He advises, he is advised. 18. He was advising, he was advised. 19. You will advise the boys. 20. The boys have been advised.

---

[1] See foot note page 5.

LESSON IV.

VERBS. — THIRD AND FOURTH CONJUGATIONS. DE-
PONENT VERBS. PERIPHRASTIC CONJUGATION.
[14–18.]

16. LESSON FROM THE GRAMMAR.

I. Third Conjugation. 209, 210 ; 213–215.

II. Fourth Conjugation. 211, 212.

III. Deponent Verbs. 221–226.

IV. Periphrastic Conjugation. 227–231.

V. Use of Adverbs. Rule LI. 582.

17. MODELS.

I. The wise live happily.

II. Diligence should be cultivated.

I. *Sapientes feliciter vivunt.*

II. *Diligentia colenda est.*

18. REMARKS.

I. The wise live happily.

1. THE WISE. Wise, *sapiens ;* the wise, *sapientes*, Nom. Plur.
See Gram. 441, 1.

2. LIVE. I live, *vivo.* But the verb must agree with the subject,
sapientes ; hence *vivunt.* Third Pers. Plur.

3. HAPPILY, *feliciter.* But the adverb in Latin generally precedes the
verb, though it generally follows it in English. See Gram. 600.

Sapientes feliciter vivunt.

II. Diligence should be cultivated.

1. DILIGENCE, *diligentia.* Nom. Sing.

2. SHOULD BE CULTIVATED, is to be cultivated. The duty or neces-

sity denoted by *should be, is to be, ought,* may be expressed by the Second Periphrastic conjugation. See Gram. 229. I cultivate, *colo.* Periphrastic conjugation, *colendus sum.* But the verb must agree with *diligentia* in number and person, and the participle in gender, number, and case. See Gram. 460, 1. Hence we have *colenda est.*

Diligentia colenda est.

19. Vocabulary.

Always, *semper,* adv.

City, *urbs, urbis,* f.

Father, *pater, tris,* m.

Follow, *sequor, i, secutus sum,* dep.

Fortify, *munio, ire, ivi, itum.*

Hannibal, *Hannibal, alis,* m.

His, her, its, their, *suus, a, um.*

Imitate, *imitor, ari, atus sum,* dep.

Instruct, *erudio, ire, ivi, itum.*

Lead, *duco, ere, duxi, ductum.*

Our, *noster, tra, trum.*

Rule, *rego, ere, rexi, rectum.*

Saguntum, *Saguntum, i,* n.

Sleep, *dormio, ire, ivi, itum.*

Take, *capio, ere, cepi, captum.*

20. Exercise.

1. He leads, he is led. 2. He will rule, he will be ruled. 3. They have ruled, they have been ruled. 4. Hannibal took Saguntum. 5. Saguntum was taken. 6. The cities had been taken. 7. He sleeps, they sleep. 8. He will sleep, they will sleep. 9. He may sleep, they may sleep. 10. Your father instructed you. 11. These boys have been instructed.

12. The boy imitates his father. 13. We will imitate our fathers. 14. You have always imitated your father. 15. We will follow you. 16. The boys followed their father. 17. We were about to praise you. 18. Diligent pupils must be praised. 19. They were about to fortify the city. 20. These cities must be fortified.

LESSON V.

AGREEMENT OF NOUNS. — NOMINATIVE AND VOCATIVE.
[19–22.]

21. LESSON FROM THE GRAMMAR.

I. Predicate Nouns. Rule I. 362.

II. Appositives. Rule II. 363.

III. Subject Nominative. Rule III. 367.

IV. Case of Address. Rule IV. 369.

22. MODELS.

I. Hear, citizens.   I. *Audīte, cives.*

II. For other models, see ■nder Lessons I. and III.

23. REMARKS.

1. HEAR. I hear, *audio ;* hear, hear ye, *audīte,* Imperative Second Pers. Plur. The subject *vos,* ye, is omitted. See Gram. 367, 2.

2. CITIZENS. Citizen, *civis ;* citizens, *cives,* Voc. Plur. See Rule IV.

3. The Vocative generally, though not always, stands after one or more words. See Gram. 602, VI.

24. VOCABULARY.

Brother, *frater, tris,* m.

Brutus, *Brutus, i,* m.

Consul, *consul, ŭlis,* m.

Diligence, *diligentia, ae,* f.

Greatly, *valde,* adv.

Herodotus, *Herodŏtus, i,* m.

History, *historia, ae,* f.

Letter, *epistŏla, ae,* f.

Many, *multi, ae, a,* plur.

Philosopher, *philosŏphus, i,* m.

Save, *servo, āre, āvi, ātum.*

Socrates, *Socrătes, is,* m.

Soldier, *miles, ĭtis,* m.

Write, *scribo, ĕre, scripsi, scriptum.*

25. Exercise.

1. Cicero was an orator.   2. The consul was an orator.
3. Cicero the consul was an orator.   4. Brutus had been
consul.   5. Brutus was consul.   6. Cicero the orator
wrote many letters.   7. The letters of Cicero the orator
have been greatly praised.   8. Socrates was a philosopher.
9. Your brother will be an orator.   10. Herodotus was
the father of history.   11. The orator praises Herodotus
the father of history.   12. Pupils, your diligence will be
praised.   13. Your diligence, boys, must be praised.   14.
The city has been fortified.   15. The city must be saved.

Lesson VI.

USE OF THE ACCUSATIVE.
[23–25.]

26. Lesson from the Grammar.

I. Accusative as Direct Object.   Rule V. 371.

II. Two Accusatives — Same Person.   Rule VI. 373.

III. Two Accusatives — Person and Thing.   Rule VII. 374.

27. Models.

I. They called the council Senate.   I. *Consilium appellavērunt Senātum.*

II. He asked me my opinion.   II. *Me sententiam rogāvit.*

III. For Model for Direct Object, see under Lesson III.

28. Remarks.

I. They called the council Senate.

1. They called. I call, *appello ;* they called, *appellavērunt* (appel-

larunt), Perf. Indic. Third Pers. Plur. The subject is omitted, being implied in the ending *erunt*. See Gram. 367, 2.

2. THE COUNCIL, *consilium*, Accus. See Rule VI.

3. SENATE, *Senātus ;* Accus. *Senātum.* See Rule VI.

4. The verb, whose usual place is at the end of the sentence, may stand between the two Accusatives, as in this Model.

II. He asked me my opinion.

1. HE ASKED. I ask, *rogo ;* he asked, *rogāvit,* Perf. Indic. Third Pers. Sing. The subject is omitted. See Gram. 367, 2.

2. ME. I, *ego ;* me, *me,* Accus. See Rule VII.

3. MY OPINION. Opinion, *sententia ;* Accus. *sententiam.* See Rule VII. The possessive *my* in this Model is not expressed in Latin, because it can be readily supplied from the context; *my opinion,* not the opinion of another. See Gram. 447.

29. VOCABULARY.

Ask, *rogo, āre, āvi, ātum.*

Call, *appello, āre, āvi, ātum.*

Catiline, *Catilīna, ae,* m.

Delight, *delecto, āre, āvi, ātum.*

Enemy, *hostis, is,* m. and f.

Island, *insŭla, ae,* f.

Judge, *judĭco, āre, āvi, ātum.*

Modesty, *verecundia, ae,* f.

Opinion, *sententia, ae,* f.

Preceptor, *praeceptor, ŏris,* m.

Rome, *Roma, ae,* f.

Sicily, *Sicilia, ae,* f.

Teach, *doceo, ēre, docui, doctum.*

Virtue, *virtus, ūtis,* f.

30. EXERCISE.

1. Your letter delights me. 2. This letter will delight your father. 3. Who wrote that letter? 4. My brother wrote that letter. 5. They call the island Sicily. 6. The island is called Sicily. 7. Sicily is an island. 8. They called Herodotus the father of history. 9. We judge you, O Catiline, an enemy. 10. You, O Catiline, will be judged an enemy. 11. We teach boys modesty. 12. We will teach our pupils wisdom. 13. The preceptor will ask you your opinion. 14. The city was called Rome. 15. Virtue must be praised.

Lesson VII.

ACCUSATIVE — Continued.
[26–29.]

31. Lesson from the Grammar.

I. Accusative of Time and Space. Rule VIII. 378.
II. Accusative of Limit. Rule IX. 379.
III. Accusative of Specification. Rule X. 380.
IV. Accusative in Exclamations. Rule XI. 381.
V. Interrogative Sentences. 346, II.

32. Models.

I. He lived thirty years.
II. Plato came to Tarentum.
III. They are not at all moved.
IV. O *deceptive* hope!

I. *Triginta annos vixit.*
II. *Plato Tarentum venit.*
III. *Nihil moventur.*
IV. *O fallācem spem!*

33. Remarks.

I. He lived thirty years.

1. He lived. I live, *vivo ;* he lived, *vixit.* See Gram. 367, 2.
2. Thirty, *triginta*, indeclinable.
3. Years. Year, *annus ;* years, Accus. Plur. *annos.* See Rule VIII.

II. Plato came to Tarentum.

1. Plato, *Plato*, Nom. See Rule III.
2. Came. I come, *venio ;* came, he came, *venit.* See Gram. 285.
3. To Tarentum. Tarentum, *Tarentum ;* to Tarentum, Accus. *Tarentum.* See Rule IX.

III. They are not at all moved.

1. They are moved. I move, *moveo ;* am moved, *moveor ;* they are moved, *moventur*, Pres. Indic. Pass. Third Pers. Plur.

2

2. NOT AT ALL, *nihil.* See Rule X.

IV. O deceptive hope !

1. O HOPE. Hope, *spes ;* O hope, *O spem.* Rule XI.

2. DECEPTIVE, *fallax ;* Acc. Sing. *fallācem.* Rule XXXIII. 438.

It is emphatic, and accordingly precedes its noun. See Gram. 598, 2.

34. VOCABULARY.

Athens, *Athēnae, ārum,* f. pl.

Come, *venio, īre, veni, ventum.*

Day, *dies, diēi,* m.

Forty-three, *tres (tria) et quadra-ginta.* G. 174, 175.

Hour, *hora, ae,* f.

How many, *quot,* indeclinable.

In, *in,* prep. with abl.

Italy, *Italia, ae,* f.

Messenger, *nuntius, ii,* m.

Month, *mensis, mensis,* m.

Move, *moveo, ēre, movi, motum.*

Not, *non,* adv. ; interrog., *nonne.* G. 346, II. 1.

Not at all, *nihil,* indeclinable. G. 128.

Numa, *Numa, ae,* m.

Reign, *regno, āre, āvi, ātum.*

Send, *mitto, ēre, misi, missum.*

Seven, *septem,* indeclinable. G. 175, 2.

Two, *duo, ae, o.* G. 176.

Wonderful, *admirabilis, e.*

Year, *annus, i,* m.

35. EXERCISE.

1. How many years did *Numa* reign? 2. Numa reigned forty-three years. 3. Were you (pl.) not two years in *Italy?* 4. We were *in Italy* seven months. 5. The consul came to Rome. 6. He was in that city seven days. 7. Was he not asked his opinion? 8. He was asked his opinion. 9. You, consul, have saved the city. 10. O wonderful virtue ! 11. You will not move the consul *at all.* 12. Did you not send a messenger to Athens? 13. I sent two messengers to Athens. 14. How many hours did you sleep? 15. I slept seven hours.

Lesson VIII.

USE OF THE DATIVE.
[30–38.]

36. Lesson from the Grammar.

I. Dative with Verbs. Rule XII. 384.

II. Two Datives — To Which and For Which. Rule XIII. 390.

III. Dative with Adjectives. Rule XIV. 391.

IV. Dative with Derivatives. Rule XV. 392.

37. Models.

I. They serve the king.	I. *Regi serviunt.*
II. It *is* a care to me.	II. *Est mihi curae.*
III. Country is dear to all.	III. *Patria omnĭbus cara est.*
IV. Obedience to laws.	IV. *Obtemperatio legĭbus.*

38. Remarks.

I. They serve the king.

1. They serve, *serviunt.*
2. The king. King, *rex;* Dat. *regi.* Rule XII.

II. It is a care to me (to me for a care).

1. It is, *est.* It is placed at the beginning of the sentence because it is emphatic. See Gram. 594, I.
2. To me. I, *ego;* to me, *mihi.* Rule XIII.
3. A care = for a care. Care, *cura;* for a care, *curae,* Dat. Rule XIII.

III. Country is dear to all.

1. Country, *patria.*
2. Is, *est.*

3. DEAR. Dear, *carus*; Fem. *cara*, to agree with *patria*.

4. To ALL. All, *omnis*; Dat. Plur. *omnĭbus*. Rule XIV.

5. Observe the order of the words in the model, though much freedom is allowable in this respect.

IV. Obedience to laws.

1. OBEDIENCE, *obtemperatio*.

2. To LAWS. Law, *lex*; to laws, *legĭbus*, Dat. Plur. Rule XV.

39. VOCABULARY.

All, *omnis, e.*	Honor, *honor, ŏris*, m.
Award, *trĭbuo, ĕre, ui, ūtum.*	Industry, *industria, ae*, f.
Citizen, *civis, civis*, m. and f.	Learning, *doctrĭna, ae*, f.
Country, one's country, *patria, ae*, f.	Obedience, *obtemperatio, ŏnis*, f.
Dear, *carus, a, um.*	Obey, *pareo, ĕre, ui, ĭtum.*
Ever = always, *semper*, adv.	Praiseworthy, *laudabĭlis, e.*
General, *imperātor, ŏris*, m.	Prefer, *praefĕro, ferre, tŭli, lātum.*
Give, *do, dare, dedi, datum.*	G. 292, 2.
Glory, *gloria, ae*, f.	Roman, *Romānus, a, um.*
Good, *bonus, a, um.*	Wealth, *divitiae, ārum*, f. pl.
Have, *sum, esse, fui*, with dat. G. 387.	

40. EXERCISE.

1. *Good* citizens will obey the laws. 2. The Romans awarded honors to their generals. 3. Industry is an honor to a pupil. 4. Virtue is a glory to all. 5. I prefer virtue to learning. 6. We prefer learning to wealth. 7. I will give you that book as a present. 8. I have seven beautiful books. 9. Will not this present be acceptable to you? 10. That present will be acceptable to me. 11. Is not the country dear to you? 12. The country has ever been very dear to me. 13. Obedience to the laws is praiseworthy.

Lesson IX.

USE OF THE GENITIVE.
[39, 40.]

41. Lesson from the Grammar.

I. Genitive with Nouns. Rule XVI. 395.

II. Genitive with Adjectives. Rule XVII. 399.

42. Models.

I. The love of truth.

II. Desirous of truth.

I. *Amor veritātis.*

II. *Veritātis cupĭdus.*

43. Vocabulary.

Athenian, *Atheniensis, is,* m. and f.

Celebrated, distinguished, *clarus, a, um.*

Demosthenes, *Demosthĕnes, is,* m.

Desirous of, *cupĭdus, a, um.*

Fond of, *amans, amantis.*

King, *rex, regis,* m.

Love, *amor, ōris,* m.

Man, *homo, ĭnis; vir,*[1] *viri,* m.

Money, *pecunia, ae,* f.

Often, *saepe,* adv.

Oration, *oratio, ōnis,* f.

Pleasure, *voluptas, ātis,* f.

Praise, *laus, laudis,* f.

Precept, *praeceptum, i,* n.

Skilled in, *perītus, a, um.*

44. Exercise.

1. The orations of Cicero have often been praised. 2. You have often praised the orations of Cicero the orator.

---

[1] *Homo* is the ordinary term for *man* as a member of the human family; while *vir* is a term of respect, a *hero*, a *man* in the full sense of the word.

3. The orations of Demosthenes, the *celebrated* orator, will always be praised. 4. Boys are fond of pleasure. 5. The pupils are fond of praise. 6. The king was desirous of glory. 7. Men are fond of money. 8. The love of country is an honor to a citizen. 9. The precepts of the *philosophers* were useful to the Athenians. 10. The general is skilled in *war*.

Lesson X.

GENITIVE — Continued.
[41–43.]

45. Lesson from the Grammar.

I. Predicate Genitive. Rule XVIII. 401.

II. Genitive with certain Verbs. Rule XIX. 406.

III. Accusative and Genitive. Rule XX. 410.

46. Models.

I. It is of small value.	I. *Parvi pretii est.*
II. He remembers *the past.*	II. *Meminit praeteritō-rum.*
III. You accuse men of crime.	III. *Viros scelĕris arguis.*

47. Remarks.

1. Model I. — Of small value, *parvi pretii.* Rule XVIII.

2. Model II. — The past = past things, events, *praeteritārum*, Gen. Plur. Neut. of *praeterĭtus*, from *praetereo*. Rule XIX. *Praeteritārum rerum* should not be used for *praeteritōrum*, except to avoid real ambiguity, as it is less euphonious.

Praeteritōrum would regularly precede the verb, but is made emphatic by being placed at the end of the sentence. See Gram. 594, II.

3. Of CRIME, *scelĕris*, Gen. of *scelus*. Rule XX.

48. VOCABULARY.

Already, *jam*, adv.

Concerns, it concerns, ~~refert~~, re-tŭlit, impers.

Esteem, *aestĭmo, āre, āvi, ātum.*

Favor, *beneficium, ii*, n.

Folly, *stultitia, ae*, f.

Forget, *obliviscor, i, oblĭtus sum,* dep.

Goodness, *bonĭtas, ātis*, f.

Grain, *frumentum, i*, n.

Great, *magnus, a, um.*

Greatly, with *intĕrest* and *refert*, *magni.*

High, at a high price, *magno*, or

magni; with verbs of valuing, *magni;* very highly, *maxĭmi.*

Integrity, *integrĭtas, ātis*, f.

Interests, it interests, ~~interest~~, in-terfuit, impers.

Never, *nunquam*, adv.

Pity, ~~misereor~~, *ēri, erĭtus sum*, dep.

Poor, *pauper, ĕris.*

Remember, ~~memĭni~~, *isse.* G. 297, I.

Repent, I repent, *me* ~~poenĭtet~~, *poenituit.* G. 299.

Sell, *vendo, ĕre, dĭdi, dĭtum.*

Theft, *furtum, i*, n.

Value, price, *pretium, ii*, n.

49. EXERCISE.

1. Virtue is a characteristic of a good man. 2. Integrity is of great value. 3. Goodness must be highly esteemed. 4. We esteem goodness very highly. 5. This book will be of great value to us. 6. We pity the poor. 7. I remember your favors. 8. We do not forget our friends. 9. We shall never forget you. 10. They accuse the boy of theft. 11. I have already repented of my folly. 12. He sells grain at a high price. 13. This greatly interests us.

LESSON XI.

USE OF THE ABLATIVE.
[44, 45.]

50. LESSON FROM THE GRAMMAR.

I. Ablative of Cause, Manner, Means. Rule **XXI.** 414.
II. Ablative of Price. Rule **XXII.** 416.

51. MODELS.

I. He is led by glory.

II. You purchased the house at a high price.

I. *Gloria ducĭtur.*

II. *Domum magno emisti.*

52. REMARKS.

1. MODEL I. — BY GLORY, *gloria*, Abl. Rule XXI.

2. MODEL II. — AT A HIGH PRICE, *magno*, Abl. Rule XXII. The Abl. of the adjective is sometimes thus used, *pretio* being understood.

53. VOCABULARY.

By, *a, ab,* prep. with abl. G. 434, 3.

Glory in, *glorior, āri, ātus sum,* dep.

Gold, *aurum, i,* n.

Happiness, success, *felicĭtas, ătis,* f.

Horse, *equus, equi,* m.

Judge, *judex, ĭcis,* m.

Mina, *mina, ae,* f.

Not, with imperatives, *ne,* adv.

One, *unus, a, um.* G. 176.

Proud, *superbus, a, um.*

Purchase, *emo, ĕre, emi, emptum.*

Rejoice, *gaudeo, ēre, gavīsus sum.* G. 272, 3.

Scipio, *Scipio, ōnis,* m.

Study, *studium, ii,* n.

Talent, *talentum, i,* n.

Thirty, *triginta,* indecl.

Valor, *virtus, ūtis,* f.

54. Exercise.

1. Socrates has often been praised for (because of) his wisdom. 2. They glory in their wealth. 3. This philosopher glories in his wisdom. 4. The pupils rejoice in their studies. 5. We are delighted with the precepts of the *philosophers.* 6. Wisdom is not purchased with gold. 7. Do not sell happiness for gold. 8. The judge has purchased a horse for one talent. 9. I will sell this horse for thirty minae. 10. He is proud of his wealth. 11. Scipio was proud of his country.

Lesson XII.

ABLATIVE — Continued.
[46–48.]

55. Lesson from the Grammar.

I. Ablative with Comparatives. Rule XXIII. 417.

II. Ablative of Difference. Rule XXIV. 418.

III. Ablative in Special Constructions. Rule XXV. 419.

56. Models.

I. Nothing is more lovely than virtue.

I. *Nihil est amabilius virtūte,* or *Nihil est amabilius quam virtus.*

II. He preceded me by two days.

II. *Biduo me antecessit.*

III. We enjoy very many things.

III. *Plurĭmis rebus fruĭmur.*

IV. Safety rests upon truth.	IV. *Salus veritāte nitĭtur.*
V. I do not need a *remedy.*	V. *Non egeo medicīna.*
VI. They are *worthy* of friendship.	VI. *Digni sunt amicitia.*
VII. We need your *authority.*	VII. *Auctoritāte tua nobis opus est.*

57. REMARKS.

1. MODEL I.—THAN VIRTUE, *quam virtus* or *virtŭte.* Rule XXIII. 417, 1. The Abl. *virtŭte* may either follow or precede the comparative, *amabilius.*

2. MODEL II. — BY TWO DAYS, *biduo*, Abl. of Dif. Rule XXIV.

3. MODEL III. — VERY MANY, *plurĭmis*, Superl. See G. 160.

4. THINGS, *rebus*, Abl. Rule XXV. *Rebus* is necessary to avoid ambiguity, because, though *plurĭma* may be used substantively, in the sense of very many things, *plurĭmis* would be ambiguous, as it would not distinguish *things* from *persons.*

5. MODELS IV. V. VI. — UPON TRUTH, A REMEDY, OF FRIENDSHIP, *veritāte, medicīna, amicitia*, Abls. Rule XXV.

6. *Medicīna* would regularly precede its verb, but is here emphatic. The regular order in Model VI. would be, *Amicitia digni sunt*, but as *digni* is emphatic, it is placed at the beginning of the sentence. See G. 594, I.

7. MODEL VII. — WE NEED = there is need to us, *nobis opus est.* See G. 419, 3. AUTHORITY, *auctoritāte*, Abl. Rule XXV. *Auctoritāte* is emphatic, and is accordingly placed at the beginning of the sentence.

58. VOCABULARY.

Abound in, *abundo, āre, āvi, ātum.*

Cato, *Cato, ōnis*, m.

Discharge, fulfil, *fungor, i, functus sum*, dep.

Duty, *officium, ii*, n.

Enjoy, *fruor, i, fructus* or *fruĭtus sum*, dep.

Five, *quinque*, indecl.

Learned, *doctus, a, um.*

Much, with comparatives, *multo,* adv.

Need, there is need, *opus est, fuit.*

Older, *major, ōris,* or *major natu.*

Relying upon, *fretus, a, um.*

Trust in, *confīdo, ĕre, fīsus sum.*

Use, *utor, uti, usus sum,* dep.

Wisely, *sapienter,* adv.

Worthy, *dignus, a, um.*

59. Exercise.

1. Cicero was more learned than Cato. 2. You are more diligent than your brother. 3. Virtue is better than wisdom. 4. Wisdom is better than gold. 5. Wisdom is dearer to us than gold. 6. You are five years older than I. 7. Your father uses his wealth wisely. 8. We enjoy our studies. 9. We will discharge our duties. 10. This city abounds in wealth. 11. We do not trust in wealth. 12. Your pupils are worthy of praise. 13. I rely (am relying) upon your friendship. 14. *We* need friends.)

Lesson XIII.

ABLATIVE — Continued.
[49–51.]

60. Lesson from the Grammar.

I. Ablative of Place. Rule XXVI. 421.

II. Ablative of Source and Separation. Rule XXVII. 425.

III. Ablative of Time. Rule XXVIII. 426, 427.

61. Models.

I. In the forum.

II. He was at Rome.

III. I ward off slaughter from you.

I. *In foro.*

II. *Romae fuit.*

III. *Caedem a vobis depello.*

IV. He died in his *eightieth* year.	IV. *Octogesĭmo anno est mortuus.*

62. REMARKS.

1. MODEL II. — AT ROME, *Romae;* why Gen. rather than Abl. *Roma?* See G. 421, II.

2. MODEL IV. — IN — YEAR, *anno.* Rule XXVIII. Why not *in anno?* See G. 426, 2. *Octogesĭmo* is emphatic, and accordingly precedes its noun. See G. 598, 2.

63. VOCABULARY.

Ago, *abhinc,* adv.
Corinth, *Corinthus, i,* f.
Danger, *pericŭlum, i,* n.
Flee, *fugio, ĕre, fugi, fugĭtum.*
Free from, *libĕro, āre, āvi, ātum.*
From, *a, ab,* prep. with abl.
Garden, *hortus, i,* m.
Greece, *Graecia, ae,* f.
Keep from, keep off, *arceo, ĕre, cui, ctum.*

Receive, *accĭpio, ĕre, cĕpi, ceptum.*
Reside, *habĭto, āre, āvi, ātum.*
See, *video, ĕre, vidi, visum.*
Sunset, *solis occāsus, us,* m.
Temple, *templum, i,* n.
Three, *tres, tria.*
Time, *tempus, ŏris,* n.
Where, *ubi,* adv.
Whole, *totus, a, um.* G. 149.
Winter, *hiems, ĕmis,* f.

64. EXERCISE.

1. There were beautiful cities *in Greece.* 2. Were you in Corinth? 3. We were in *Corinth* the whole winter. 4. In *Athens* we saw beautiful temples. 5. Does not your friend reside at Rome? 6. He resides in Athens. 7. He fled from Rome to Athens. 8. I have received two letters *from your father.* 9. The city has been freed from great dangers. 10. Where were you at *sunset?* 11. I was in the garden *at that time.* 12. I was in Rome three years ago. 13. We will keep the enemy from the city.

Lesson XIV.

ABLATIVE — Continued.
[52–55.]

65. Lesson from the Grammar.

I. Ablative of Characteristic. Rule XXIX. 428.

II. Ablative of Specification. Rule XXX. 429.

III. Ablative Absolute. Rule XXXI. 430, 431.

IV. Cases with Prepositions. Rule XXXII. 432–435.

66. Models.

I. Piso, a man of the *highest* virtue.

II. Piso was a man of the *highest* virtue.

III. They are similar in character.

IV. They flourished in the reign of Servius.

V. I have written to a friend.

I. *Piso, vir summa virtūte.*

II. *Piso summa virtūte fuit.*

III. *Morĭbus simĭles sunt.*

IV. *Servio regnante viguērunt.*

V. *Ad amīcum scripsi.*

67. Remarks.

1. Model I. — A man of the highest virtue, *vir summa virtūte;* but in the predicate, as in the second model, Piso was a man, etc., *vir* is omitted. See G. 428. 1, 2). As *summa* is emphatic, it is placed before its noun. See G. 598. 2.

2. Model III. — In character. Character, manners, *mores;* in character, *morĭbus;* Abl. of Specification. Rule XXX.

3. Model IV. — In the reign of Servius = Servius reigning, *Servio regnante;* Abl. Absol. Rule XXXI.

68. Vocabulary.

Ancus, *Ancus, i*, m.	Light, *lux, lucis*, f.
Before, *ante*, prep. with acc.	Marcius, *Marcius, ii*, m.
Conspiracy, *conjuratio, ōnis*, f.	Remarkable, *singulāris, e.*
Courage, *virtus, ūtis*, f.	Spain, *Hispania, ae*, f.
Eloquence, *eloquentia, ae*, f.	Surpass, *supĕro, āre, āvi, ātum.*
Form, make, *facio, ĕre, feci, factum.*	Tarquin, *Tarquinius, ii*, m.
Greek, *Graecus, i*, m.	To, *ad*, prep. with acc.

69. Exercise.

1. The general, a man of *remarkable* courage, will save the city. 2. The general is a man of remarkable courage. 3. Cicero, a man of remarkable eloquence, was consul. 4. The Greeks surpassed the Romans in learning. 5. The Romans surpassed the Greeks in valor. 6. Tarquin came to Rome in the reign of Ancus Marcius. 7. A conspiracy was formed in Rome when Cicero was consul. 8. Scipio was in Spain. 9. Tarquin came into Italy. 10. The boy came to me *before light*.

Lesson XV.

ADJECTIVES. PRONOUNS.
[56–62.]

70. Lesson from the Grammar.

I. Agreement of Adjectives. Rule XXXIII. 438, 439.

II. Agreement of Pronouns. Rule XXXIV. 445.

     Personal and Possessive Pronouns. 446–449.

     Demonstrative Pronouns. 450–452.

Relative Pronouns. 453.

Interrogative Pronouns. 454.

Indefinite Pronouns. 455–459.

71. MODELS.

I. Fortune is blind.	I. *Fortūna caeca est.*
II. I who encourage you.	II. *Ego qui te confirmo.*
III. Wash your hands.	III. *Manus lava.*
IV. He loves himself.	IV. *Se dilĭgit.*
V. The guardian of this city.	V. *Custos hujus urbis.*
VI. Who am I?	VI. *Quis ego sum?*
VII. A certain rhetorician.	VII. *Quidam rhetor.*

72. REMARKS.

1. MODEL I. — BLIND, *caeca*, Fem. Sing. Nom. to agree with *fortūna*. Rule XXXIII.

2. MODEL II. — ENCOURAGE, *confirmo*, First Pers. to agree with *qui*, which is of the First Pers. to agree with the antecedent *ego*. Rule XXXIV.

3. MODEL III. — YOUR HANDS, *manus*. The possessive, *tuas*, your, is omitted. See G. 447.

4. MODEL V. — OF THIS CITY. This city, *haec urbs;* of this city, *hujus urbis.*

5. MODEL VI. — WHO, *quis?* Why not *qui?* See G. 454.

73. VOCABULARY.

Have, *habeo, ĕre, ui, ĭtum.*

Instructor, *praeceptor, ōris,* m.

Make, *facio, ĕre, feci, factum.*

Modest, *modestus, a, um.*

Peace, *pax, pacis,* f.

Some one, a certain one, *quidam, quaedam, quiddam* or *quoddam.* G. 191.

Yesterday, *heri,* adv.

74. Exercise.

1. Peace will be acceptable to us. 2. The city will be beautiful. 3. I have seen *beautiful* cities. 4. The pupils are diligent. 5. Your friendship delights me. 6. Your instructor praises you. 7. Which book have you? 8. I have *your* book. 9. *True* wisdom makes men modest. 10. This precept will be useful to me. 11. The precepts of your instructor will be useful to you. 12. Some boys praise themselves. 13. The letter which you wrote yesterday will delight your father.

Lesson XVI.

AGREEMENT OF VERBS. — INDICATIVE.
[63–67.]

75. Lesson from the Grammar.

I. Agreement of Verb with Subject. Rule XXXV. 460–463.

II. Use of Indicative. Rule XXXVI. 474.

Present. 466, 467.

Imperfect. 468, 469.

Future and Future Perfect. 470, 473.

Perfect and Pluperfect. 471, 472.

76. Models.

I. Cato praised this law.

I. *Cato hanc legem laudāvit.*

II. Cicero and I are well.

II. *Ego et Cicĕro va-lēmus.*

III. I will write to you.

III. *Scribam ad te.*

77. REMARKS.

1. MODEL I. — PRAISED, *laudāvit*, Historical Perfect (G. 471, II.), Third Pers. Sing. to agree with *Cato*. Rule XXXV.

2. MODEL II. — CICERO AND I, *ego et Cicĕro*. In Latin the First Pers. stands before the Second.

3. ARE WELL, *valēmus*, First Pers. Plur. to agree with *ego et Cicĕro*. See G. 463, 1.

4. MODEL III. — I WILL WRITE, *scribam*, Fut. Why not *ego scribam?* See G. 367, 2; 446.

5. To YOU, *ad te*. This may stand either before or after the verb, though the modifiers of verbs more frequently stand before them. See G. 600.

78. VOCABULARY.

At, *ad*, or *apud*, prep. with accus.

Conquer, *vinco, ĕre, vici, victum.*

For his (her, its) own sake, *propter sese (se).*

Love, *amo, āre, āvi, ātum.*

Macedonia, *Macedonia, ae,* f.

Perseus, *Perseus,˙i,* m.

Pydna, *Pydna, ae,* f.

Servius, *Servius, ii,* m.

Ten, *decem,* indecl.

To-morrow, *cras,* adv.

Tried, *spectātus, a, um.*

Wise, *sapiens, entis.*

79. EXERCISE.

1. By whom was *Saguntum* taken? 2. This city was taken by Hannibal. 3. How many books have you? 4. *I* have ten good books. 5. Cato was a man of *tried* virtue. 6. We rejoice in your happiness. 7. Who was reigning at that time? 8. King Servius was reigning at Rome. 9. Will you not write to me? 10. I will write

to you to-morrow.　11. Virtue must be loved for its own sake.　12. Socrates was judged the wisest of men.　13. Herodotus has been called the father of history.　14. Perseus, the king of Macedonia, was conquered at Pydna.

Lesson XVII.

TENSES AND USE OF THE SUBJUNCTIVE.
[68–74.]

80. Lesson from the Grammar.

I. Sequence of Tenses.　Rule XXXVII.　480, 481.

II. Potential Subjunctive.　Rule XXXVIII.　485, 486.

III. Subjunctive of Desire.　Rule XXXIX.　487, 488.

IV. Subjunctive of Purpose or Result.　Rule XL.　489–492; 494; 497–500.

81. Models.

I. Perhaps you may inquire.

II. Who doubts?

III. Let us *love* our country.

IV. He strives that he may conquer.

V. I allowed *no day* to pass without giving something.

I. *Forsĭtan quaerātis.*

II. *Quis dubĭtet?*

III. *Amēmus patriam.*

IV. *Enitĭtur ut vincat.*

V. *Nullum intermīsi diem quin alĭquid darem.*

82. Remarks.

1. Model I. — You may inquire, *quaerātis,* Subj.　Rule XXXVIII. Subject *vos,* omitted.　See G. 367, 2.

2. MODEL II. — WHO DOUBTS, or would doubt? = no one doubts, *quis dubĭtet?* question of appeal, Subj. See G. 486, II.

3. MODEL III. — LET US LOVE, *amēmus*, Subj. of Desire. Rule XXXIX. The verb is made emphatic by standing at the beginning of the sentence. See G. 594, I.

4. OUR COUNTRY, *patriam*, possessive omitted. See G. 447.

5. MODEL IV. — THAT HE MAY CONQUER, *ut vincat*, Subj. of Purpose. Rule XL. Present tense, because it depends upon a Principal tense, *enitĭtur*. Rule XXXVII.

6. MODEL V. — I ALLOWED — TO PASS, *intermīsi*.

7. WITHOUT GIVING SOMETHING = but that I gave something, *quin alĭquid darem. Darem*, Subj. with *quin*, Imperfect tense, dependent upon *intermĭsi*. See G. 498, 3; 481, II. 1.

8. *Nullum — diem* are made emphatic by separation. See G. 594, III.

83. VOCABULARY.

Doubt, *dubĭto, āre, āvi, ātum.*
So, *tam ; ĭta,* adv.

That, expressing purpose or result, *ut,* conj.

That = but that, *quin,* conj.

84. EXERCISE.

1. He praises you (pl.) that he may be praised by you.
2. He praised you (pl.) that he might be praised by you.
3. They will praise us that they may be praised by us. 4. I do not doubt that you (pl.) have been diligent. 5. We did not doubt that you (pl.) had been diligent. 6. The judge may be accused of folly. 7. Let us obey the laws. 8. May our pupils love virtue. 9. May they be diligent. 10. The pupils are so diligent that they are praised by their preceptor. 11. Let us praise virtue. 12. Let virtue be praised.

LESSON XVIII.

SUBJUNCTIVE — CONTINUED.
[75–82.]

85. LESSON FROM THE GRAMMAR.

I. Subjunctive of Condition. Rule XLI. 503–513.

II. Subjunctive of Concession. Rule XLII. 515, 516.

III. Subjunctive of Cause. Rule XLIII. 517–520.

IV. Subjunctive of Time with Cause. Rule XLIV. 521–523.

86. MODELS.

I. If this is a state, I am a citizen.

II. The day would fail me, if I should recount.

III. Wisdom would not be sought, if it accomplished nothing.

IV. Though he may deride.

V. Since life is full of fear.

VI. You are waiting till he speaks.

I. *Si haec civĭtas est, civis sum ego.*

II. *Dies deficiat, si numĕrem.*

III. *Sapientia non expeterētur, si nihil efficĕret.*

IV. *Licet irrideat.*

V. *Quum vita metus plena sit.*

VI. *Exspectas dum dicat.*

87. REMARKS.

1. MODEL I. — In *civis sum ego*, regularly *ego sum civis*, or *ego civis sum*, *civis* is emphatic, and is accordingly placed at the beginning of the clause. See G. 594, I.

2. MODEL II. — WOULD FAIL, SHOULD RECOUNT, *deficiat, numĕrem*, Subj. Rule XLI. 509.

3. MODEL III. — WOULD BE SOUGHT, ACCOMPLISHED, *expeteretur*, *efficěret*, Subj. Rule XLI. 510, Imperfect, 510, 1.

4. MODEL IV. — MAY DERIDE, *irrideat*, Subj. of Concession. Rule XLII.

5. MODEL V. — SINCE — IS, *quum — sit*, Subj. of Cause. Rule XLIII.

6. MODEL VI. — TILL HE SPEAKS, that he may speak; *dum dicat*, Subj. of Cause and Time. Rule XLIV.

88. VOCABULARY.

Although, *quamquam ; licet, etsi,* conj.	Read, *lego, ěre, legi, lectum.*
Because, *quod,* conj.	Until, *dum, donec,* conj.
However, *quamvis,* adv.	Wait, *exspecto, āre, āvi, ātum.*
If, *si,* conj.	When, *quum,* conj.
Just, *justus, a, um.*	Yet, *tamen,* adv.

89. EXERCISE.

1. If they are good, they are happy. 2. If you will be diligent, you will be praised. 3. If you would be diligent, you would be praised. 4. If you (pl.) were diligent, you would be praised. 5. If they had been good, they would have been happy. 6. Although the judge is just, he is yet often blamed. 7. However just he may be, he will often be blamed. 8. You will be praised, because you are diligent. 9. The citizens will praise the judge, because (on the ground that) he is just. 10. We will wait until you read the letter (i. e. that you may read it). 11. We saw beautiful temples, when we were in Rome.

Lesson XIX.

SUBJUNCTIVE — Continued.
[83–85.]

90. Lesson from the Grammar.

I. Subjunctive in Indirect Questions. Rule XLV. 525.

II. Subjunctive by Attraction. Rule XLVI. 527.

III. Subjunctive in Indirect Discourse. Rule XLVII. 529.

91. Models.

I. What a day may bring forth is uncertain.

    I. *Quid dies ferat, incertum est.*

II. I fear I shall increase the *labor*, while I wish to diminish it.

    II. *Vereor ne, dum minuĕre velim labōrem, augeam.*

III. He boasted that he had made the *ring* which he wore.

    III. *Gloriātus est, annŭlum quem habēret se confecisse.*

92. Remarks.

1. Model I. — May bring forth, *ferat*, Subj. Rule XLV.

2. Uncertain, *incertum*, Nom. Sing. Neut., to agree with the clause *quid — ferat*. See G. 438, 3; 35, III.

3. Model II. — I shall increase = lest I may increase, *ne augeam*, Subj. See G. 492, 4.

4. While I wish, *dum velim*. *Velim* is attracted into the Subjunctive by the Subjunctive *augeam*. Rule XLVI.

5. In the arrangement of words and clauses in Model II., observe (1) that the clause *dum — labōrem* is inserted in the clause *ne — augeam* (G. 604, I.), and (2) that the object *labōrem* is expressed in the in-

serted clause, *dum — labōrem*, but omitted after *augeam*. A literal rendering of the Latin would be, *I fear lest, while I wish to diminish the labor, I may increase (it)*. Emphasis places *labōrem* at the end of the clause. See G. 594, II.

6. MODEL III. — THAT HE HAD MADE, *se confecisse*, Infinitive with Subject Accusative, depending upon *gloriātus est*. See G. 550. *Se*, not *eum*, must be used, according to G. 449, I.

7. WHICH HE WORE, had, *quem habēret*. *Habēret*, Subj., because in Indirect Discourse. Rule XLVII. The Imperfect is used, because it depends upon an Historical tense, *gloriātus est*, and denotes Incomplete action. See G. 481, II. 1. In the language of the one who made the boast, the Indicative would be used, *quem habeo*.

8. The object *annŭlum* would regularly follow the subject *se*, but is here placed at the beginning of the clause because it is emphatic.

93. VOCABULARY.

Ask (a question), *interrŏgo, āre, āvi, ātum*.	Please, *placeo, ēre, ui, ĭtum*, dat. G. 385.
Do, *facio, ĕre, feci, factum*.	Say, *dico, ĕre, dixi, dictum*.
Know, *scio, ire, ivi, itum*.	Whether, *num*, adv. G. 526, I.
Not to know, *nescio, ire, ivi, ĭtum*.	Who, which (relative), *qui, quae, quod*.

94. EXERCISE.

1. What did your father say? 2. I do not know what he said. 3. He asks what I have done. 4. He asked what I had done. 5. They ask what I am doing. 6. They asked what I was doing. 7. He asked me to read the letter which he had received. 8. The preceptor praises the pupils, because they are diligent. 9. He says that he praises the pupils, because they are diligent. 10. Did not that letter please your father? 11. I asked whether that letter pleased your father.

Lesson XX.

IMPERATIVE. INFINITIVE.
[86–91.]

95. Lesson from the Grammar.

I. Imperative. Rule XLVIII. 535.
II. Subject of Infinitive. Rule XLIX. 545.
III. Infinitive as Subject. 549.
IV. Infinitive as Object. 550.

96. Models.

I. Practise justice.	I. *Justitiam cole.*
II. That a *citizen should be bound*, is a crime.	II. *Facĭnus est vincīri civem.*
III. I find that Plato came to Tarentum.	III. *Platōnem Tarentum venisse reperio.*

97. Remarks.

1. Model II. — That a citizen should be bound, *vincīri civem*, or *civem vincīri.* The latter is the common order, but in the former *vincīri* and *civem* are made emphatic. *Vincīri civem* is the subject of *est* (G. 549), and *civem* is the subject of *vincīri.* Rule XLIX.

2. Model III. — That Plato came to Tarentum, *Platōnem Tarentum venisse*, object of the active verb, *reperio.* See G. 550.

3. To Tarentum, *Tarentum.* Rule IX.

98. Vocabulary.

Ancient, *antĭquus, a, um.*	Guard, *custōdio, īre, īvi, ītum.*
Break, offend against, *viŏlo, āre, āvi, ātum.*	Parent, *parens, entis,* m. and f.
	People = nation, *popŭlus, i,* m.

Practise, *colo, ĕre, colui, cultum.* | See that, take care that, *curo, āre,*
Safe, *salvus, a, um.* | *āvi, ātum.*

99. EXERCISE.

1. Boys, obey the laws, love your parents, imitate the good. 2. Soldiers, see that you guard the city. 3. Remember the ancient valor of the Roman people. 4. It is the part of a *good* citizen to obey the laws. 5. It is the part of a wise man to practise virtue. 6. Ancus was reigning. 7. They say that Ancus was reigning. 8. We know that the city is safe. 9. Do not break the laws. 10. Imitate your father. 11. They say that the city has been taken. 12. It is true that *good* laws are useful.

LESSON XXI.

GERUNDS, SUPINES, PARTICIPLES. — PARTICLES.
[92-99.]

100. LESSON FROM THE GRAMMAR.

I. Gerunds and Gerundives. 559–566.

II. Supines. 567–570.

III. Supine in *um.* Rule L. 569.

IV. Participles. 571–581.

V. Use of Adverbs. Rule LI. 582–585.

VI. Use of Conjunctions. 587, 588.

101. MODELS.

I. The art of living. | I. *Ars vivendi.*
II. We are inclined to learn. | II. *Ad discendum propensi sumus.*

3

III. For cultivating the fields.	III. *Ad colendos agros.*
IV. By reading the orators.	IV. *Legendis oratorĭbus.*
V. He has come to congratulate you.	V. *Venit tibi gratulātum.*
VI. Plato died while writing.	VI. *Plato scribens mortuus est.*
VII. Laelius was living happily.	VII. *Laelius beāte vivēbat.*
VIII. You and Tullia are well.	VIII. *Tu et Tullia valētis.*

102. REMARKS.

1. MODEL I. — OF LIVING, *vivendi*, Gen. of Gerund, depending upon *ars.* Rule XVI.

2. MODEL III. — FOR CULTIVATING THE FIELDS, *ad colendos agros ; colendos*, Gerundive agreeing with *agros.* See G. 562. *Ad colendum agros* should not be used. See G. 562, 3 ; 565, 2.

3. MODEL IV. — *Legendis* is Gerundive, agreeing with *oratorĭbus. Legendo oratōres* may also be used.

4. MODEL V. — TO CONGRATULATE, *gratulātum*, Sup. Rule L.

5. MODEL VI. — WHILE WRITING, *scribens*, Participle, G. 578, I.

6. MODEL VIII. — ARE WELL, *valētis*, Second Pers. Plur., G. 463, 1.

103. VOCABULARY.

Act, *ago, ĕre, egi, actum.*

Agreeable, *jucundus, a, um.*

Ambassador, *legātus, i, m.*

And, *et; atque; que*, enclitic. G. 587, I. 2.

Ask for, seek, *peto, ĕre, petīvi, petītum.*

Either — or, *aut — aut*, conj.

Happily, *beāte,* adv.

Hear, *audio, īre, īvi, ītum.*

Inclined, *propensus, a, um.*

Learn, *disco, ĕre, didĭci.*

Live, *vivo, ĕre, vixi, victum.*

Neither — nor, *neque — neque ; nec — nec.*

Play, *ludo, ĕre, lusi, lusum.*

Terrify, *terreo, ĕre, ui, ītum.*

104. Exercise.

1. We are desirous of living happily. 2. The art of reading will be useful to us. 3. Are you (pl.) not desirous of learning wisdom? 4. We are desirous of learning wisdom. 5. Boys are inclined to play. 6. Men are inclined to act. 7. We learn by teaching. 8. They will send ambassadors to ask for *peace*. 9. This is agreeable *to hear*. 10. The soldiers, being terrified, fled. 11. Let us imitate the good and wise. 12. He is either in Rome or in Athens. 13. They were neither in Rome nor in Athens.

Lesson XXII.

GENDER. FORMATION OF CASES.
[106–111.]

105. Lesson from the Grammar.

I. Gender. 44, 47; 99–115, 118, 120.

II. Formation of Cases. 55–90.

106. Models.

I. He yields to the time.	I. *Tempŏri cedit.*
II. In winter and summer.	II. *Hĭĕme et aestāte.*
III. *Cato's* orations.	III. *Catōnis oratiōnes.*

107. Remarks.

1. Model I. — To the time, *tempŏri*, Dat. Rule XII.

2. Model II. — In winter, *hĭĕme*, Abl. Rule XXVIII.

3. Model III. — Cato's, *Catōnis*, Gen. Rule XVI. The Genitive

more commonly follows its noun, but may precede, especially when emphatic. G. 598, 2.

4. Give the Gender of all the nouns in the Models.

108. Vocabulary.

Battle, *proelium, ii*, n.

Brave, *fortis, e.*

Demand, *postŭlo, āre, āvi, ātum.*

Despair of, *despēro, āre, āvi, ātum,*
    with acc., or *de* with abl.

From, *a* or *ab; e* or *ex.*

Incite, *incĭto, āre, āvi, ātum.*

Incursion, *incursio, ōnis*, f.

Reward, *merces, ĕdis*, f.

Safe, secure, *tutus, a, um.*

Safety, *salus, ūtis*, f.

Small, *parvus, a, um.*

Timid, *timĭdus, a, um.*

Trumpeter, *tubĭcen, ĭnis*, m.

109. Exercise.

1. The trumpeter incites the brave soldiers to battle. 2. The brave soldiers are incited to battle by the trumpeter. 3. The citizens have despaired of safety. 4. Let us not despair *of safety.* 5. *Timid* men often despair of safety. 6. *Brave* soldiers will never despair of their country. 7. The citizens are safe from the incursions of the enemy. 8. Let us not be timid in danger. 9. A reward must be demanded. 10. We will demand a small reward.

Lesson XXIII.

GENDER AND FORMATION OF CASES — Continued.
[112–147.]

110. Vocabulary.

Admonish, *admŏneo, ēre, ui, ĭtum.*

Another, *alius, a, ud; alter, altĕ-*

ra, *altĕrum.* G. 149; 149, 3.

Bravely, *fortĭter*, adv.

Common, *commūnis, e.*
Content, *contentus, a, um.*
Easy, *facilis, e.*
Ennius, *Ennius, ii,* m.
Fight, *pugno, āre, āvi, ātum.*
Herald, *praeco, ōnis,* m.
Hope, *spes, spei,* f.
Liberate, *libĕro, āre, āvi, ātum.*
Name, *nomen, ĭnis,* n.

Not yet, *nondum,* adv.
Poem, *poēma, ătis,* n.
Proclaim, *proclāmo, āre, āvi, ātum.*
Rule, *dominatio, ōnis,* f.
Son, *filius, ii,* m.   G. 45, 5, 2).
Tyrant, *tyrannus, i,* m.
Victor, *victor, ōris,* m.
Xenophon, *Xenŏphon, ontis,* m.

111. Exercise.

1. Hope is common to all men.   2. It is easy to admonish another.   3. The *brave* soldiers fought most bravely.   4. The son of Xenophon fought bravely.   5. Xenophon heard that his son had fought bravely.   6. Herald, proclaim the name of the *victor*.   7. The names of the *victors* will be proclaimed by the heralds.   8. Have you not read the poems of Ennius?   9. I have not yet read them.   10. They liberated the city from the rule of the *tyrants*.   11. Let us be content with our books.

Lesson XXIV.

SYNOPSIS OF CONJUGATION.   FORMATION OF THE PARTS OF THE VERB.
[148–168.]

112. Lesson from the Grammar.

I. Synopsis of Conjugation.   216–226.
II. Formation of the Parts of the Verb.   240–242; 246–260.

113. Models.

I. I will write to you what I think.

II. He *will conquer* his disposition and command himself.

I. *Ad te scribam quid sentiam.*

II. *Vincet ănĭmum sibī-que imperābit.*

114. Remarks.

1. Model I. — I think, *sentiam*, Subj. in Indirect Question. See G. 525.

2. Model II. — His. The possessive should here be omitted in Latin. See G. 447.

3. Give the Principal Parts and the Synopsis of the Verbs in the Models.

115. Vocabulary.

Alba Longa, *Alba Longa, Albae Longae*, f.

Ascanius, *Ascanius, ii*, m.

Citadel, *arx, arcis*, f.

Early, ancient, *antīquus, a, um.*

Enlarge, *amplio, āre, āvi, ātum.*

Found, *condo, ĕre, dĭdi, dĭtum.*

Priscus, *Priscus, i*, m.

Romulus, *Romŭlus, i*, m.

Saturnia, *Saturnia, ae*, f.

Succeed, *succēdo, ĕre, cessi, cessum,* dat. G. 386.

Tullius, *Tullius, ii*, m.

116. Exercise.

1. The citadel was called Saturnia. 2. Did not Ascanius found a city in Italy? 3. He founded a city in *very early* times. 4. He is said to have founded a city in very early times. 5. They say that he founded a city. 6. The city was called Alba Longa. 7. Who founded Rome? 8. Romulus founded Rome. 9. Who enlarged

the city? 10. King Ancus enlarged the city. 11. Whom did *Servius Tullius* succeed? 12. King Servius succeeded Tarquinius Priscus.

LESSON XXV.

FORMATION OF THE PARTS OF VERBS — CONTINUED.
[169–184.]

117. VOCABULARY.

Against, *contra, in,* prep. with acc.

Camillus, *Camillus, i,* m.

Conspire, *conjūro, āre, āvi, ātum.*

Fable, *fabŭla, ae,* f.

Field, *ager, agri,* m.

Fire, *ignis, ignis,* m.

Lay waste, *vasto, āre, āvi, ātum.*

Porsena, *Porsĕna, ae,* m.

Relate, *narro, āre, āvi, ātum.*

Sword, *ferrum, i,* n., lit. *iron ;* with fire and sword, *ferro ignĕque.*

With, *cum,* prep. with abl.

Youth, *juvĕnis, is,* m. and f.

118. EXERCISE.

1. What ought to be done? 2. I will ask thy father what ought to be done. 3. Ask your father what ought to be done. 4. Who conquered the enemy? 5. Camillus is said to have conquered the enemy. 6. They were conquered in a great battle. 7. The youths conspired against king Porsena. 8. Will you (pl.) not make peace with the enemy? 9. We are making peace with the enemy. 10. I will relate to you this fable. 11. The enemy will lay waste the fields with fire and sword.

LESSON, XXVI.

FORMATION OF THE PARTS OF VERBS — CONTINUED.
[185–200.]

119. VOCABULARY.

Be subject to, obey, *pareo, ēre, ui, ĭtum*, dat.

Cannae, *Cannae, ārum*, f. pl.

Carthaginian, *Poenus, i*, m.; *Carthaginiensis, is*, m. and f.

Fight, battle, *pugna, ae*, f.

Formerly, *quondam*, adv.

Friendly, *amĭcus, a, um*.

In vain, *frustra*, adv.

Naval, *navālis, e ;* naval battle,

naval engagement, *pugna navālis*.

New Carthage, *Carthāgo Nova, Carthagĭnis Novae*, f.

Once, *semel*, adv.

Publius, *Publius, ii*, m.

State, *civĭtas, ātis*, f.

Try, *tento, āre, āvi, ātum*.

Victory, *victoria, ae*, f.

Village, *vicus, i*, m.

120. EXERCISE.

1. Who took New Carthage? 2. Publius Scipio is said to have taken that city. 3. Peace will be tried in vain. 4. We will try peace once. 5. They called the village Cannae. 6. Many states of Italy were formerly subject to the Romans. 7. Saguntum was friendly to the Romans. 8. The Romans conquered the Carthaginians in (by) a naval battle. 9. This victory was most acceptable to the soldiers. 10. Victory is always acceptable to soldiers.

Lesson XXVII.

FORMATION OF THE PARTS OF VERBS — Continued.
[201–214.]

121. Vocabulary.

Among, *inter*, prep. with acc.

Booty, *praeda, ae,* f.

Caesar, *Caesar, ăris,* m.

Capua, *Capua, ae,* f.

Cleopatra, *Cleopătra, ae,* f.

Coat of mail, *lorīca, ae,* f.

Come to the relief of, *subvĕnio, īre, vēni, ventum.*

Divide, *divĭdo, ĕre, vīsi, vīsum.*

Egypt, *Aegyptus, i,* f.

Find, *invĕnio, īre, vēni, ventum.*

Golden, *aureus, a, um.*

Mithridates, *Mithriddtes, is,* m.

Nile, *Nilus, i,* m.

Ptolemy, *Ptolemaeus, i,* m.

Queen, *regīna, ae,* f.

School, *ludus, i,* m.

Sulla, *Sulla, ae,* m.

122. Exercise.

1. Will you not come to the relief of your country? 2. We ask you to come to the relief of your country. 3. He says that he will come to the relief of his country. 4. By whom was *Mithridates* conquered? 5. He was conquered in many battles by Sulla. 6. He was conquered in Greece. 7. This school was at Capua. 8. Cleopatra was queen of Egypt. 9. The soldiers will divide the booty among themselves. 10. Ptolemy, king of Egypt, was conquered by Caesar. 11. The king's golden coat of mail was found in the Nile.

Lesson XXVIII.

IRREGULAR, DEFECTIVE, AND IMPERSONAL VERBS.
[215–221.]

123. Lesson from the Grammar.

I. Irregular Verbs.   287–296.

II. Defective Verbs.   297.

III. Impersonal Verbs.   298–301.

124. Models.

I. Who proposed the law ?

II. I should prefer to be Phidias.

III. They began to be credulous.

IV. It is proper that this should be done.

I. *Quis legem tulit?*

II. *Ego me Phidiam esse mallem.*

III. *Credŭli esse coepērunt.*

IV. *Hoc fĭĕri oportet.*

125. Remarks.

1. Model II. — Should prefer, *mallem*, Potential Subj. See G. 485.

2. To be = that I should be, *me esse*, depending upon *mallem*. See G. 551, II.

3. Model III. — Credulous, *credŭli*, Nom., agreeing with the subject of *coepērunt*. See G. 547, I.

4. Model IV. — That this should be done, *hoc fĭĕri*, subject of *oportet*. See G. 549, 1.

5. Give the Synopsis of the Irregular, Defective, and Impersonal Verbs in the Models.

126. Vocabulary.

Approve, *probo, āre, āvi, ātum.*

Be able, can, *possum, posse, potui.*

Forces, *copiae, ārum,* f. pl.

From, out of, *e, ex,* prep. with abl. G. 434, 3.

Gaul, the country, *Gallia, ae,* f.

Gaul, a Gaul, *Gallus, i,* m.

Lacedaemonian, *Lacedaemonius, ii,* m.

Lead out, *edūco, ĕre, duxi, ductum.*

Leonidas, *Leonĭdas, ae,* m.

Occupy, *occŭpo, āre, āvi, ātum.*

Plan, *consilium, ii,* n.

Renew, *instauro, āre, āvi, ātum.*

Return, go back, *redeo, ĭre, ii, ĭtum.*

So, so greatly, to such an extent, *adeo,* adv.

Thermopylae, *Thermopўlae, ārum,* f. pl.

Wage against, *infĕro, ferre, tŭli, illātum.*

127. Exercise.

1. Caesar was waging war against the Gauls.   2. War has been waged against us.   3. Caesar had returned from Gaul to Rome.   4. Leonidas was king of the Lacedaemonians.   5. The Lacedaemonians sent their king Leonidas to occupy Thermopylae.   6. We led out our forces from the city.   7. The enemy were so terrified that they fled.   8. Were they able to renew the war?   9. They were not able to renew the war.   10. Do you (pl.) not approve my plan?   11. We approve it.   12. It will be approved by all.

Lesson XXIX.

IRREGULAR, DEFECTIVE, AND IMPERSONAL VERBS —
CONTINUED.
[222–229.]

128. Vocabulary.

Begin, *coepi, coepisse.*

Engagement, fight, *proelium, ii,* n., *pugna, ae,* f.

Finish, bring to a close, *finio, īre, īvi, ītum.*

Leuctra, *Leuctra, ōrum,* n. pl.

Observe, *servo, āre, āvi, ātum.*

Six, *sex,* indecl.

Wish, *volo, velle, volui.*

129. Exercise.

1. Did not the enemy fortify the city? 2. They began to fortify the city. 3. Do you (pl.) not *wish* to fortify the city? 4. We *wish* to fortify it. 5. *Shall* we not *be able* to fortify it? 6. You (pl.) *will be able* to fortify it. 7. The war was brought to a close (finished) by a *naval* engagement. 8. Will you (pl.) not give me this book as a present? 9. We will give you *six books* as a present. 10. This peace will be observed many years. 11. The Lacedaemonians were conquered at Leuctra.

Lesson XXX.

IRREGULAR, DEFECTIVE, AND IMPERSONAL VERBS —
CONTINUED.
[230–245.]

130. Vocabulary.

Agis, *Agis, ĭdis,* m.

Chaeronea, *Chaeronēa, ae,* f.

Conceal, *celo, āre, āvi, ātum.*

Joy, *gaudium, ii,* n.

Liberty, *libertas, ātis*, f.

Pericles, *Pericles, is*, m.

Philip, *Philippus, i*, m.

Prefer, would rather, *malo, malle, malui*.

Present, *dono, āre, āvi, ātum.*

Preside over, *praesum, esse, fui.*

Recover, *recupĕro, āre, āvi, ātum.*

Republic, *res publĭca, rei publĭcae*, f.

131. EXERCISE.

1. Pericles at that time presided over the republic. 2. He is said to have presided over the republic many years. 3. Philip wished to wage war against the Athenians. 4. War was waged by Philip against the Athenians. 5. Philip conquered the Athenians at Chaeronea. 6. The victor wished to conceal his joy. 7. Many wish to rule. 8. I prefer to obey. 9. The Athenians wished to present the general with a golden crown. 10. The Lacedaemonians wished to recover their liberty.

PART SECOND.

LATIN SYNTAX.

Lesson XXXI.

SUBJECT AND PREDICATE.
[1, 3.][1]

132. Lesson from the Grammar.

I. Case of Subject. 367.

II. Agreement of Verb. 460.

III. Arrangement of Subject and Predicate. 593.

IV. Effect of Emphasis and Euphony. 594.

133. Models.

I. Scipio was made consul.

II. Demosthenes himself does not satisfy *us*.

I. *Scipio factus est consul.*

II. *Nobis non satisfăcit ipse Demosthĕnes.*

---

[1] This portion of the work is intended to accompany the reading of Caesar's Commentaries on the Gallic War. The enclosed numerals standing at the beginning of each lesson refer to Books and Chapters in that work. Thus [1, 3] denotes Book I. Chap. III., and shows that this lesson is to be learned after the pupil has read the first three Chapters of the first Book.

134. REMARKS.

1. MODEL II. — DEMOSTHENES HIMSELF, *ipse Demosthĕnes.* These words, which would regularly stand at the beginning of the sentence, are placed at the end because emphatic. See G. 594, II.

2. Us, *nobis*, Dative depending upon *satisfăcit.* Rule XII. See also G. 385, 2. *Nobis*, being emphatic, stands at the beginning of the sentence. G. 594, I.

135. VOCABULARY.

Accomplish, *confĭcio, ĕre, fēci, fec-tum.*

Adjacent, nearest, *proxĭmus, a, um.* G. 166.

Among, with, near to, *apud*, prep. with acc.

Belgians, *Belgae, ārum*, m. pl.

Borders, territory, *fines, finium,* m. pl.

Eloquent, *elŏquens, entis.*

Establish, *confirmo, āre, āvi, ātum.*

German, *Germānus, i*, m.

He, she, it, *is, ea, id.* G. 451.

Keep from, *prohĭbeo, ĕre, ui, ĭtum.* G. 425, 2, 2).

Wage, *gero, ĕre, gessi, gestum.*

136. EXERCISE.

1. The Romans surpassed the Gauls in valor. 2. The Gauls were surpassed in valor by the Romans. 3. The Romans praised their own valor. 4. Cicero was the most eloquent of the Romans. 5. He was the most eloquent *among the Romans.* 6. The Belgians waged many wars with the Germans. 7. All these things must be accomplished by us at the same time. 8. Peace must be established with the adjacent states. 9. The enemy must be kept from our borders. 10. War must be waged in the territory of the enemy.

Lesson XXXII.

FORMS OF SUBJECT.
[1, 6.]

137. Lesson from the Grammar.

I. Subject — Noun or Pronoun, expressed or implied. 367, 1.

II. Subject — Infinitive, Clause with Conjunction, Indirect Question. 549, 492, 495, 525, 2.

III. Subject — Simple, Complex, Compound. 351, 352, 361, 1.

IV. Agreement of Verb with Compound Subject. 463.

138. Models.

I. Glory follows virtue.	I. *Gloria virtūtem sequĭtur.*
II. They are led by glory.	II. *Gloria ducuntur.*
III. That an orator should be angry is by no means becoming.	III. *Oratōrem irasci minĭme decet.*
IV. It remains for me to supplicate you (that I should supplicate you).	IV. *Relĭquum est, ut te orem.*
V. It is asked what ought to be done.	V. *Quaerĭtur quid agendum sit.*
VI. Habit and reason have made you gentle.	VI. *Consuetūdo et ratio te lenem fecērunt.*
VII. Marcus and I are well.	VII. *Ego et Marcus valēmus.*

139. Remarks.

1. Model II. — They are led, *ducuntur*. The subject is omitted, being implied in the ending of the verb. See G. 367, 2.

2. By glory, *gloria*, Abl. Rule XXI.

3. Model III. — That an orator should be angry, *oratōrem irasci*, an Infinitive with a subject, used as the subject of *decet*. See G. 549, 1.

4. By no means, *minǐme*, least, least of all things. It qualifies *decet*. Rule LI.

5. Model IV. — It remains = is left, *relǐquum est*.

6. For me to supplicate you = that I should supplicate you, *ut te orem*, a clause expressing both subject and result. See G. 495, 2. Such clauses usually follow the predicate.

7. Model V. — What ought to be done, *quid agendum sit*, indirect question, subject of *quaerǐtur*. See G. 525, 2. For the Subjunctive, see G. 525.

8. Model VII. — Marcus and I, *ego et Marcus*. In compound subjects and objects, the Latin places the first person before the second or third.

9. Are well, *valēmus*. For person, see G. 463, 1.

140. Vocabulary.

Burn, burn up, *exūro, ěre, ussi, ustum*.

Encounter, *subeo, ǐre, ii, ǐtum*. G. 295.

Helvetians, *Helvetii, ōrum*, m. pl.

Marcus, *Marcus, i*, m.

Of, concerning, *de*, prep. with abl.

Persuade, *persuādeo, ěre, suāsi, suāsum*, dat. G. 385.

Prepared, *parātus, a, um*.

Remains, it remains, *relǐquum est* (*ut* with subj.)

Speak, *dico, ěre, dixi, dictum*.

Town, *oppǐdum, i*, n.

Uncertain, *incertus, a, um*.

141. Exercise.

1. The Helvetians will burn their towns and villages.
2. *All* the towns and villages will be burned. 3. The

soldiers are prepared to encounter these dangers.   4. Marcus and I were prepared to encounter all dangers.   5. We have seen the beautiful city.   6. You and Marcus did not see that city.   7. It will be easy to persuade *your* father.   8. You and Marcus will easily persuade *my* father.   9. Whether that city was taken is uncertain. 10. It remains for me to speak of this city.

Lesson XXXIII.

FORMS OF PREDICATE.
[1, 9.]

142. Lesson from the Grammar.

I. Predicate — Verb, Noun, Adjective, Infinitive. 353, 553, I.

II. Predicate — Simple, Complex, Compound. 353, 354–356, 361, 2.

III. Agreement of Predicate with Subject. 460, 362, 438.
    1. Verb with Subject. 460.
    2. Predicate Noun with Subject. 362.
    3. Predicate Adjective with Subject. 438, 2.

143. Models.

I. The world is subject to God.

I. *Mundus Deo paret.*

II. Gorgias was a rhetorician.

II. *Gorgias fuit rhetor.*

III. The reasons are most just.

III. *Causae justissĭmae sunt.*

IV. To live is to think.

IV. *Vivĕre est cogitāre.*

V. He stated his opinion.

VI. These things are acceptable and agreeable to the people.

V. *Sententiam dixit.*

VI. *Haec popŭlo grata atque jucunda sunt.*

144. REMARKS.

1. MODEL III. — MOST JUST, *justissĭmae*, superlative, in the Nom. Fem. Plur. to agree with *causae*. Rule XXXIII. It may stand either before or after *sunt*.

2. MODEL IV. — To LIVE, *vivĕre*, subject of *est*. See G. 549.

3. To THINK, *cogitāre*, predicate nominative after *est*. See G. 553, I.

145. SYNONYMES.

Leader, commander; *dux, imperātor.*

1. *Dux, ducis*, m.; LEADER, GENERAL, — considered simply in his capacity as the *leader* of troops.

2. *Imperātor, ōris*, m.; COMMANDER, GENERAL, — with special reference to his authority and rank as commander, — a higher title than *dux*.

146. VOCABULARY.

Call, *appello, nomĭno, voco, āre, āvi, ātum*. See Syn. 184.

Celts, *Celtae, ārum*, m. pl.

Commander, *imperātor, ōris*, m.

Fear, *metuo, ĕre, ui*. G. 274.

Language, tongue, *lingua, ae*, f.

Leader, *dux, ducis*, m. and f.

Not only — but also, *non solum — sed etiam*.

147. EXERCISE.

1. The Gauls were the enemies of the Romans. 2. We have been called the friends of the *Gauls*. 3. The Gauls were called in their language Celts. 4. The Belgi-

ans were very brave.   5. Caesar was the commander of the Romans.   6. The Romans did not fear the leaders of the *enemy*.   7. The Romans called Cicero the father of his country.   8. Peace and friendship will be established with the enemy.   9. It is easy to encounter these dangers. 10. The Romans not only waged war with the Gauls, but also conquered them.

Lesson XXXIV.

FORMS OF MODIFIERS.
[1, 12.]

148. Lesson from the Grammar.

I. Modifiers of Subject — Adjectives, Nouns, 352.

II. Modifiers of Verb Predicate — Objective Modifiers, Adverbial Modifiers.   354.

III. Modifiers of Predicate Noun.   352, 355.

IV. Modifiers of Predicate Adjective.   356.

V. Position of Modifiers in the Sentence.   598–601.

149. Models.

I. Good men love equity.

I. *Viri boni aequitātem amant.*

II. The name of peace is pleasing.

II. *Nomen pacis est dulce.*

III. I greatly feared the voyage.

III. *Navigatiōnem valde timēbam.*

IV. Justice is the queen of virtues.

IV. *Justitia est regīna virtūtum.*

| V. Virtue is productive of pleasure. | V. *Virtus est efficiens voluptātis.* |

150. REMARKS.

1. MODEL III. — GREATLY, *valde.* An adverb used with an object generally stands directly before the verb, *valde timēbam.*

2. I FEARED, *timēbam* or *timui.* The latter would express simply the *fact*, I feared, while the former denotes the *continuance* of the fear, I feared = I was fearing.

3. MODEL V. — OF PLEASURE, *voluptātis.* Rule XVII. Such a genitive may either precede or follow its adjective.

151. VOCABULARY.

Arar, *Arar, āris,* m.; acc. *Arārim.*	Lead across, *tradūco, ĕre, duxi, ductum.*
Army, *exercĭtus, us,* m.	
Endeavor, *conor, āri, ātus sum,* dep.	Order, *jubeo, ĕre, jussi, jussum.*
	Orgetorix, *Orgetŏrix, ĭgis,* m.
Labienus, *Labiēnus, i,* m.	River, *flumen, ĭnis,* n.

152. EXERCISE.

1. The soldiers greatly feared the valor of the *brave* Helvetians. 2. Caesar, the commander of the *Roman army*, conquered the enemy. 3. The leaders of the enemy were conquered in many battles. 4. He *ordered* the beautiful towns to be burned. 5. Orgetorix formed this conspiracy. 6. He *endeavored* to persuade all the states to wage war with Caesar. 7. He said that this plan would be useful to all the states. 8. Cicero was called the father of his country. 9. This state formerly waged war with the Roman people. 10. Labienus led his forces across the river Arar.

Lesson XXXV.

INTERROGATIVE AND IMPERATIVE SENTENCES.
[1, 15.]

153. Lesson from the Grammar.

I. Interrogative Sentences. 346, II.
    1. Single Questions. 346, II. 1.
    2. Double Questions. 346, II. 2.
    3. Answers. 346, II. 3.

II. Imperative Sentences. 346, III.

III. Moods in Imperative Sentences — Imperative, Subjunctive. 535, 488, II.

154. Models.

I. What is better than goodness?

II. Is that your fault, or ours?

III. Did he state the cause? He did.

IV. Save yourselves.

V. Use your strength.

I. *Quid est melius bonitāte?*

II. *Utrum ea vestra, an nostra culpa est?*

III. *Dixitne causam? Dixit.*

IV. *Conservāte vos.*

V. *Robŏre utāre.*

155. Remarks.

1. Model I. — Than goodness, *quam bonĭtas*, or *bonitāte*. We will use the latter form, which may stand either before or after *melius*. For the ablative, see Rule XXIII.

2. Model III. — He did = he did state it, *dixit*. See G. 346, II. 3.

156. SYNONYMES.

Road, way, path; *via, iter, semĭta.*

1. *Via, ae,* f.; ROAD, WAY, — the usual route.

2. *Iter, itinĕris,* n.; (1), ROAD, WAY, — the direct route; (2), JOURNEY, MARCH, — the progress made.

3. *Semĭta, ae,* f.; PATH, FOOT-PATH.

157. VOCABULARY.

Four, *quattuor,* indecl.

Helvetian, *Helvetius, a, um.*

How large, *quantus, a, um.*

Journey, *iter, itinĕris,* n.

Narrow, *angustus, a, um.*

Path, *semĭta, ae,* f.

Province, *provincia, ae,* f.

Road, *via, ae,* f.

Route, *iter, itinĕris,* n.

Show, *monstro, āre, āvi, ātum.*

Through, *per,* prep. with acc.

158. EXERCISE.

1. Did you call Caesar the friend of the Gauls? 2. We cannot call Caesar the friend of the Gauls. 3. How large a force had Caesar? 4. I do not know how large a force he had. 5. Did he not make a journey through the Roman province? 6. How many roads are there to the city? 7. There are four roads to the city. 8. I will show you the *nearest* route. 9. This path is very narrow. 10. Was Orgetorix a Roman or a Helvetian? 11. He was a Helvetian. 12. Who was the *bravest* of the Helvetians? 13. Orgetorix. 14. Do not wage war with the Romans. 15. Let us bravely encounter these dangers.

• LESSON XXXVI.

COMPLEX AND COMPOUND SENTENCES.
[1, 19.]

159. LESSON FROM THE GRAMMAR.

I. Complex Sentences. 357–359.

II. Compound Sentences. 360.

III. Compound Sentences — Abridged. 361.

160. MODELS.

I. The reasons which you mention are most just.

II. The name of peace is delightful, and the thing itself beneficial.

III. *Preserve* yourselves, *your* wives, your children, and your fortunes.

IV. Who would seek honor (as eagerly) as he would avoid ignominy?

V. We love equity and right.

I. *Causae quas comměmŏras justissĭmae sunt.*

II. *Nomen pacis dulce est, et ipsa res salutāris.*

III. *Conservāte vos, conjŭges, libĕros, fortunasque vestras.*

IV. *Quis honōrem tam expĕtat quam ignominiam fugiat?*

V. *Aequitātem et jus amāmus.*

161. REMARKS.

1. Observe that the first model is a complex sentence with the relative clause, *quas commemŏras;* that the second is a compound sentence, consisting of two members connected by *et*, and that the third has a compound object, *vos — vestras.*

2. MODEL I. — WHICH, *quas*, in the Fem. Plur. to agree with its antecedent, according to Rule XXXIV., and in the Accus. as the object of *commemŏras*, according to Rule V.

3. MODEL II. — THE THING ITSELF, *ipsa res*. *Res* is the subject of *est*, understood.

4. MODEL III. — YOURSELVES, *vos*. *Ipsos* need not be added. For this reflexive use of *vos*, see G. 448.

5. YOUR, *vestras*, expressed but once; here with the last object, *fortūnas*. If not emphatic, it would here be omitted. See G. 447.

162. VOCABULARY.

Aeduans, *Aedui, ōrum*, m. pl.

Ancient, *antiquus, a, um, pristīnus, a, um*.[1]

Cavalry, *equitātus, us*, m.

Command, be in command of, *praesum, esse, fui*, dat. G. 386.

Cross, *transeo, īre, ii, ītum*.

Dumnorix, *Dumnŏrix, īgis*, m.

Flow into, *influo, ĕre, fluxi, fluxum*.

Into, *in*, prep. with acc.

Lake, *lacus, us*, m.

Lemannus, *Lemannus, i*, m.

Remember, *reminiscor, i*, dep. G. 406, II.

Rhone, *Rhodănus, i*, m.

163. EXERCISE.

1. *How large a force* Caesar had at that time is uncertain. 2. Whether those cities could be taken was uncertain. 3. They say that the Gauls were surpassed in valor by the Romans. 4. We crossed the river which flows into lake Lemannus. 5. The river which we crossed is called the Rhone. 6. The enemy must be conquered and their cities must be taken. 7. Dumnorix, who commanded the cavalry of the *Aeduans*, fled. 8. Let us not establish peace and friendship with the enemy. 9. *Let us remember* the ancient valor of the Romans.

---

[1] *Antiquus* refers to the remote past; while *pristīnus* generally refers to the more recent past, or else has the force of *primitive, pristine*.

4

Lesson XXXVII.

AGREEMENT OF NOUNS.
[1, 24.]

164. Lesson from the Grammar.

I. Agreement of Predicate Nouns.   362.

II. Agreement of Appositives.   363.

165. Models.

I. Virtues are the attendants and companions of wisdom.

I. *Virtūtes sunt ministrae comitesque sapientiae.*

II. Artemisia was the wife of *Mausolus,* king of Caria.

II. *Artemisia Mausŏli, Cariae regis, uxor fuit.*

III. Two most powerful cities, Carthage and Numantia, were destroyed by Scipio.

III. *Duae urbes potentissĭmae, Carthāgo atque Numantia, a Scipiōne sunt delētae.*

IV. He learned when a boy what deserved to be learned.

IV. *Puer didĭcit, quod discendum fuit.*

166. Remarks.

1. Model I. — Attendants, *ministrae,* not *ministri,* to agree in gender with *virtūtes.* See G. 362, 1, 1).

2. Model II. — King of Caria, *Cariae regis,* or *regis Cariae. Regis* is in the Gen. in apposition with *Mausŏli.* The whole sentence could be arranged in the English order: *Artemisia fuit uxor Mausŏli, regis Cariae.* But in that form it would lose not only in point of euphony, but also of compactness; the modifier, *regis Cariae,* would be merely an

awkward addition to the sentence, while in the model it is incorporated into the very structure of the sentence itself.

3. Model III. — Two most powerful cities, *duae urbes potentissĭmae.* Here *potentissĭmae* qualifies *urbes,* while *duae* qualifies the complex idea, *urbes potentissĭmae;* not *two cities,* but *two most powerful cities.* In such cases one adjective often precedes the noun, while the other follows it, as in the model, though both may either precede or follow the noun.

4. Model IV. — When a boy, *puer,* in apposition with the omitted subject of *didĭcit.* See G. 363, 2 and 3.

5. Deserved to be learned, *discendum fuit,* Periphrastic Conjugation. See G. 231.

167. Synonymes.

Custom, usage, habit; *consuetūdo, mos.*

1. *Consuetūdo, ĭnis,* f.; custom, usage, habit, — the generic word for custom of any kind.

2. *Mos, moris,* m.; custom, — used chiefly of approved and established customs, especially if national. *Mores,* plur., character.

168. Vocabulary.

Caria, *Caria, ae,* f.	Nature, *natūra, ae,* f.
Custom, habit, *consuetūdo, ĭnis,* f.;	Numantia, *Numantia, ae,* f.
mos, moris, m.	Powerful, *potens, entis.*
Destroy, *deleo, ēre, ēvi, ētum.*	Second, another, *alter, ĕra, ĕrum.*
Excellent, *praeclārus, a, um.*	G. 149; 149, 2.
Mausolus, *Mausōlus, i,* m.	

169. Exercise.

1. Mausolus was at that time king of *Caria.* 2. Rome was for many years a most powerful city. 3. They say that Carthage was formerly a most powerful city. 4. Did

you not say that Caesar was the commander of the *Roman army*? 5. Cicero says that the two cities, Carthage and Numantia, were destroyed by Scipio, the commander of the *Roman army*. 6. Habit is a second nature. 7. We say that habit is a second nature. 8. From whom (pl.) did you receive that *excellent* custom? 9. We received this *excellent* custom from our fathers.

Lesson XXXVIII.

NOMINATIVE AND VOCATIVE.
[1, 29.]

170. Lesson from the Grammar.

I. Nominative as Subject. 367.

II. Nominative in Agreement with another Nominative. 368.

III. Vocative. 369.

171. Models.

I. Socrates was condemned.	I. *Socrătes damnātus est.*
II. Themistocles the commander liberated Greece from servitude.	II. *Themistŏcles imperātor servitūte Graeciam liberāvit.*
III. I approve your decision, Brutus.	III. *Tuum, Brute, judicium probo.*

172. Remarks.

1. Model II. — The commander, *imperātor*, Nom. in apposition with the Nom. *Themistŏcles.* Rule II.

2. From servitude, *servitūte*, Abl. of Separation. Rule XXVII.

See also G. 425, 3. *Servitūte* may stand either before or after the direct object, *Graeciam.*

3. Model III. — Your, *tuum.* The possessive should here be expressed to avoid ambiguity.

4. Brutus, *Brute.* For the place of the Vocative in the sentence, see G. 602, VI.

173. Vocabulary.

Allobroges, *Allobrŏges*, um, m. pl.	Junius, *Junius*, ii, m.
Collatinus, *Collatīnus*, i, m.	Lucius, *Lucius*, ii, m.
Condemn, *damno*, āre, āvi, ātum.	Lucullus, *Lucullus*, i, m.
Crassus, *Crassus*, i, m.	Mercury, *Mercurius*, ii, m.
First, *primus*, a, um. G. 166.	Numitor, *Numĭtor*, ōris, m.
Geneva, *Genēva*, ae, f.	Quintus, *Quintus*, i, m.
God, *deus*, dei, m. G. 45, 6.	Rich, *dives*, ĭtis. G. 165, 2.
Grandson, *nepos*, ōtis, m.	When, interrog., *quando*, adv.

174. Exercise.

1. Crassus and Lucullus were the richest of the Romans. 2. Mercury was the messenger of the *gods.* 3. Romulus, the first king of the Romans, was the grandson of *Numitor.* 4. We *have praised* the good, and we *have been praised* by the good. 5. Caesar says that Geneva is a town of the Allobroges. 6. Lucius Junius Brutus and Lucius Tarquinius Collatinus were made consuls. 7. When, Labienus, will you cross the river? 8. Why, O judges, did you condemn Socrates? 9. Marcus Tullius Cicero and Quintus Tullius Cicero were brothers.

Lesson XXXIX.

ACCUSATIVE AS DIRECT OBJECT.
[1, 32.]

175. Lesson from the Grammar.

Accusative as Direct Object. 371.
    1. Cognate Accusative. 371, 1.
    2. Accusative with other Cases. 371, 2.
    3. Transitive and Intransitive Verbs. 371, 3.
    4. Accusative with Compounds. 371, 4.
    5. Clause as Object. 371, 5.
    6. Passive Construction. 371, 6.

176. Models.

I. Brutus freed his country.	I. *Brutus patriam liberāvit.*
II. They live a secure life.	II. *Tutam vitam vivunt.*
III. They wrote laws for their states.	III. *Leges civitatĭbus suis scripsērunt.*
IV. They were sighing over these things.	IV. *Haec gemēbant.*
V. He crossed the Euphrates.	V. *Euphrātem transiit.*
VI. You know that I think the same.	VI. *Scis me idem sentīre.*

177. Remarks.

1. Model III. — Their states, *civitatĭbus suis*, Dat. Rule XII. See also 371, 2. These words may stand either before or after the direct object, *leges*. See G. 600, 3. *Suis* must be expressed to avoid ambiguity.

2. Model IV. — These things, *haec* or *has res*. The former is preferable, because it is shorter and equally clear.

3. Model V. — *Euphrātem.* See G. 371, 4.

4. Model VI. — That I think the same, *me idem sentire*, object of *scis*. G. 371, 5. For the case of *me*, see G. 545; for that of *idem*, 371, 1, 3).

178. Synonymes.

Army; *exercĭtus, agmen, acies.*

1. *Exercĭtus, i,* m. (*exerceo*) ; army, — the generic word for army, as composed of disciplined men.

2. *Agmen, agmĭnis,* n. (*ago*) ; army on the march.

3. *Acies, ēi,* f.; army in battle array; line of battle.

179. Vocabulary.

Army (on the march), *agmen, ĭnis,* n.

Arrange (a line of battle), *instruo, ĕre, struxi, structum.*

As, relat. after *idem, qui, quae, quod.*

Attack, *adorior, ĭri, ortus sum,* dep.

Base, *turpis, e.*

Boast, make a boast, *glorior, āri, ātus sum,* dep.

Both — and, *et — et.*

Camp, *castra, ōrum,* n. pl. G. 132.

Encamp, *castra pono, ĕre, posui, posĭtum.*

Ford, *vadum, i,* n.

Immense, *ingens, entis.*

Laelius, *Laelius, ii,* m. G. 45, 5, 2).

Large, *magnus, a, um.*

Lead (a life), live, *vivo, ĕre, vixi, victum.*

Life, *vita, ae,* f.

Line of battle, *acies, aciēi,* f.

March, journey, *iter, itinĕris,* n.; on the march, *in itinĕre.*

Now, *nunc,* adv.

Number, *numĕrus, i,* m.

Place, *locus, i,* m. G. 141.

Rhine, *Rhenus, i,* m.

Take, carry, *porto, āre, āvi, ātum.*

Think, judge, *sentio, ĭre, sensi, sensum.*

Useless, *inutĭlis, e.*

180. EXERCISE..

1. Have you not many friends? 2. Both you and I have a very large number of friends. 3. An *immense* army crossed the Rhine and encamped in Gaul. 4. The commander of the *enemy* arranged his line of battle. 5. The enemy will attack our army on the march. 6. At *this place* the Rhine is crossed by a ford. 7. *You,* Laelius, have lived a *most happy* life. 8. Has he not led a *useless* life? 9. Do not lead a *base* life. 10. Did you not make that boast? 11. I made the *same* boast as you. 12. We will endeavor to take with us all the *grain* which we now have. 13. You think the same as all *good* men. .

LESSON XL.

TWO ACCUSATIVES.
[1, 37.]

181. LESSON FROM THE GRAMMAR.

I. Two Accusatives — Same Person. 373.
    1. Predicate Accusative. 373, 1.
    2. Verbs with Predicate Accusative. 373, 2.
    3. Adjective as Predicate Accusative. 373, 3.
    4. Passive Construction. 373, 4.

II. Two Accusatives — Person and Thing. 374.
    1. Person and Thing — Active and Passive. 374, 1.
    2. Verbs with two Accusatives. 374, 2.

182. Models.

I. Panaetius calls Plato the Homer of philosophers.	I. *Panaetius Platōnem Homērum philosophōrum appellat.*
II. Panaetius calls Plato divine.	II. *Panaetius Platōnem divīnum appellat.*
III. I was asked my opinion.	III. *Ego sententiam rogātus sum.*
IV. I ask of you this favor.	IV. *Te hoc beneficium rogo.*
V. We will surely retain in memory that which you have taught us.	V. *Quod nos docuisti, id certe memoria retinebĭmus.*

183. Remarks.

1. Model III. — My opinion, *sententiam.* Rule VII. The Possessive is omitted. See G. 447.

2. Model V. — In memory = by means of memory, *memoria*, Abl. of Means. Rule XXI. The relative clause often precedes the antecedent clause, as in this model (G. 604, II.), and then the antecedent itself generally stands at the beginning of its own clause.

184. Synonymes.

To call, to name; *appello, voco, nomĭno.*

1. *Appello, āre, āvi, ātum;* (1) TO CALL, TO NAME, — especially with the idea of calling a person (or thing) by his true name, or of giving him a characteristic title; (2) TO ADDRESS.

2. *Voco, āre, āvi, ātum;* (1) TO CALL, — generally with special reference to *pronouncing* or *speaking* the name; (2) TO SUMMON, INVITE.

3. *Nomĭno, āre, āvi, ātum;* TO NAME, — to give a name.

185. Vocabulary.

Ariovistus, *Ariovistus, i,* m.
Blind, *caecus, a, um.*
Calamity, *calamitas, atis,* f.
Conceal, *celo, are, avi, atum.*
Dinner, *coena, ae,* f.
Favor, *faveo, ere, favi, fautum.*
Fortune, *fortuna, ae,* f.

Invite, *voco, are, avi, atum.*
Make, *efficio, ere, feci, fectum.*
Mourn over, *maereo, ere.* G. 268.
Name, *nomen, inis,* n.
Name, to name, call, *nomino; ap-
pello; voco, are, avi, atum.*
Senate, *senatus, us,* m.

186. Exercise.

1. The senate called Ariovistus king and friend. 2. Let us call the commander of the army by his own name. 3. I have invited your brother to dinner. 4. Romulus ordered the city to be called Rome from his own name. 5. Fortune often makes those whom she favors *blind*. 6. You have made your life happy and useful. 7. Who taught the Belgians the arts of war? 8. Were not the Germans taught the arts of war by Ariovistus? 9. Why were we not asked our opinion? 10. Let us ask them their opinion. 11. They will mourn over this calamity. 12. I will not conceal from you my opinion.

Lesson XLI.

TWO ACCUSATIVES — Continued. SPECIAL CONSTRUCTIONS.
[1, 40.]

187. Lesson from the Grammar.

I. Special Constructions. 374, 3.
    1. With *Celo.* 374, 3, 1).

2. With Verbs of Teaching. 374, 3, 2).

3. With Verbs of Asking, Demanding. 374, 3, 3).

4. With *Peto, Postŭlo, Quaerq.* 374, 3, 4).

II. Infinitive, or Clause, as Accusative of Thing. 374, 4.

III. Neuter Pronoun, or Adjective, as Accusative of Thing. 374, 5.

IV. Two Accusatives with Compounds. 374, 6.

188. Models.

I. You were kept ignorant of the most important things.	I. *Maxĭmis de rebus celātus es.*
II. He taught Socrates to play on the lyre.	II. *Socrătem fidĭbus docuit.*
III. I ask you in regard to the same things.	III. *Te iisdem de rebus interrŏgo.*
IV. He asks this from the king.	IV. *Hoc a rege petit.*
V. He teaches you to be wise.	V. *Te sapĕre docet.*
VI. Philosophy taught us to know ourselves.	VI. *Philosophia nos docuit ut nosmet ipsos noscerēmus.*
VII. He admonished me of it.	VII. *Id me monuit.*
VIII. He led his forces over the Rhone.	VIII. *Rhodănum copias trajēcit.*

189. Remarks.

1. Model I. — Of = concerning, in regard to, *de.* G. 434.

2. The most important, greatest, things, *maxĭmis rebus.* *Maxĭmis* alone would not distinguish *things* from *persons.* An emphatic adjective belonging to a noun with a preposition is often placed before

the preposition. Hence *maxĭmis de rebus;* also *iisdem de rebus,* in Model III.

3. MODEL II. — To PLAY UPON THE LYRE, in the Latin idiom WITH THE LYRE, *fidĭbus,* Abl. of Means. Rule XXI.

4. MODEL V. — To BE WISE, *sapĕre.* This simply supplies the place of one accusative after *docet.* He teaches you to be wise, i. e. teaches you wisdom. G. 374, 4.

5. MODEL VI. — To KNOW OURSELVES = that we should know ourselves, *ut nosmet ipsos noscerēmus.* G. 374, 4. For the mood of *noscerēmus,* see G. 492, and for the tense, 481, II. 1. For the difference in force between this clause and the infinitive, as used in Model V., see G. 554, II. and III.

6. MODEL VIII. — HE LED OVER, *trajēcĭt,* lit. *threw over,* or *across.*

7. HIS FORCES, *copias;* possessive omitted.

190. VOCABULARY.

Across, *trans,* prep. with acc.

Admonish, *moneo, ēre, ui, ĭtum.*

Demand, *postŭlo, āre, āvi, ātum.*

Depart, *discēdo, ĕre, cessi, cessum.*

Home, *domus, us* or *i,* f. G. 117, 1.

In regard to, *de,* prep. with abl.

Inform, teach, *doceo, ēre, docui, doctum.*

It is permitted, *licet, licuit* or *licĭtum est,* impers. G. 299.

Keep in ignorance, *celo, āre, āvi, ātum.* To keep ignorant of (in regard to), *celo de.*

Multitude, *multitŭdo, ĭnis,* f.

No, *nullus, a, um.* G. 149.

Of = from, *a, ab,* prep. with abl.

191. EXERCISE.

1. Did they not ask these favors from Caesar? 2. We will ask no favors from Marcus. 3. We will not keep you in ignorance *in regard to this calamity.* 4. Caesar was not kept ignorant of these plans. 5. They informed Caesar in regard to the plans of the enemy. 6. The soldier will ask from his commander to be permitted to

depart to his home.   7. Of what will he admonish them?
8. What did he at the same time demand of Ariovistus?
9. He demanded *of him* that he should not lead the Germans into Gaul.   10. The king had already led a multitude of Germans across the Rhine into Gaul.   .

Lesson XLII.

ACCUSATIVE AS SUBJECT OF INFINITIVE.   IN AGREEMENT WITH ANOTHER ACCUSATIVE.
[1, 44.]

192. Lesson from the Grammar.

I. Accusative as Subject of an Infinitive.   545.

II. Accusative in Agreement with another Accusative.   362, 363.

    1. As Predicate Accusative.   362; 373, 1.

    2. As Appositive.   363.

193. Models.

I. You know that I speak Latin.

I. *Scis me Latine loqui.*

II. I rejoice that you recommend that to me.

II. *Gaudeo id te mihi suadēre.*

III. They called Cicero the father of his country.

III. *Cicerōnem patrem patriae nominavērunt.*

IV. Marcellus took the city of Syracuse.

IV. *Marcellus urbem Syracūsas cepit.*

194. REMARKS.

1. MODEL I. — THAT I SPEAK, *me loqui*, object of *scis*. See Rule V., also G. 371, 5; 550. ME, subject of *loqui*. Rule XLIX.

2. LATIN = in Latin, *Latīne*, adverb qualifying *loqui*. Rule LI. Observe the difference of idiom between the English and the Latin.

3. MODEL II. — *Id*, being emphatic, is placed at the beginning of the infinitive clause, even before the subject *te*. G. 594, I.

4. MODEL IV. — THE CITY OF SYRACUSE, Latin idiom, THE CITY SYRACUSE, *urbem Syracūsas*. Rule II.

195. VOCABULARY.

For, in behalf of, *pro*, prep. with abl.

Gracchus, *Gracchus, i*, m.

Greek, in Greek, *Graece*, adv.

Latin, in Latin, *Latīne*, adv.

Nasica, *Nasīca, ae*, m.

Tiberius, *Tiberius, ii*, m.

Twice, *bis*, adv.

196. EXERCISE.

1. The Roman people made Cicero consul. 2. Did you not say that Cicero was consul at that time? 3. I said that Tiberius Gracchus was at that time consul. 4. They say that Publius Scipio Nasica was twice consul. 5. We know that you have been called wise. 6. Do you not know that Cicero spoke both Latin and Greek? 7. They say that Marcus already speaks Latin. 8. Why did you teach him to speak Latin? 9. He will come *with a large army* to take the city of Geneva. 10. We know that you are always prepared to encounter dangers for your country.

Lesson XLIII.

ACCUSATIVE IN AN ADVERBIAL SENSE. IN EXCLA-
MATIONS.
[1, 49.]

197. Lesson from the Grammar.

I. Accusative of Time and Space. 378.
    1. Accusative with *Per.* 378, 1.

II. Accusative of Limit. 879.
    1. Accusative with *Ad.* 379, 1.
    2. *Urbs* or *Oppĭdum* with Preposition. 379, 2.
    3. Words like Names of Towns. 379, 3.
    4. Other Names of Places. 879, 4.

III. Accusative of Specification. 380.
    1. In good prose only in its freer sense. 380, 2.

IV. Accusative in Exclamations. 381.

198. Models.

I. *At Athens* Pericles was for very many years the leader of the public council.

I. *Athēnis Perĭcles plurĭmos annos princeps consilii publĭci fuit.*

II. Hippias came to Olympia.

II. *Hippias Olympiam venit.*

III. There are *three* roads to Mutina.

III. *Tres sunt viae ad Mutĭnam.*

IV. Demaratus betook himself to Tarquinii, a city of Etruria.

IV. *Demarātus se contŭlit Tarquinios in urbem Etruriae.*

V. Scipio was conducted home.	V. *Scipio domum reductus est.*
VI. Latona fled to *Delos.*	VI. *Latōna confūgit Delum.*
VII. He came into Epirus.	VII. *In Epīrum venit.*
VIII. My letter will not profit you at all.	VIII. *Nihil tibi meae littĕrae prodĕrunt.*
IX. O *welcome* arrival!	IX. *O gratum adventum!*

199. REMARKS.

1. MODEL I. — AT ATHENS, *Athēnis*, Abl. of Place. Rule XXVI. Emphasis places it at the beginning of the sentence. G. 594, I.

2. MODEL III. — THERE ARE, *sunt.* ` In this signification, — *there is, there are,* — the verb *sum* generally stands before its subject, as in the model, and indeed generally at the beginning of the sentence; but here *tres* is emphatic, and takes the first place.

3. MODEL IV. — A CITY OF ETRURIA, *in urbem Etruriae.* Observe the difference of idiom. In the English, *city* is in apposition with *Tarquinii*, while in Latin *in urbem* is treated simply as a modifier of *contŭlit,* — betook himself into a city of Etruria. *Tarquinios — Etruriae* would regularly precede *contŭlit ;* but, being emphatic, it stands at the end of the sentence.

4. MODEL VIII. — NOT AT ALL, *nihil.* Rule X. It is emphatic.

200. SYNONYMES.

Letter, epistle ; *littĕra, littĕrae, epistŏla.*

1. *Littĕra, ae,* f. ; LETTER, — of the alphabet.

2. *Littĕrae, ārum,* f. plur. ; LETTER, EPISTLE, — regarded simply as a written communication without any reference to its epistolary character.

3. *Epistŏla, ae,* f. ; LETTER, EPISTLE, — with special reference to its epistolary character.

201. Vocabulary.

Betake one's self, *se conferre; confĕro, ferre, tŭli, collātum.*

Fortunate, *fortunātus, a, um.*

Greek, *Graecus, a, um.*

Letter of the alphabet, *littĕra, ae,* f.

Letter, epistle, *littĕrae, ārum,* f.; *·epistŏla, ae,* f.

Move, *commŏveo, ĕre, mōvi, mōtum.*

Pronounce, speak, *dico, ĕre, dixi, dictum.*

Request, *rogātus, vs,* m.

202. Exercise.

1. Caesar waged war in Gaul ten years. 2. Did not the soldiers wish to return home? 3. Did you not say that Ariovistus sent ambassadors to Caesar? 4. I said so. 5. The soldiers betook themselves to the city of Geneva. 6. They betook themselves to their camp *at Geneva.* 7. Did not the Allobroges send ambassadors to the senate at Rome? 8. Cicero wrote many letters to his brother Quintus. 9. Demosthenes, when a boy, was not able to pronounce the letter R. 10. Your brother knows one Greek letter. 11. I read your letter at Rome. 12. The commander will *not* be *at all* moved by this request. 13. O happy country! 14. O fortunate city!

Lesson XLIV.

DATIVE WITH VERBS.
[1, 54.]

203. Lesson from the Grammar.

I. Dative with Verbs. 384.
    1. Dative of Advantage and Disadvantage. 385.

204. MODELS.

I. We yield to the sacred laws of our country.	I. *Sanctis patriae legĭbus obsequĭmur.*
II. I do not look with envy upon *your advantages.*	II. *Non ego invideo tuis commŏdis.*
III. My Cicero sends you greeting.	III. *Cicĕro meus tibi salūtem dicit.*
IV. *Provide for* your country.	IV. *Prospicĭte patriae.*
V. The *fountain* has the name Arethusa.	V. *Fonti nomen Arethūsa est.*
VI. What should be done by us?	VI. *Quid nobis agendum est?*
VII. What does the law mean?	VII. *Quid sibi lex vult?*
VIII. The house was an *ornament* to the city.	VIII. *Domus urbi fuit ornamento.*

205. REMARKS.

1. MODEL I. — For the order of words, see G. 598, 3.

2. MODEL II. — NON : see G. 602, IV. Why is the possessive (*tuis*) expressed with *commŏdis*, but omitted with *patriae* in Model I.? See G. 447.

3. MODEL III. — SENDS GREETING, *salūtem dicit*, lit. *says safety,* i. e. expresses his desire for your safety and health.

4. MODEL V. — THE FOUNTAIN HAS, *fonti est*, lit. *is to the fountain.*

5. MODEL VI. — BY US, *nobis*, lit. *to us.* See G. 388.

6. MODEL VII. — MEAN, *sibi vult*, lit. *wish for itself*, i. e. propose to itself.

7. MODEL VIII. — AN ORNAMENT, *ornamento*, lit. *for an ornament.* Observe the difference of idiom, but remember that the Latin sometimes employs the nominative, like the English. See G. 390, 2.

206. VOCABULARY.

Ally, *socius, ii*, n.

Be in command of, *praesum, esse, fui.*

Business, *negotium, ii*, n. To have business, *negotium, sum, esse, fui*, with dat.

Defence, *praesidium, ii*, n.

Envy, to look upon with envy, *invideo, ēre, vīdi, vīsum.*

Ephesus, *Ephĕsus, i*, f.

Especially, *maxime*, adv.

It is the intention, *in animo est, esse, fuit*, with dat. It is my intention, *mihi est in animo.*

Mean, *volo, velle, volui*, with dat.

Mind, *animus, i*, m.

207. EXERCISE.

1. I have ever favored both you and your brother. 2. The good and wise never envy the rich. 3. Praise and glory are especially envied. 4. Caesar, who is in command of the army, is especially envied. 5. It is our intention to wage war against the Romans and their allies. 6. *Ariovistus* at that time had a large army. 7. *That beautiful city* had the name of Ephesus. 8. What did these presents mean? 9. The good and wise must be praised by all. 10. What business had the Helvetians in the Roman province? 11. Virtue is a glory to all. 12. The cavalry of the Aeduans was a defence to the Roman army.

Lesson XLV.

DATIVE WITH VERBS. SPECIAL CONSTRUCTIONS.
[2, 5.]

208. Lesson from the Grammar.

I. Double Construction. 384, 1.

II. *To* or *For*, how rendered into Latin. 384, 2.

III. Accusative or Dative with a Difference of Meaning. 385, 3.

209. Models.

I. He presents gifts to the citizens.	I. *Munĕra civĭbus donat.*
II. The Tarentines presented Archias the poet with citizenship.	II. *Tarentīni Archiam poētam civitāte donavērunt.*
III. We came to Delos.	III. *Delum venĭmus.*
IV. I yield to the time.	IV. *Tempŏri cedo.*
V. They fight for liberty.	V. *Pro libertāte dimĭcant.*
VI. He wrote laws for the state.	VI. *Leges civitāti scripsit.*
VII. I consult you.	VII. *Ego vos consŭlo.*
VIII. *Consult* for yourselves.	VIII. *Consulĭte vobis.*
IX. He feared danger.	IX. *Pericŭlum metuēbat.*
X. He feared for himself.	X. *Sibi metuēbat.*

210. Remarks.

1. MODEL I. — For the arrangement of two or more objects with the same verb, see G. 600, 3.

2. MODELS III. AND IV. — Why is *to Delos* rendered by the Accus. *Delum*, and *to the time*, by the Dative, *tempŏri?* See G. 379, 3; 383, •384.

3. MODELS V. AND VI. — Why is *for liberty* rendered by *pro* with the Abl., *pro libertāte*, and *for the state* by the Dative, *civitāti?* See G. 384, 2, 2); 383, 384.

211. VOCABULARY.

Consult, *consŭlo, ĕre, sului, sultum.*
Detriment, *detrimentum, i,* n.
Distinguished, *clarus, a, um.*
Near, near to, *ad,* prep. with acc.
Ought, *debeo, ĕre, ui, ĭtum.*
Supplicate, *supplĭco, āre, āvi, ātum.*

Surround, *circumdo, āre, dĕdi, dā-tum.* G. 264, 1.
Often, *saepe,* adv.
Wall, *murus, i,* m.
Winter quarters, *hiberna, ōrum,* n. adj. used as subs.

212. EXERCISE.

1. Servius Tullius the king surrounded the city of Rome with a wall. 2. The Athenians presented Demosthenes the orator with a golden crown. 3. Demosthenes, the distinguished orator, was presented with a golden crown. 4. We ought to encounter all dangers *for our country.* 5. We will all supplicate the commander in behalf of this soldier. 6. Whom did you (pl.) consult in regard to this plan? 7. We consulted Caesar the commander of the army. 8. For whom did *Caesar* consult? 9. He consulted for the safety of his whole army. 10. Let us lead our forces *into winter quarters* near Geneva. 11. The friendship of the Roman people was often a detriment, not a defence, to their allies.

Lesson XLVI.

DATIVE WITH ADJECTIVES AND DERIVATIVES.
[2, 12.]

213. Lesson from the Grammar.

I. Dative with Adjectives. 391, 391, 2.
II. Dative with Derivatives. 392.

214. Models.

I. The soil *of their country* is dear to all.

I. *Patriae solum omnĭbus carum est.*

II. Pleasure is especially unfriendly to *virtue*.

II. *Voluptas maxĭme est inimīca virtūti.*

III. Your letters are acceptable to me.

III. *Tuae epistŏlae mihi gratae sunt.*

IV. We *are seeking* a Latin word equivalent to the Greek.

IV. *Quaerĭmus verbum Latīnum par Graeco.*

V. *Very kind* to his father.

V. *Perindulgens in patrem.*

VI. Useful for many things.

VI. *Multas ad res utĭlis.*

VII. *Liberty* is characteristic of the *Roman people*.

VII. *Romāni popŭli est propria libertas.*

VIII. Justice is obedience to the laws.

VIII. *Justitia est obtemperatio legĭbus.*

IX. They speak consistently with themselves.

IX. *Sibi constanter dicunt.*

215. REMARKS.

1. MODEL II. — Why is *virtūti* placed at the end of the sentence? G. 594, II.

2. MODEL IV. — Why is *quaerĭmus* placed at the beginning of the sentence? G. 594, I.

3. MODEL VI. — FOR MANY THINGS, *multas ad res.* For the order of words, see Rem. 189, 2 [1]. With *utĭlis* observe the difference of meaning between the Dative and the Accus. with *ad*; *mihi utĭlis,* useful to me; *multas ad res utĭlis,* useful for many things, purposes.

4. MODEL VII. — OF THE ROMAN PEOPLE, *Romāni popŭli,* Gen. depending upon *propria.* See Rule XVII.; also G. 399, 3. This genitive is emphatic, and therefore stands at the beginning of the sentence. G. 594, I. The emphatic *Romāni* precedes its noun. The emphatic subject, *libertas,* is placed at the end of the sentence. G. 594, II.

5. MODEL IX. —, WITH THEMSELVES, *sibi,* Dative depending upon *constanter,* which admits the Dative after the analogy of its primitive *constans,* from *consto.*

216. SYNONYMES.

Acceptable, agreeable; *acceptus, gratus, jucundus.*

1. *Acceptus, a, um;* ACCEPTABLE, WELCOME, — for whatever reason.

2. *Gratus, a, um;* GRATEFUL, ACCEPTABLE, — especially because of value or worth.

3. *Jucundus, a, um;* AGREEABLE, PLEASANT, DELIGHTFUL.

Acceptus implies simply that the object to which it is applied is *acceptable, gratus* that it is acceptable because of its value, whether agreeable or not, and *jucundus,* that it is in itself agreeable.

217. VOCABULARY.

A battle is fought, *pugnātur, pugnātum est,* impers.

Acceptable, *acceptus, a, um; gratus, a, um.*

---

[1] See Explanation of References, page xi.

Admonition, *admonitio, ōnis,* f.

Although, *etiamsi,* conj.

Approach, *appropinquo, āre, āvi, ātum.*

But, *sed; autem.*   G. 587, III. 2.

Near, *prope, propius, proxĭme,* adv.

Peculiar to, *proprius, a, um.*

Spirited, in a spirited manner, *acrĭter,* adv.

Word, *verbum, i,* n.

218. EXERCISE.

1. The friendship of the Aeduans was acceptable to Caesar.   2. Your letters will always be acceptable to me.   3. Your admonition, although it is not agreeable, is yet acceptable to me.   4. Your words are very agreeable to me.   5. The books which you sent were very acceptable to me.   6. At that time the study of eloquence was not common to Greece, but peculiar to Athens.   7. We have endeavored to persuade the citizens.   8. *At the same time* the Aeduans were approaching the borders of the Belgians, who are nearest to the Germans.   9. A spirited battle was fought very near the camp of *Caesar.*

LESSON XLVII.

GENITIVE WITH NOUNS AND ADJECTIVES.
[2, 19.]

219. LESSON FROM THE GRAMMAR.

I. Genitive with Nouns.   395.
    1. Varieties of Genitive with Nouns.   396.
    2. Peculiarities.   397.
    3. Other Constructions.   398.
II. Genitive with Adjectives.   399.

220. MODELS.

I. The glory of *virtue* is eternal.	I. *Virtūtis gloria est sempiterna.*
II. Socrates in the judgment of Greece was the wisest of all men.	II. *Socrătes judicio Graeciae omnium sapientissĭmus fuit.*
III. *Compare* the life of Trebonius with that of Dolabella.	III. *Conferte vitam Trebonii cum Dolabellae.*
IV. Love of (to) country.	IV. *Amor in patriam.*
V. He is desirous of victory.	V. *Victoriae avĭdus est.*
VI. The mind is capable of all virtues.	VI. *Mens virtūtum omnium capax est.*
VII. No one will be found like you.	VII. *Nemo tui simĭlis inveniētur.*

221. REMARKS.

1. MODEL II. — IN THE JUDGMENT, i. e. in accordance with, by the judgment, *judicio.* Rule XXI.

2. OF ALL MEN, *omnium,* used substantively. G. 441.

3. MODEL III. — WITH THAT OF DOLABELLA, *cum Dolabellae,* — *vita* being omitted. G. 397, 1, (1).

4. MODEL IV. — OF COUNTRY, *patriae,* or *in* or *erga patriam.* G. 398, 4.

5. MODEL VII. — LIKE YOU, *tui simĭlis,* or *tibi simĭlis.* G. 391, 1; 399, 3.

222. SYNONYMES.

Avaricious, desirous, devoted to, pursuing; *avārus, cupĭdus, avĭdus, studiōsus.*

5

1. *Avārus, a, um ;* AVARICIOUS, — desirous of money and gain.

2. *Cupĭdus, a, um ;* DESIROUS, EAGERLY DESIROUS, — often with the idea of haste and impatience.

3. *Avĭdus, a, um ;* DESIROUS, EARNESTLY DESIROUS, VERY DESIROUS, GREEDY, — often involving the idea of an excessive or selfish desire.

4. *Studiōsus, a, um ;* STUDIOUS, DEVOTED TO, STUDENT OF, PURSUING, — involving zeal in the pursuit of a study, or in the support of a person or cause.

223. VOCABULARY.

Affair, thing, *res, rei,* f.

Avaricious, *avārus, a, um.*

For, *enim,* conj. G. 587, V. 3.

Greedy, very desirous, *avĭdus, a, um.*

Literature, letters, *littĕrae, ārum,* f. pl.

Military, *militāris, e ;* military affairs, *res militāris,* sing.

Revolution, *res novae,* f. pl.; lit. *new things.*

Science, learning, *doctrīna, ae,* f.

Skilful in, *perītus, a, um.*

Student of, *studiōsus, a, um.*

Three days, *triduum, i,* n.

Unmindful, *immĕmor, ŏris.*

Zeal, *studium, ii,* n.

224. EXERCISE.

1. We will now make a journey into the territory of the Belgians. 2. We have persuaded the soldiers to make a journey of three days through the territory of the Helvetians. 3. The Belgians were very skilful in military affairs. 4. They were *never* unmindful of their ancient valor, and were always desirous of a revolution. 5. But at this time they had more zeal than wisdom ; for they were conquered by the Romans in *many* battles. 6. The

soldiers are very desirous of victory and glory. 7. The avaricious are ever greedy for *money*. 8. We are students of literature.

Lesson XLVIII.

GENITIVE WITH VERBS.
[2, 26.]

225. Lesson from the Grammar.

I. Predicate Genitive. 401.
    1. Predicate Genitive and Predicate Nominative. 401, 1.
    2. Predicate Genitive and Predicate Adjective. 401, 2.
    3. Varieties of Predicate Genitive. 402.
    4. Verbs with Predicate Genitive. 403.
    5. Other Constructions for the Genitive. 404.

II. Genitive of Place. 421, II.

III. Genitive with certain Verbs. 406, 409.
    1. Other Constructions. 407.
    2. *Refert* and *Intĕrest*. 408.

IV. Accusative and Genitive. 410.

226. Models.

I. Murena was a man of much industry.	I. *Murēna multae industriae fuit.*
II. The field is now of more value than it then was.	II. *Ager nunc pluris est quam tunc fuit.*
III. It is your duty to understand.	III. *Tuum est intelligĕre.*

IV. It is the duty of an orator to speak.	IV. *Oratōris officium est dicĕre.*
V. You were in the mean time at Rome.	V. *Tu interea Romae fuisti.*
VI. To do right *is the interest* of all.	VI. *Intĕrest omnium recte facĕre.*
VII. It greatly interests me.	VII. *Magni intĕrest mea.*
VIII. I repent of my error.	VIII. *Me errōris mei poenĭtet.*

227. REMARKS.

1. MODEL I. — WAS A MAN OF, Latin idiom, *was of*, MAN omitted in rendering into Latin. G. 402, III.

2. MODEL II. — IS OF MORE VALUE, *pluris est*, lit. *is of more*. G. 402, III. 1.

3. MODEL III. — IT IS YOUR DUTY TO UNDERSTAND, Latin idiom, *to understand is yours*. *Tuum*, not *tui*, must be used. G. 404, 1.

4. MODEL IV. — IT IS THE DUTY OF AN ORATOR, *oratōris est*, or *oratōris officium est*. G. 404, 2.

5. MODEL V. — AT ROME, *Romae*. G. 423, II.

6. MODEL VII. — GREATLY, *magni*, lit. *of much, of great*. G. 408, 3.

7. IT INTERESTS ME, *intĕrest mea*, not *mei*. G. 408, 1, 2).

8. MODEL VIII. — I REPENT OF MY ERROR, Latin idiom, *it repents me of my error.*

228. VOCABULARY.

Be ashamed, *pudet, puduit* or *pudĭtum est,* impers. I am ashamed, *me pudet.* G. 299.

Bitterly, *acerbe,* adv.

Pity, *misĕret, miserĭtum est,* impers. I pity, *me misĕret.* G. 299.

Repent, *poenĭtet, poenituit,* impers. I repent, *me poenĭtet.* G. 299.

Treachery, *proditio, ōnis,* f.

229. Exercise.

1. The Romans did not forget the ancient valor of the Helvetians. 2. The Gauls were very brave. 3. The Belgians were of *great* valor. 4. It is characteristic of *true* valor to encounter all dangers in behalf of the republic. 5. It is the interest of all to obey the laws. 6. It is important to the glory of the state to consult for the safety of all the citizens. 7. The Germans were not ashamed of their valor. 8. The Helvetians bitterly repented of their conspiracy. 9. Do you not pity them? 10. We do not accuse *you* of conspiracy. 11. This soldier has already been accused of treachery.

Lesson XLIX.

ABLATIVE.
[2, 35.]

230. Lesson from the Grammar.

I. Ablative of Cause, Manner, Means. 414.
    1. Various Expressions for Cause. 414, 2, 2) and 3).
    2. Means and Agent distinguished. 414, 4 and 5.

II. Ablative of Price. 416.

III. Ablative with Comparatives. 417.
    1. Comparatives with *Quam*. 417, 1.
    2. Ablative, when admissible. 417, 2.
    3. Construction with *Plus* and *Minus*. 417, 3.

231. MODELS.

I. An art is praised because of its usefulness.

I. *Ars utilitāte laudā-tur.*

II. *By my right* I ask of you this favor.

II. *Meo jure te hoc beneficium rogo.*

III. Terentia was delighted with *your letter.*

III. *Terentia delectāta est tuis littĕris.*

IV. Friendship is to be sought for its own sake.

IV. *Amicitia est propter se expetenda.*

V. Cato was praised by all.

V. *Cato ab omnĭbus laudātus est.*

VI. It was done through the agency of Fabricius.

VI. *Per Fabricium factum est.*

VII. He purchased the senatorial rank with money.

VII. *Ordĭnem senatorium pretio mercātus est.*

VIII. What is more desirable than wisdom?

VIII. *Quid est optabilius sapientiā, or quam sapientiā.*

IX. He lived with you more than a year.

IX. *Tecum plus annum vixit.*

232. REMARKS.

1. MODEL I. — BECAUSE OF ITS USEFULNESS, *utilitāte*, Abl. of Cause. Rule XXI.

2. MODEL II. — I ASK OF YOU, *te rogo.* Rule VII.

3. MODEL III. — WITH YOUR LETTER, *tuis littĕris*, or *tua epistŏla.* Rule XXI. See also Synonymes, 200.

4. MODEL IV. — FOR ITS OWN SAKE = on account of itself, *propter*

se. These words, it will be observed, stand between *est* and *expetenda.* Modifiers are not unfrequently thus placed between the two parts in the compound forms of verbs.

5. MODEL VI. — THROUGH THE AGENCY OF FABRICIUS, *per Fabricium,* lit. *through Fabricius.* G. 414, 5, 1).

6. MODEL IX. — WITH YOU, *tecum.* G. 434, 5.

7. MORE THAN A YEAR, *plus annum,* not *plus anno.* G. 417, 3.

233. SYNONYMES.

Celebrated, distinguished, illustrious, noble ; *celĕber, clarus, illustris, nobĭlis.*

1. *Celĕber, bris, bre ;* CELEBRATED, MUCH FREQUENTED, — applied mostly to places.

2. *Clarus, a, um ;* DISTINGUISHED, CONSPICUOUS, CELEBRATED, — especially for brilliant achievements.

3. *Illustris, e ;* ILLUSTRIOUS, RENOWNED, — a stronger term than *clarus,* applied especially to those who are distinguished for rank and worth.

4. *Nobĭlis, e ;* WELL KNOWN, FAMOUS, NOBLE, — with special reference to high birth and ancestry.

234. VOCABULARY.

Aid, *auxĭlium, ii,* n.	Noble, *nobĭlis, e.*
Antioch, *Antiochīa, ae,* f.	Solon, *Solon* or *Solo, ŏnis,* m.
Celebrated, *celĕber, bris, bre.*	Themistocles, *Themistŏcles, is,* m.
High, great (price), *magnus, a, um.*	Thousand, *mille,* indecl. adj.; pl.
Illustrious, *illustris, e.*	*millia, ium,* n. subst. G. 178.
Lead on, *addŭco, ĕre, duxi, ductum.*	

235. EXERCISE.

1. The soldiers were led on by the hope of a reward.
2. The Aeduans were sent with all their forces as aid to

Caesar. 3. Why did they not come with cavalry? 4. More than five thousand came *in one day*. 5. Who was there at Rome more distinguished than Cicero? 6. Antioch was formerly a celebrated city. 7. The name of Themistocles is more illustrious than that of Solon. 8. The Athenians sent three most noble philosophers to Rome. 9. He has purchased a house at a high price. 10. The safety of the *country* is dear to *me*.

Lesson L.

ABLATIVE — Continued.
[3, 8.]

236. Lesson from the Grammar.

I. Ablative of Difference. 418.
II. Ablative in Special Constructions. 419.

237. Models.

I. Longer by *one* day.	I. *Uno die longior.*
II. The wise man makes the best use of reason.	II. *Sapiens ratiōne optĭme utĭtur.*
III. I am *intimate* with Trebonius.	III. *Trebonio utor familiarĭter.*
IV. Nature is content with little.	IV. *Natūra parvo contenta est.*
V. What need have you of our aid?	V. *Quid tibi opĕra nostra opus est?*
VI. No one trusts in the stability of *fortune*.	VI. *Nemo fortūnae stabilitāte confīdit.*
VII. I trust in virtue.	VII. *Virtūti confīdo.*

238. REMARKS.

1. MODEL II. — MAKES THE BEST USE OF REASON, Latin idiom, *uses reason best.*

2. MODEL III. — I AM INTIMATE WITH, *utor familiariter.*

3. MODEL V. — WHAT NEED HAVE YOU, Latin idiom, *as to what is there need to you,* — *quid tibi opus est.* Quid, see G. 380, 2. OF OUR AID, *opĕra nostra,* Abl. G. 419, 3.

4. MODEL VII. — I TRUST IN VIRTUE, *virtŭti* or *virtŭte confĭdo.* With the Dative the idea of *trust* is prominent, I trust in virtue, i. e. trust it, trust to it; while with the Abl., the idea of *means* is prominent, I trust in virtue, i. e. am confident because of or by means of virtue.

239. SYNONYMES.

I. To need, to be without, to be free from; *egeo, indigeo, careo, vaco.*

1. *Egeo, ēre, ui* — ; TO NEED, TO BE DESTITUTE OF, — to be without something which one needs.

2. *Indigeo, ēre, ui* — ; TO NEED, TO FEEL NEED, — involving a deep *sense* of need, while *egeo* refers rather to the need itself.

3. *Careo, ēre, ui, ĭtum;* TO BE WITHOUT, — with little reference to the character of the object as desirable or undesirable.

4. *Vaco, āre, āvi, ātum;* TO BE FREE FROM, TO BE WITHOUT, — especially to be without that which is undesirable.

II. Man, hero; *homo, vir.*

1. *Homo, homĭnis,* m. and f.; MAN, — a member of the human family, man or woman.

2. *Vir, viri,* m.; HERO, TRUE MAN, — as a term of respect.

240. Vocabulary.

Advice, counsel, *consilium, ii,* n.

Affection, love, *amor, ōris,* m.

Be destitute of, need, *egeo, ĕre, ui ; indĭgeo, ĕre, ui.*

Be free from, be without, *vaco, āre, āvi, ātum ; careo, ĕre, ui, ĭtum ; egeo, ĕre, ui.*

Be intimate with, *familiarĭter utor, i, usus sum.*

Be needful (there needs, is need of), *opus est, fuit.*

Best, in the best manner, *optĭme,* adv.

Enjoyment, *delectatio, ōnis,* f.

Familiarly, *familiarĭter,* adv.

Fault, *culpa, ae,* f.

Feel the need of, *indĭgeo, ĕre, ui.*

Fidelity, faith, *fides, ĕi,* f.

Highest, of the highest degree, *summus, a, um,* sup. of *supĕrus.*

Kindness, *benignĭtas, ātis,* f.

Nothing, *nihil,* n. indecl.

Pain, *dolor, ōris,* m.

Use, make use of, *utor, i, usus sum,* dep.

Very, *valde,* adv.

241. Exercise.

1. Laelius was for many years very intimate with Scipio. 2. He was at that time both without pain and without enjoyment. 3. We are *now* destitute of (need) many things. 4. I feel the need of your advice. 5. Now your counsels, your affection, and your fidelity are needful to us. 6. There was no need of so many words. 7. Let us make the best use of our time. 8. The *Roman* soldiers were always worthy of the highest praise. 9. Nothing is more worthy of a *great* and *distinguished* man than kindness. 10. What is there in man better than virtue? 11. The safety of the *country* is much dearer to you than life.

Lesson LI.

ABLATIVE — Continued.
[3, 13.]

242. Lesson from the Grammar.

I. Ablative of Place. 421–424.
    1. Places not Towns. 422.
    2. Names of Towns. 423.
    3. Like Names of Towns. 424.

II. Ablative of Source and Separation. 425; 425, 3.

III. Construction of Names of Places.
    1. The Place in which. 421, I. and II.
    2. The Place from which. 421, I. and II.
    3. The Place to which. 379; 379, 4.

243. Models.

I. In what city do we live ?
    I. *In qua urbe vivĭmus ?*

II. He died at Babylon.
    II. *Babylōne mortuus est.*

III. I withdrew from the forum.
    III. *De foro discessi.*

IV. Aeschines withdrew from *Athens*.
    IV. *Aeschĭnes cessit Athēnis.*

V. He fled from home.
    V. *Domo profūgit.*

VI. You have freed your country from perils.
    VI. *Pericŭlis patriam liberavistis.*

VII. He came into the province.
    VII. *In provinciam advēnit.*

VIII. I came to Capua.
    VIII. *Capuam veni.*

244. REMARKS.

1. Why is the preposition used in models I. III. VII., and omitted in all the others? G. 421; 424; 425, 3; 379; 379, 4.

2. MODEL IV. — Emphasis places *Athĕnis* at the end of the sentence.

245. SYNONYMES.

Country; *patria, ager, rus.*

1. *Patria, ae,* f.; NATIVE COUNTRY, — the country of one's birth.

2. *Ager, agri,* m.; COUNTRY, — as consisting of fields, THE OPEN COUNTRY; — in this sense generally plural.

3. *Rus, ruris,* n.; THE COUNTRY, — as distinguished from the city.

246. VOCABULARY.

Capable, *capax, ăcis.*

Country, *rus, ruris,* n.; *patria, ae,* f.; *ager, agri,* m.

Fear, *metus, us,* m.

Few, *pauci, ae, a,* pl.

Forced marches, *magna itinĕra,* n. pl.; lit. *great marches.*

Go, *eo, ire, ivi, itum.*

Hasten, *contendo, ĕre, tendi, tentum.*

Land, *terra, ae,* f.

Mind, the mental faculty, *mens, mentis,* f.

Obtain, *potior, ĭri, ĭtus sum,* dep. G. 419, I.

Remain, *maneo, ĕre, mansi, mansum.*

Sea, *mare, is,* n.; on sea and land, *terra marĭque.*

Servitude, *servĭtus, ūtis,* f.

Sovereignty, *imperium, ii,* n.

247. EXERCISE.

1. We lived in Geneva more than three months. 2. From Geneva we hastened with forced marches into Italy.

3. Now let us go from the city into the country. 4. He went from home a few days ago, and will remain in the country two months. 5. We made a journey of three days through the country. 6. The *brave* soldiers have encountered many dangers in behalf of their country. 7. War must be waged against the Carthaginians on sea and land. 8. It was the intention of the Helvetians to obtain the sovereignty of all Gaul. 9. Will you not free this city from the fear of servitude? 10. To man God has given a mind capable of all virtues.

Lesson LII.

ABLATIVE — Continued.
[3, 20.]

248. Lesson from the Grammar.

I. Ablative of Time. 426.
   1. Time within which. 426, 2.
   2. Time since an event, or between two events. 427, 427, 1–4.

II. Ablative of Characteristic. 428.
   1. Genitive and Ablative distinguished. 428, 4; 396, IV.

III. Ablative of Specification. 429.

249. Models.

I. Plato died in his eighty-first year.

I. *Plato uno et octogesimo anno mortuus est.*

II. I have leisure at this time for philosophy.

II. *Hoc tempŏre philoso-phiae vaco.*

III. He smiled *once* in his life.

III. *Semel in vita risit.*

IV. Homer lived many years *before Romulus.*

IV. *Homērus annis mul-tis fuit ante Romŭ-lum.*

V. He was slain some months after.

V. *Alĭquot post menses occīsus est.*

VI. You are of a cheerful spirit.

VI. *Tu hilări anĭmo es.*

250. REMARKS.

1. MODEL I. — HIS — omitted in rendering.

2. MODEL III. — IN HIS LIFE, *in vita.* Why is the preposition *in* used? G. 426, 2.

3. MODEL IV. — HOMER LIVED MANY YEARS BEFORE ROMULUS, Latin idiom, *Homer was before Romulus by many years. Annis,* Abl. of Difference. Rule XXIV. *Ante Romŭlum* at the end of the sentence because emphatic.

4. MODEL V. — SOME MONTHS AFTER, Latin idiom, *after some months.* For the order of the words, see G. 427, 2.

5. MODEL VI. — OF A CHEERFUL SPIRIT, or WITH A CHEERFUL SPIRIT, *hilări anĭmo,* Abl. of Characteristic. Rule XXIX.

251. VOCABULARY.

Afterwards, *post,* adv.

Equal, *par, paris.* go to shell

Fifth day of the month, *nonae, ārum,* f. pl. For exception see G. 708, I. 2.

Fiftieth, *quinquagesĭmus, a, um.*

First day of the month, *calendae, ārum,* f. pl.

Fourth, *quartus, a, um.*

Greatly, *magnopĕre,* adv.

Ides, *idus, iduum,* f. pl. G. 708,
I. 3.

June, of June, *Junius, a, um.* G.
708, III. 2.

March, of March, *Martius, a, um.*

May, of May, *Maius, a, um.*

Punic, *Punicus, a, um.*

Put to death, *occido, ĕre, cĭdi, ci-
sum.*

Pythagoras, *Pythagŏras, ae,* m.

Refinement, *humanĭtas, ātis,* f.

Return, come back, *reverto* or *revertor, ĕre* or *i, reverti, re-
versum.* See G. 273, III.,
verto.

Sixth, *sextus, a, um.*

Sixtieth, *sexagesĭmus, a, um.*

Such, so great, *tantus, a, um.*

Third, *tertius, a, um.*

252. EXERCISE.

1. Pythagoras was in Italy at the same time in which Lucius Junius Brutus liberated his country. 2. Publius Scipio took Carthage in the third Punic war. 3. The ambassadors returned to Rome on the first day of May. 4. I received your letter *on the fifth day* of June. 5. Caesar was put to death in his fifty-sixth year, on the ides of March. 6. *Two years afterwards* Cicero was put to death, in his sixty-fourth year. 7. The Belgians were equal to the Germans in valor. 8. They were surpassed by the *Romans* both in valor and in refinement. 9. The Romans surpassed the Greeks in the arts of *war.* 10. The Greeks surpassed the Romans in the arts of *peace.* 11. Herodotus is a man of such eloquence that he greatly delights us.

LESSON LIII.

ABLATIVE — CONTINUED.
[3, 29.]

253. LESSON FROM THE GRAMMAR.

I. Ablative Absolute. 431.

II. Cases with Prepositions. 432.
    1. Accusative. 433.
    2. Ablative. 434.
    3. Accusative or Ablative. 435.

254. MODELS.

I. When many opinions had already been expressed, I was asked my opinion.

I. *Multis sententiis jam dictis, rogātus sum sententiam.*

II. Many orators flourished in the *time of Cato.*

II. *Vivo Catōne multi oratōres floruērunt.*

III. Socrates brought philosophy down to common life.

III. *Socrătes philosophiam ad vitam commūnem adduxit.*

IV. He wrote the book with great care.

IV. *Magna cum cura librum scripsit.*

V. He has retired from office.

V. *Magistrātu abiit.*

VI. What are you to do with this man?

VI. *Quid hoc homĭne facias?*

VII. He fled into Asia.

VII. *In Asiam profūgit.*

VIII. *In this island* is a fountain of sweet water.

VIII. *In hac insŭla est fons aquae dulcis.*

255. REMARKS.

1. MODEL I. — WHEN MANY OPINIONS HAD BEEN EXPRESSED, Latin idiom, *many opinions having been spoken*. *Sententiam*. Rule VII.

2. MODEL II. — IN THE TIME OF CATO, *vivo Catōne*, lit. *Cato alive*. Rule XXXI. Observe the position of these words at the beginning of the sentence. G. 594, I.

3. MODEL VI. — WITH THIS MAN, *hoc homĭne*. G. 434, 2. *Facias*, G. 486, II.

256. SYNONYMES.

Battle, engagement, conflict; *pugna, proelium*.

1. *Pugna, ae*, f.; BATTLE, ENGAGEMENT, FIGHT, STRIFE, — the generic term for a conflict of any kind, whether between individuals or armies, whether with the fist, with words, or with arms.

2. *Proelium, ii*, n.; BATTLE, ENGAGEMENT, — a conflict in a military sense.

257. VOCABULARY.

Aquitanians, *Aquitāni, ōrum*, m.

Arrive, *pervĕnio, ĭre, vēni, ventum*.

Become, *fio, fiĕri, factus sum*. G. 294.

Betake one's self, *se recipĕre ; recĭpio, ĕre, cēpi, ceptum*.

Cassius, *Cassius, ii*, m.

Eager, *alăcer, cris, cre*.

Fight, to fight, *pugno, āre, āvi, ātum*. To fight (lit. *make*) a battle, *proelium (pugnam) facio, ĕre, feci, factum*.

How great, *quantus, a, um*.

Living, alive, *vivus, a, um*.

Reduce to a state of peace, *paco, āre, āvi, ātum*.

Result, *exĭtus, us*, m.

Rout, *pello, ĕre, pepŭli, pulsum*.

Strife, *pugna, ae*, f.

Successful, *secundus, a, um*.

Vicinity, in the vicinity of, *ad*, prep. with acc.

Within, *intra*, prep. with acc.

Yoke, *jugum, i*, n.

258. Exercise.

1. In the consulship of Lucius Cassius the Helvetians routed the Roman army and sent it under the yoke. 2. Within five days we shall arrive in the vicinity of Geneva. 3. Having routed the army of the enemy, the Aquitanians betook themselves to the town. 4. *Our* soldiers, having fortified their camp, became more eager to fight. 5. Caesar, having reduced all Gaul to a state of peace, led his army into winter quarters. 6. How great is the strife of orators! 7. Caesar fought many successful battles. 8. The result of this battle is uncertain. 9. These wars were waged against the Gauls in the time of Cicero.

Lesson LIV.

ADJECTIVES.
[1, 4.]¹

259. Lesson from the Grammar.

I. Agreement of Adjectives. 438; 438, 1–8.
    1. With Clause. 438, 3.
    2. Construction according to Sense. 438, 6.
    3. With two or more Nouns. 439.

II. Use of Adjectives. 440.
    1. With the Force of Nouns. 441.

---

¹ The enclosed numerals standing at the beginning of the following lessons refer to Cicero's Orations against Catiline. Thus [1, 4] shows that this lesson is to be learned after the pupil has read the first four Chapters of the first Oration against Catiline.

2. Equivalent to Clauses. 442.
3. Instead of Adverbs. 443.
4. Comparison of Adjectives. 444.

260. MODELS.

I. An *upright* life is a *happy* life.	I. *Honesta vita beāta vita est.*
II. It is true that there is friendship among the good.	II. *Verum est amiciti- am inter bonos esse.*
III. Castor and Pollux were seen.	III. *Castor et Pollux visi sunt.*
IV. Honors and victories are accidental.	IV. *Honōres et victoriae fortuĭta sunt.*
V. I loved Hortensius when he was alive.	V. *Hortensium vivum amāvi.*
VI. Roscius was frequently at Rome.	VI. *Roscius erat Romae frequens.*
VII. Nothing is more beautiful than virtue.	VII. *Nihil est virtūte formosius.*
VIII. Aristides was without exception the most just of all.	VIII. *Aristīdes unus omnium justissĭmus fuit.*

261. REMARKS.

1. MODEL II. — *Verum* agrees with the infinitive clause, *amicitiam — esse.* G. 438, 3; 35, III. AMONG, BETWEEN THE GOOD, *inter bonos. Bonos* used substantively, *the good.* G. 441.

2. MODEL IV. — ARE ACCIDENTAL, i. e. accidental things, *fortuĭta sunt.* G. 439, 2, 3).

3. MODEL V. — I LOVED HORTENSIUS WHEN HE WAS ALIVE, or *when alive,* Latin idiom, *I loved Hortensius alive.*

4. MODEL VI. — ROSCIUS WAS FREQUENTLY AT ROME, Latin idiom, *Roscius was frequent at Rome.* G. 443.

5. MODEL VIII. — WITHOUT EXCEPTION THE MOST JUST OF ALL, *unus omnium justissĭmus,* lit. *alone of all the most just, the most just one of all.* G. 444, 3.

262. VOCABULARY.

Assemble, *convĕnio, ĭre, vĕni, ventum.*

Capture, *capio, ĕre, cepi, captum.*

Certain, *certus, a, um.*

Frequently, *frequens, entis,* adj. G. 443.

Full, in full numbers, *frequens, entis.*

Jupiter, *Jupĭter, Jovis,* m.

Openly, *palam,* adv.

Stator, *Stator, ŏris,* m.

Treason, *proditio, ŏnis,* f.

Wicked, *scelerātus, a, um.*

Without exception, alone, *unus, a, um.* G. 176, 1.

263. EXERCISE.

1. We will now read the orations of Cicero the *celebrated* orator. 2. Cicero was consul in the same year in which Catiline formed his wicked conspiracy. 3. There were many orators in Rome at that time, but Cicero was without exception the most eloquent of all. 4. Catiline had frequently heard him in the senate. 5. The senate assembled in full numbers in the temple of Jupiter Stator. 6. Cicero was the first who openly accused Catiline of treason. 7. It is certain that a conspiracy was formed. 8. Many thousands of the enemy were captured in the first Punic war. 9. Scipio and Laelius were often praised by *Cicero.*

Lesson LV.

PRONOUNS.
[1, 7.]

264. Lesson from the Grammar.

I. Agreement of Pronouns. 445.
   1. Agreement of Pronoun used as Adjective. 445, 1.
   2. Agreement with Personal Pronoun. 445, 2.
   3. With two Antecedents. 445, 3.
   4. With Predicate Noun or Appositive. 445, 4.
   5. Construction according to Sense. 445, 5.
   6. Antecedent omitted. 445, 6.
   7. Clause as Antecedent. 445, 7.

II. Personal and Possessive Pronouns. 446, 447.
   1. Nominative of Personal Pronouns omitted. 446.
   2. Possessive Pronouns omitted. 447.
   3. Reflexive Use of Pronouns. 448, 449.

265. Models.

I. *Every* virtue attracts us to itself.

I. *Omnis virtus nos ad se allicit.*

II. From your letter I have received *incredible pleasure.*

II. *Ex littĕris tuis cepi incredibĭlem voluptātem.*

III. They will live a *more secure* life under my protection.

III. *Tutiōrem vitam meo praesidio vivent.*

IV. You are the one who commended me.

IV. *Tu es is qui me ornasti.*

V. The produce and fruits which the earth yields.

V. *Fruges atque fructus quos terra gignit.*

VI. They reject glory, which is the fruit of virtue.	VI. *Gloriam qui est fructus virtūtis repudiant.*
VII. There are some who think.	VII. *Sunt qui censeant.*
VIII. Our country delights us, as it ought.	VIII. *Nos, id quod debet, patria delectat.*
IX. I console myself.	IX. *Me consōlor.*

266. REMARKS.

1. MODEL III. — UNDER MY PROTECTION, *meo praesidio*, lit. *by means of*, or *because of*, *my protection*. Rule XXI. *Vitam*, G. 371, 1, 3).

2. MODEL IV. — THE ONE WHO, *is qui*, not *unus qui*.

3. MODEL V. — WHICH, *quos*, masculine. G. 445, 3.

4. MODEL VI. — *Qui* agrees with *fructus*, rather than with *gloriam*. G. 445, 4.

5. MODEL VII. — THERE ARE SOME, *sunt*. G. 445, 6. *Censeant*, for the Subjunctive, see G. 501, 1.

6. MODEL VIII. — AS IT OUGHT, Latin idiom, *that which it owes, ought*, — *id quod debet*. G. 445, 7. Emphasis places *nos* at the beginning of the sentence.

267. VOCABULARY.

As, relat., *qui, quae, quod.* As it ought, *id quod debet.* G. 445, 7.

Ascertain, *cognosco, ĕre, nōvi, nĭtum.*

Condemn, *condemno, āre, āvi, ātum.*

Defend, *defendo, ĕre, fendi, fensum.*

Depart from, *exeo, īre, ii, ĭtum.*

Devote one's self to, *studeo, ēre, ui,* dat. G. 385.

Divine, *divīnus, a, um.*

Gift, *donum, i,* n.

Oppose, *obsisto, ĕre, stĭti, stĭtum.* G. 386.

Remissness, *nequitia, ae,* f.

Sometimes, *interdum,* adv.

Vigilant, *vigilans, antis.*
You, thou, *tu, tui.*

Your, thy, companions, friends,
&c., *tui, ōrum.* G. 441, 1.

268. Exercise.

1. I have said that Cicero accused Catiline of treason.
2. Did you not condemn yourself for remissness? 3. I
have often condemned myself for remissness. 4. Cicero
said that he condemned the consuls for remissness. 5.
You, Catiline, and all your companions, ought to depart
from the city. 6. You and I, who oppose this conspiracy,
ought to be vigilant. 7. There are some who fear Catiline. 8. We will *defend*, as we ought, the safety of the
Roman people. 9. *Let us send* the cavalry to ascertain
where the *enemy* are. 10. Cicero devoted himself to eloquence, which is sometimes called a *divine gift.*

Lesson LVI.

PRONOUNS — Continued.
[1, 10.]

269. Lesson from the Grammar.

I. Demonstrative Pronouns. 450–452.

II. Relative Pronouns. 453.
    1. Relative Clause = Ablative with *Pro.* 453, 4.
    2. Relative with Adjective. 453, 5.

III. Interrogative Pronouns. 454.

IV. Indefinite Pronouns. 455–459.

270. MODELS.

I. *One* thing I will ex-
   plain, and that too a
   most important one.

I. *Unam rem explicā-
   bo, eamque maxĭ-
   mam.*

II. Nothing is useful
    which is not also
    honorable.

II. *Nihil est utĭle, quod
    non idem hones-
    tum.*

III. We are such as we
     ought to be.

III. *Iĭ sumus, qui esse
     debēmus.*

IV. I hope you are well,
    such is your pru-
    dence.

IV. *Spero, quae tua pru-
    dentia est, te va-
    lēre.*

V. The most beautiful vessels which he had
   seen.

V. *Vasa, quae pulcher-
   rĭma vidĕrat.*

VI. What kind of a man
    was he?

VI. *Qui vir fuit?*

VII. One party contends,
     the other fears.

VII. *Altĕri dimĭcant, al-
     tĕri timent.*

VIII. One thing seems best
      to some, another to
      others.

VIII. *Aliud aliis vidētur
      optĭmum.*

IX. The *best* men ever ren-
    der the greatest ser-
    vice to posterity.

IX. *Optĭmus   quisque
    maxĭme   posteri-
    tāti servit.*

271. REMARKS.

1. MODEL I. — AND THAT TOO A MOST IMPORTANT ONE, Latin idiom,
and that the greatest, — eamque maxĭmam. G. 451, 2.

2. MODEL II. — WHICH ALSO, *quod idem,* lit. *which the same.*

3. MODEL IV. — SUCH IS YOUR PRUDENCE, Latin idiom, *which is
your prudence, — te valĕre* being the antecedent of *quae.* What other
forms may be used? G. 453, 4.

4. MODEL V. — THE MOST BEAUTIFUL VESSELS WHICH, Latin idiom, *the vessels, which the most beautiful.* G. 453, 5.

5. MODEL VIII. — ONE THING SEEMS BEST TO SOME, ANOTHER TO OTHERS, Latin idiom, *another thing seems best to others.*

6. MODEL IX. — THE BEST MEN EVER, Latin idiom, *every best man.* RENDER THE GREATEST SERVICE, *maxĭme servit*, lit. *serves most* or *especially.*

272. SYNONYMES.

Dinner, feast, entertainment ; *coena, epŭlae, convivium.*

1. *Coena, ae,* f. ; DINNER, — as the principal family meal.

2. *Epŭlae, ārum,* f. pl. ; FEAST, ENTERTAINMENT, — with special reference to its *sumptuous* character.

3. *Convivium, ii,* n. ; lit. *a living together* (*con, vivo*) ; FEAST, ENTERTAINMENT, — with special reference to its *social* character.

273. VOCABULARY.

Audacity, *audacia, ae,* f.

Best, *optĭmus, a, um.*

Choice, *conquisĭtus, a, um.*

Conversation, *sermo, ōnis,* m.

Daily, of increase or decrease, *in dies ; in dies singŭlos.* See Syn. 399.

Deliver (an oration), *habeo, ēre, ui, ĭtum ;* lit. *to have.*

Each, one each, *singŭli, ae, a,* distrib. num.

Eighth of November, *ante diem sextum idus Novembres.* G. 708.

Entertainment, *convivium, ii,* n.

Feast, viands, *epŭlae, ārum,* f. pl.

Increase, intrans., *cresco, ĕre, crevi, cretum.*

Load, pile up, *exstruo, ĕre, struxi, structum.*

Madness, *furor, ōris,* m.

On account of, *propter,* prep. with acc.

6

Pleasure, enjoyment, *delectatio, ōnis,* f.

Presence, in the presence of, *apud,* prep. with acc.

Put to death, *interfĭcio, ĕre, fēci, fectum.*

Squander, *profundo, ĕre, fūdi, fūsum.*

Such, sometimes rendered by *qui, quae, quod,* relat. pron. G. 453, 4.

Sumptuous, *sumptuōsus, a, um.*

Table, *mensa, ae,* f.

Unbridled, *effrenātus, a, um.*

274. EXERCISE.

1. The oration which we are now reading was delivered in the temple of Jupiter Stator. 2. It was delivered by Cicero on the 8th of November, *in the presence of the senate.* 3. The unbridled audacity of Catiline was *at that time* increasing daily. 4. Catiline, such was his unbridled madness, endeavored to put Cicero to death. 5. I will give you the best books which I have. 6. The judge has invited us to dinner. 7. There are some who squander their money upon sumptuous feasts. 8. The tables are loaded with the *choicest* viands. 9. Many are delighted with entertainments on account of their enjoyment of conversation.

LESSON LVII.

VERBS — AGREEMENT, VOICE, TENSE. INDICATIVE MOOD.
[I, 13.]

275. LESSON FROM THE GRAMMAR.

I. Agreement of Verbs. 460–463.

II. Use of Voices. 464, 465.

III. Tenses of the Indicative. 466–473.

IV. Use of the Indicative. 474.

276. Models.

I. You assume the name of virtue.	I. *Nomen virtūtis usurpas.*
II. All things were made *by* God.	II. *A Deo omnia facta sunt.*
III. I will explain as I shall be able those things which you desire.	III. *Ea quae vis, ut potĕro, explicăbo.*
IV. Mithridates has already reigned upwards of twenty-two years.	IV. *Mithridātes annum jam tertium et vicesĭmum regnat.*
V. It would be tedious to enumerate the uses.	V. *Longum est persĕqui utilitātes.*

277. Remarks.

1. MODEL II. — ALL THINGS, *omnia*. *Res* is not necessary, as there is no ambiguity. Emphasis determines the position of *a Deo.*

2. MODEL IV. — HAS REIGNED UPWARDS OF TWENTY-TWO YEARS, *annum tertium et vicesĭmum regnat*, lit. *is reigning the twenty-third year*, or *plus viginti duo annos regnāvit.*

3. MODEL V. — IT WOULD BE TEDIOUS, Latin idiom, *it is long*, a long task, *longum est.*

278. Vocabulary.

Against, *in*, prep. with acc.

Better, *melior, ius*, compar. of *bonus.*

Can, could, *possum, posse, potui.*

Decree, *consultum, i*, n.

Entertain the same sentiments, *eădem sentio, ĭre, sensi, sensum.*

Founding of the city, *urbs condīta.* G. 580.

In accordance with, *e, ex*, prep. with abl., lit. *from.*
Inactivity, *inertia, ae,* f.
Keep, *servo, āre, āvi, ātum.*
Ninetieth, *nonagesĭmus, a, um.*
Now = already, *jam*, adv.
Promise, *promissum, i,* n.

Rightly, *recte*, adv.
Six hundredth, *sexcentesĭmus, a, um.*
Tedious, long, *longus, a, um.*
Thing, *res, rei,* f.
Think, feel, perceive, *sentio, ĭre, sensi, sensum.*

279. EXERCISE.

1. It would be better not to keep those promises. 2. It would be tedious to speak of these things. 3. The city should have been liberated from fear. 4. Can we rightly accuse Cicero of inactivity and remissness? 5. Could he not, in accordance with the decree of the senate, have ordered Catiline to be put to death? 6. Did he not wish to do this? 7. So many entertained the same sentiments as Catiline, that he did not judge this the best thing to do. 8. We have *now* read the first oration of *Cicero* against Catiline. 9. In what year was it delivered? 10. *It was delivered* in the six hundred and ninety-first year from the founding of the city.

LESSON LVIII.

SUBJUNCTIVE MOOD.
[2, 4.]

280. LESSON FROM THE GRAMMAR.

I. Tenses of the Subjunctive. 476–479.
  1. Sequence of Tenses. 480; 481.
  2. Exceptions in Sequence. 482.

II. The Potential Subjunctive.   485; 486, 1–7.

III. The Subjunctive of Desire.   487; 488, 1–5.

IV. The Subjunctive of Purpose or Result.   489.

281. MODELS.

I. They strive to conquer.	I. *Nītuntur ut vincant.*
II. May I be able to accomplish my endeavors.	II. *Utĭnam conāta effĭcĕre possim.*
III. Would that I had been able to accomplish my endeavors.	III. *Utĭnam conāta effĭcĕre potuissem.*
IV. Let us avoid pride, haughtiness, and arrogance.	IV. *Superbiam, fastidium, arrogantiamque fugiāmus.*
V. Who would seek glory as he would shun infamy?	V. *Quis gloriam tam expĕtat quam infamiam fugiat?*
VI. I collect all things, that I may write something *new to you.*	VI. *Omnia collĭgo, ut novi scribam alĭquid ad te.*
VII. The house was so furnished that it was an *ornament* to the city.	VII. *Domus sic ornāta fuit ut urbi esset ornamento.*

282. REMARKS.

1. MODEL I. — THEY STRIVE TO CONQUER, Latin idiom, *they strive that they may conquer.*

2. MODEL II. — MAY I BE ABLE, *possim,* or *utĭnam possim.*

3. MODEL III. — WOULD THAT I HAD BEEN ABLE, *utĭnam potuissem.*

4. MODEL V. — WOULD SEEK, WOULD SHUN, *expĕtat, fugiat,* Potential Subjunctives.

5. MODEL VI.—SOMETHING NEW, *novi aliquid*, lit. *something of new*. G. 441, 2; 396, III. 2, 3). *Novi*, being emphatic, is at the beginning of the clause.

6. MODEL VII.—WAS AN ORNAMENT, *esset ornamento*. For the mood and tense of *esset*, see G. 489; 494; 481, II. 1. For the case of *ornamento*, see G. 390.

283. SYNONYMES.

Rest, repose, tranquillity; *quies, requies, tranquillitas*.

1. *Quies, quiētis*, f.; REST, REPOSE, — in itself considered.

2. *Requies, ētis*, f.; REST, REPOSE, — as a means of refreshing and invigorating the exhausted powers, whether of body or of mind.

3. *Tranquillitas, ātis*, f.; TRANQUILLITY, CALMNESS, REPOSE, — involving freedom from care and anxiety.

284. VOCABULARY.

Affair, business, *negotium, ii*, n.

Civil, domestic, *domesticus, a, um*.

Dare, *audeo, ēre, ausus sum.* G. 272, 3.

Even, *etiam*, adv.

Highest welfare of the state, *summa res publica*.

Like, *similis, e.* G. 391, 2, 4), (2).

Long for, *expeto, ēre, petivi, petitum*.

Neglect, *negligo, ēre, lexi, lectum*.

O that! *utinam*, interj.

Public, *publicus, a, um*.

Repose, *tranquillitas, ātis*, f.

Rest, *quies, ētis*, f.; *requies, ētis*, f.

Seek, *quaero, ēre, quaesivi, quaesitum*.

Strive, *nitor, niti, nisus* and *nixus sum*, dep.

Vigilantly, sharply, *acriter*, adv.

Watch, *vigilo, āre, āvi, ātum*.

Weary, *defatigo, āre, āvi, ātum*.

Withdraw, *se removēre; removeo, ēre, mōvi, mōtum*.

285. EXERCISE.

1. There were *in Rome* so many like Catiline that they even dared to defend him. 2. O that we may be able to

conquer the leader *of this civil war!* 3. Would that I had received your letter. 4. Cicero the consul strove to defend the name and safety of the Roman people. 5. Let us strive to defend the republic. 6. Cicero, when consul, watched so vigilantly for the safety of the republic, that he has often been called the father of his country. 7. Many long for repose. 8. Many, longing for repose, withdraw from public affairs. 9. Rest does not always delight us. 10. Your wearied mind now seeks rest. 11. Who would neglect the highest welfare of the state?

Lesson LIX.

SUBJUNCTIVE OF PURPOSE OR RESULT — Continued.
[2, 8.]

286. Lesson from the Grammar.

I. Subjunctive of Purpose with *Ut* and *Ne*. 490.
    1. Pure Purpose. 491.
    2. Mixed Purpose. 492; 492, 1–4.
    3. Peculiarities. 493; 493, 1–4.

II. Subjunctive of Result with *Ut* and *Ut Non*. 490.
    1. Pure Result. 494.
    2. Mixed Result. 495; 495, 1–3.
    3. Peculiarities. 496; 496, 1–3.

III. Subjunctive with *Quo, Quin, Quominus*. 497–499; 498, 1–3.

287. Models.

I. It is necessary to eat that you may live.

I. *Esse oportet ut vivas.*

II. I ask you to aid him.

III. I fear that you will not endure the labors.

IV. It is necessary that virtue should attract you.

V. *There is* no one present who does not see.

VI. I cannot but send a letter.

VII. *Death does not deter* a wise man from deliberating for the republic.

II. *Te rogo ut eum juves.*

III. *Timeo ut labōres sustineas.*

IV. *Te oportet virtus trahat.*

V. *Adest   nemo,   quin videat.*

VI. *Facĕre non possum, quin littĕras mittam.*

VII. *Non deterret sapientem mors, quomĭnus rei publĭcae consŭlat.*

288. Remarks.

1. Model I. — To eat, *esse*, from *edo*, G. 291, subject of *oportet*.

2. Model III. — That you will not endure, *ut sustineas*. G. 492, 4.

3. Model IV. — *Trahat :* for the mood and for the omission of *ut*, see G. 495 ; 496, 1.

4. Model V. — Who does not see, *quin videat*, but that he sees. G. 498, 2.

5. Model VI. — I cannot but send, Latin idiom, *I am not able to do but that I may send.*

6. Model VII. — From deliberating, Latin idiom, *by which the less he may deliberate.* Emphasis places *mors* at the end of its clause.

289. Vocabulary.

Arms, *arma, ōrum*, n. pl.   G. 131, 1, 4).

Attend to, to serve, *servio, īre, īvi, ītum.* G. 385.

Behooves, it behooves, *oportet, oportuit.* G. 299.

Deter, *deterreo, ěre, ui, ĭtum.*

Diligently, *dīligenter,* adv.

Fear, to fear, *timeo, ěre, ui, ĭtum.*

For = to secure, *ad,* prep. with acc.

Forefathers, *majōres, um,* m. pl.

Free, *liber, ěra, ěrum.*

From, after verbs of hindering, *quomĭnus,* conj.

Greater, *major, us,* comparative of *magnus.* G. 165.

Health, *valetūdo, ĭnis,* f.

Homer, *Homērus, i,* m.

Implore, *oro, āre, āvi, ātum.*

Not only — but also, *non modo — sed etiam.*

Poet, *poēta, ae,* m.

Profit, to profit, *condūco, ěre, duxi, ductum ;* in this sense only in Third Pers. G. 385.

Punishment, penalty, *poena, ae,* f.

Rule, *impěro, āre, āvi, ātum.*

Studiously, *studiōse,* adv.

Take, take up, *capio, ěre, cepi, captum.*

Take care, to take care, *caveo, ěre, cavi, cautum.*

Than, *quam,* conj.

290. Exercise.

1. Our forefathers took up arms that they might be free. 2. The *Romans* took up arms not only that they might be free, but also that they might rule. 3. Cicero exhorts us to read studiously his orations. 4. Care must be taken that the punishment may not be greater than the fault. 5. I implore you to attend to your health most diligently. 6. We cannot doubt that virtue especially profits the state. 7. We cannot doubt that there were *poets* before Homer. 8. I fear that these dangers may increase. 9. It behooves us all to watch for the safety of the republic. 10. Nothing deterred Cicero from defending the republic.

Lesson LX.

RELATIVE CLAUSES OF PURPOSE OR RESULT.
[2, 13.]

291. Lesson from the Grammar.

I. Relative Clauses of Purpose. 500 ; 500, 1.

II. Relative Clauses of Result. 500 ; 500, 2.

III. Special Constructions in Relative Clauses. 501.
    1. After Indefinite Antecedents. 501, I.
    2. After *Unus, Solus*, and the like. 501, II.
    3. After *Dignus, Indignus, Idoneus, Aptus.* 501, III.

292. Models.

I. I sent one to state this.

II. I am not such a one as to use these things.

III. I see nothing else which we can do.

IV. There are some who are feared.

V. *True* wisdom is the only thing which dispels sadness.

VI. The fables are worthy to be read.

I. *Misi qui hoc dicĕret.*

II. *Non is sum qui his utar.*

III. *Nihil aliud video, quod agĕre possī̆mus.*

IV. *Sunt qui timeantur.*

V. *Vera sapientia est una, quae moestitiam pellat.*

VI. *Fabŭlae dignae sunt quae legantur.*

293. Remarks.

1. Model I. — One to state this, Latin idiom, *who should state this.*

2. MODEL II. — AS TO USE, *qui utar*, lit. *who may use.*

3. MODEL III. — WHICH WE CAN DO, *quod agĕre possĭmus*, lit. *which we may be able to do.*

4. MODEL V. — THE ONLY THING, *una*, agreeing with *sapientia.*

5. MODEL VI. — WORTHY TO BE READ, *dignae quae legantur*, lit. *worthy which may be read.*

294. SYNONYMES.

Joy, gladness, joyousness; *gaudium, laetitia, hilarĭtas.*

1. *Gaudium, ii*, n.; JOY, THE EMOTION OF JOY, — in itself considered.

2. *Laetitia, ae*, f.; GLADNESS, JOY, — as shown in the countenance or in action.

3. *Hilarĭtas, ātis*, f.; JOYOUSNESS, CHEERFUL, HAPPY DISPOSITION, — not a momentary feeling, but a characteristic of the temperament.

295. VOCABULARY.

Be elated, *effĕror, efferri, elātus sum ;* pass. of *effĕro.*

Cheerfulness, *hilarĭtas, ātis,* f.

Deny, *nego, āre, āvi, ātum.*

Excessive, *nimius, a, um.*

Faesulae, *Faesŭlae, ārum,* f. pl.

Fill, *compleo, ēre, ēvi, ētum.*

Forever, *in perpetuum.*

Greatest, *maxĭmus, a, um.* G. 165.

Lose, *amitto, ĕre, mĭsi, missum.*

On the part of, often rendered by the *Genitive.*

Perpetual, *perpetuus, a, um.*

Rejoicing, *laetitia, ae,* f.

Sad, *tristis, e.*

Whole, *cunctus, a, um.*

296. EXERCISE.

1. *Many* states sent ambassadors to Rome to establish peace and friendship with the Roman people. 2. There

were some, both *in Rome* and *at Faesulae*, who denied that Catiline was forming a conspiracy against the republic. 3. Let us not lose our cheerfulness. 4. I fear you will lose your cheerfulness forever. 5. There were some in the temple of Jupiter Stator who were filled with the greatest joy. 6. *In so great rejoicing* on the part of the whole state, you alone are sad. 7. We cannot doubt that the king was elated with excessive joy. 8. The orations of *Cicero* are worthy to be read by all.

·Lesson LXI.

SUBJUNCTIVE OF CONDITION.
[3, 4.]

297. Lesson from the Grammar.

I. Rule for the Subjunctive of Condition. 503.
    1. Condition Supplied. 503, 2.
    2. Force of Tenses. 504.
    3. *Dum, modo, dummŏdo.* 505.
    4. *Ac si, ut si, quasi,* etc. 506.

II. Conditions with *Si, Nisi, Ni, Sin.* 507–510.
    1. Mixed Forms. 511.
    2. Subjunctive and Indicative. 512.

298. Models.

I. Mental powers *remain,* if only *industry* remains.

I. *Manent ingenia, modo permaneat industria.*

II. If I should deny it, I should speak falsely.

II. *Si negem, mentiar.*

III. You *cannot* retain your *manhood*, if you arrange all things with reference to pleasure.

III. *Non potestis, voluptāte omnia dirigentes, retinēre virtūtem.*

IV. No one without hope would expose himself *to death.*

IV. *Nemo sine spe se offerret ad mortem.*

V. As if they should appropriate others' possessions to their own use.

V. *Ut si in suam rem aliēna convertant.*

VI. If it was not lawful, it was not necessary.

VI. *Si non licēbat, non necesse erat.*

VII. You would do wrong, if you should not give warning.

VII. *Imprŏbe fecĕris, nisi monuĕris.*

VIII. Eloquence would not be praised, if it accomplished nothing.

VIII. *Eloquentia non laudarētur, si nihil efficĕret.*

IX. If we shun folly, let us pursue wisdom.

IX. *Si stultitiam fugĭmus, sapientiam sequāmur.*

X. They would have abandoned their fields, had he not sent a letter.

X. *Relictūri agros erant, nisi littĕras misisset.*

299. REMARKS.

1. MODEL III. — IF YOU ARRANGE ALL THINGS WITH REFERENCE TO PLEASURE, *voluptāte omnia dirigentes*, lit. *arranging all things by pleasure.* G. 503, 2.

2. MODEL IV. — Observe the position of *ad mortem.*

3. MODEL V. — TO THEIR OWN USE, *in suam rem*, lit. *into their own affair.*

4. MODEL IX. — LET US PURSUE, *sequāmur.* G. 487.

5. MODEL X. — THEY WOULD HAVE ABANDONED, *relictūri erant,* lit. *were about to abandon.* G. 512, 2, 2).

300. VOCABULARY.

Be willing, to wish, *volo, velle, volui.*

Conscript Fathers, *Patres Conscripti,* m. pl.

Depart, set out, *proficiscor, i, fectus sum,* dep.

Exile, *exsilium, ii,* n.

Gladly, *laete,* adv.

Inaction, *inertia, ae,* f.

If only, *dummŏdo,* conj.

Leisure, at leisure, *otiōsus, a, um.*

Provide for, *provĭdeo, ēre, vīdi, vīsum,* with dat.

Suppress, *comprĭmo, ēre, pressi, pressum.*

Tell, *dico, ēre, dixi, dictum.*

Unless, *nisi,* conj.

301. EXERCISE.

1. What would you have said, if Cato had been ordered to go into exile? 2. If you were willing to hear me; I would tell you. 3. I would gladly hear you, if only I were at leisure. 4. Unless you suppress this conspiracy, Conscript Fathers, you will be condemned for inaction. 5. If you (pl.) will watch for the safety of the republic, you will be praised by all the citizens. 6. If Cicero had not provided for the state, he would have been condemned by all. 7. If Catiline would only depart from the city, we should all be liberated from fear. 8. O that he had not formed this conspiracy against the republic!

Lesson LXII.

SUBJUNCTIVE OF CONCESSION.
[3, 7.]

302. Lesson from the Grammar.

I. Rule for the Subjunctive of Concession. 515.

II. Classes of Concessive Clauses. 516.
1. With *Quamquam.* 516, I.
2. With *Licet, Quamvis, Quantumvis,* etc. 516, II.
3. With the Compounds of *Si.* 516, III.

303. Models.

I. Though he may deride, reason will yet avail more.

I. *Licet irrideat, plus tamen ratio valēbit.*

II. Though they understand, they never speak.

II. *Quamquam intellĭgunt, tamen nunquam dicunt.*

III. *Acquit* Verres, though he confesses that he has accepted moneys.

III. *Absolvĭte Verrem, qui se fateātur pecunias cepisse.*

IV. Though *pain* may not be the greatest evil, it is certainly an evil.

IV. *Ne sit summum malum dolor, malum certe est.*

V. Though *glory* may not possess anything in itself, yet it follows virtue.

V. *Etsi nihil habeat in se gloria, tamen virtūtem sequĭtur.*

304. REMARKS.

1. MODEL III. — THOUGH HE CONFESSES, *qui fateātur*, lit. *who may confess*. G. 515, II. The verb on which an infinitive clause depends is often inserted in that clause directly after the subject, as *fateātur* after *se*. See Part Third, 601.

2. MODEL IV. — *Ne sit*. G. 516, II. 1. Observe also the order of words, as affected by emphasis.

3. MODEL V. — Emphasis places *gloria* at the end of the clause.

305. SYNONYMES.

Fear, alarm; *metus, timor, formīdo*.

1. *Metus, us*, m.; FEAR, A RATIONAL FEAR, — arising from real danger.

2. *Timor, ōris*, m.; FEAR, — a fear arising either from timidity or from imminent danger, and accordingly less under the control of reason than *metus*.

3. *Formīdo, ĭnis*, f.; ALARM, DREAD, CONSTERNATION, — a great and overwhelming fear.

306. VOCABULARY.

Aid, means, *opes, opum*, f. pl. G. 133, 1.

Although, *quamquam, licet, quamvis*, etc. G. 516.

Banish, throw off, *abjĭcio, ĕre, jēci, jectum*.

Conceal, *occulto, āre, āvi, ātum*.

Consternation, *formīdo, ĭnis*, f.

Disgraceful, *turpis, e*.

Emolument, *emolumentum, i*, n.

Even if, *etĭamsi*, conj.

Fear, *timor, ōris*, m.; *metus, us*, m.

Follow, *consĕquor, i, secūtus sum*, dep.

Honorable, *honestus, a, um*.

Right, *rectus, a, um*.

Sudden, *subĭtus, a, um*.

Way, manner, *modus, i*, m.

307. EXERCISE.

1. The *best* men do what is right, even if they see that no emolument will follow. 2. Although they fear him, they deny it. 3. Even if they feared him, they would deny it. 4. That which is disgraceful, although it may. be concealed, can in no way be honorable. 5. *With your aid*, even if we were timid, we would banish all fear. 6. Let not fear deter us from watching for the safety of the republic. 7. Let us liberate the state both from danger and from fear. 8. Let not this *sudden* consternation deter us from doing what is right.

LESSON LXIII.

SUBJUNCTIVE OF CAUSE AND TIME.
[3, 11.]

308. LESSON FROM THE GRAMMAR.

I. Rule for the Subjunctive of Cause. 517.
   1. Clauses with *Quum.* 518.
   2. Relative Clauses denoting Cause. 519.
   3. Clauses with *Quod, Quia, Quoniam, Quando.* 520.
II. Rule for the Subjunctive of Time with Cause. 521.
   1. Clauses with *Dum, Donec, Quoad.* 522.
   2. Clauses with *Antĕquam* and *Priusquam.* 523.

309. MODELS.

I. Since these things are so, proceed.

I. *Quae quum ita sint, perge.*

II. O the *power* of truth, since it defends itself!

II. *O vis veritātis, quae se defendat!*

III. I heard Zeno when I was at Athens.

III. *Zenōnem, quum Athēnis essem, audiēbam.*

IV. Since I have spoken of the kind of war, I will now speak of its magnitude.

IV. *Quoniam de genĕre belli dixi, nunc de magnitudĭne dicam.*

V. No one shuns pleasure itself because it is pleasure.

V. *Nemo ipsam voluptātem, quia voluptas sit, fugit.*

VI. You will keep them till I see you.

VI. *Ea continēbis quoad te videam.*

VII. While the laws were in force.

VII. *Dum leges vigēbant.*

VIII. They are present before it is light.

VIII. *Priusquam lucet, adsunt.*

IX. Before he comes, he will send a letter.

IX. *Antĕquam veniat, littĕras mittet.*

310. Remarks.

1. Model I. — *Quae quum.* G. 602, III. 1.

2. Model II. — Since it defends, *quae defendat*, lit. *which may defend.* G. 519.

3. Model III. — When I was, *quum essem.* G. 518, II. 1.

4. Model IV. — Of its magnitude, *de magnitudĭne*, concerning the magnitude. The possessive *its* should not be rendered.

5. Model IX. — Before he comes, *antĕquam veniat.* G. 521, 1.

311. Vocabulary.

Be in force, *vigeo*, *ēre*, *ui*.

Curtius, *Curtius*, *ii*, m.

Decree, *consultum*, *i*, n.; a decree of the senate, *senātus consultum*.

Drive, cast out, *ejīcio*, *ēre*, *jēci*, *jectum*.

Hate, *odi*, *odisse*. G. 297, I.

Lycurgus, *Lycurgus*, *i*, m.

Record, *perscrībo*, *ēre*, *scripsi*, *scriptum*.

Scarcely, scarcely yet, *vixdum*, adv.

Since, as, *quum*, conj.

Strong, ample, *amplus*, *a*, *um*; in the strongest terms, *amplissimis verbis*.

Thank, *gratias ago*, *ēre*, *egi*, *actum*.

Thanks, *gratiae*, *ārum*, f. pl. G. 132.

While, *dum*, conj.

312. Exercise.

1. I had scarcely read your letter when Curtius came to me. 2. They often heard *Cicero*, when they were in Rome. 3. Many hate the consul because he has driven Catiline into exile. 4. I praise the consul because he has driven this man into exile. 5. The senate thanked Cicero in the strongest terms, because he had liberated the republic from the greatest dangers. 6. Since these things are so, let us defend the consul. 7. The Lacedaemonians were brave while the laws of Lycurgus were in force. 8. Let us wait until this decree of the senate is recorded.

LESSON LXIV.

SUBJUNCTIVE IN INDIRECT QUESTIONS.
[4, 2.]

313. LESSON FROM THE GRAMMAR.

I. Rule for the Subjunctive in Indirect Questions. 525.

II. Single and Double Questions. 526.

314. MODELS.

I. I understood what the law meant.

I. *Intellexi quid sibi lex vellet.*

II. It is uncertain *how long* the life *of each one of us* will be.

II. *Incertum est, quam longa nostrum cujusque vita futūra sit.*

III. It is asked whether virtue is sought for its own worth, or for certain advantages.

III. *Quaerĭtur, virtus suamne propter dignitātem, an propter fructus alĭquos expetātur.*

IV. It is asked whether *virtue* can be produced by nature or by education.

IV. *Quaerĭtur natūra an doctrīna possit effĭci virtus.*

V. Let us inquire whether or not there was need of a fleet.

V. *Opus fuĕrit classe necne quaerāmus.*

315. REMARKS.

1. MODEL I. — MEANT, *sibi vellet,* lit. *wished for itself.* For mood and tense, see G. 525; 481, II. The order *quid sibi lex* is more euphonious than *quid lex sibi.*

2. Model III. — Whether — or, *ne — an.* But in models IV. and V. the particle is omitted in the first member. G. 526, II.

3. Model IV. — Emphasis places *virtus* at the end of the sentence.

4. Model V. — Let us inquire, *quaerămus.* G. 487. Or not, *necne*, G. 526, II. 2, 1). Of a fleet, *classe*, G. 419, V.

316. Vocabulary.

Command, *impĕro, āre, āvi, ātum.*
Depart, go, *eo, ire, ivi, ĭtum.*
Difficult, *difficĭlis, e.*
Disagree, *dissentio, ĭre, sensi, sensum.*
False, *falsus, a, ŭm.*
Hesitate, *dubĭto, āre, āvi, ātum.*
Important, great, *magnus, a, um.*
Inquire, *quaero, ĕre, quaesĭvi or ĭi, quaesĭtum.*
Or not, *an non ; necne.* G. 526, II. 2, 1); 346, II. 2, 3).
Preserve, *servo, āre, āvi, ātum.*

Presume, believe, *credo, ĕre, dĭdi, dĭtum.*
Question, *quaestio, ōnis, f.*
Report, *rumor, ōris, m.*
School, *schola, ae, f.*
Subject, thing, *res, rei, f.*
Think, *puto, āre, āvi, ātum.*
Upon, concerning, *de*, prep. with abl.
Whether — not, *nonne.*
Whether — or, *utrum — an.*
Wonder, *miror, āri, ātus sum,* dep.

317. Exercise.

1. Let us ask Catiline whether he hesitates to depart from the city.   2. Cicero asked him whether he hesitated to depart from the city at the command of the consul.   3. I wonder why philosophers disagree upon the most important subjects.   4. It is difficult to say whether this report is true or false.   5. They inquired of me whether I did not think that Cicero would preserve the republic.   6. Whether or not riches make us happy, is the question. 7. When you were in Athens, you *were* often, I presume, in the schools of the philosophers.

Lesson LXV.

SUBJUNCTIVE BY ATTRACTION. SUBJUNCTIVE IN INDIRECT DISCOURSE.

[4, 6.]

318. Lesson from the Grammar.

I. Subjunctive by Attraction. 527.

II. Subjunctive in Indirect Discourse. 529.

319. Models.

I. I formed the plan, to depart before it was light.

I. *Cepi consilium ut antĕquam lucēret exīrem.*

II. You were saying that you wished those things which I had done, to result prosperously.

II. *Dicēbas te velle, quae egissem felicĭter evenīre.*

320. Remarks.

1. Model I. — Before it was or should be light, *antĕquam lucĕret*, Subj. by Attraction because of its connection with *exīrem*.

2. Model II. — Those things which I had done, *quae egissem*, antecedent omitted. G. 451, 1. *Egissem*, Subj. by Attraction.

321. Synonymes.

Safe, unharmed, secure; *salvus, incolŭmis, tutus.*

1. *Salvus, a, um ;* safe, preserved, rescued from danger, — applicable both to persons and to things.

2. *Incolŭmis, e ;* SAFE, UNHARMED, — especially applicable to persons. *Incolŭmis* involves more than *salvus.* He who escapes *salvus*, escapes with his life, though not necessarily without injury; but he who escapes *incolŭmis*, escapes unhurt.

3. *Tutus, a, um ;* SECURE, FREE FROM DANGER.

322. VOCABULARY.

Believe, *credo,* *ĕre, dĭdi, dĭtum.* G. 385.

Children, *lĭbĕri, ōrum,* m. pl. G. 131, 1, 1).

Desire, *cupio, ĕre, īvi, ĭtum.*

Dine, *coeno, āre, āvi, ātum.*

Doubtful, *dubius, a, um.* There is no doubt = it is not doubtful, *non dubium est.*

Unharmed, *incolŭmis, e.*

With, at the house of, *apud,* prep. with acc.

323. EXERCISE.

1. He says that he was dining with the consul when he received your letter. 2. They say that he was reading your letter when the messenger came to him. 3. We have said that the Lacedaemonians were brave while the laws of Lycurgus were in force. 4. Did you not say that many hated Cicero because he had driven Catiline into exile? 5. I said that I praised the consul because he had driven this man into exile. 6. There is no doubt that there were many who did not believe Cicero while Catiline was in the city. 7. There is no one who does not desire that his children should be unharmed and happy. 8. The republic is at length safe. 9. There is no doubt that this city is secure.

Lesson LXVI.

INDIRECT DISCOURSE.
[4, 10.]

324. Lesson from the Grammar.

I. Moods in the Oratio Obliqua. 530, 531.

II. Tenses in the Oratio Obliqua. 532.

III. Pronouns in the Oratio Obliqua. 533.

325. Models.

I. Democritus says that there are *innumerable worlds*.

II. They say that Plato entertained the same opinion of the immortality of the soul as Pythagoras.

III. Hippias boasted that there was nothing in any art which *he* did not know.

I. *Democrĭtus dicit innumerabĭles esse mundos.*

II. *Platōnem ferunt de animōrum aeternitāte sensisse idem quod Pythagŏram.*

III. *Hippias gloriātus est nihil esse ulla in arte quod ipse nescīret.*

326. Remarks.

1. MODEL II. — OF (on the subject of) THE IMMORTALITY OF THE SOUL (of souls), *de animōrum aeternitāte.* G. 602, II. 3. ENTERTAINED THE SAME OPINION AS PYTHAGORAS, Latin idiom, *thought the same thing which Pythagoras* (thought). *Pythagŏram*, subject of *sensisse* understood. G. 551, 5.

2. MODEL III. — WHICH HE DID NOT KNOW, *quod ipse nescīret.* For mood and tense of *nescīret*, see G. 531; 481, II. 1.

327. SYNONYMES.

Courage, fortitude; *virtus, fortitūdo.*

1. *Virtus, ūtis,* f.; COURAGE, VALOR, ENERGY, — as shown in action.

2. *Fortitūdo, ĭnis,* f.; FORTITUDE, FIRMNESS, — as shown in resistance.

328. VOCABULARY.

Africa, *Afrĭca, ae,* f.

Ask, inquire, *quaero, ĕre, quaesīvi, sĭtum ;* it is asked, *quaerĭtur, quaesītum est.*

Attract, *allĭcio, ĕre, lexi, lectum.*

Compel, *cogo, ĕre, coēgi, coactum.*

Fortitude, *fortitūdo, ĭnis,* f.

Go from, *exeo, īre, ii, ĭtum.*

Here, *hic,* adv.

Mention, *commemŏro, āre, āvi, ātum.*

Second time, *itĕrum,* adv.

There, *illic,* adv.

Why, *quid.* G. 380, 2.

329. EXERCISE.

1. Why should *I* here mention the Roman senators? 2. He asked why he should there mention the Roman senators. 3. We have said that the orations of Cicero are worthy to be read by all. 4. It is *often* asked whether the letters of Cicero are worthy to be read a second time. 5. They say that Catiline would not have gone from the city unless he had feared the consul. 6. Your brother says that he will write to you when he comes to Rome. 7. Cicero says that Hannibal was compelled by the valor of Scipio to return into Africa. 8. There is no doubt that virtue attracts to itself the good and wise. 9. It is the part of fortitude to bear all things bravely.

7

Lesson LXVII.

IMPERATIVE.
[4, 11.]

330. Lesson from the Grammar.

I. Tenses of the Imperative. 534.

II. Use of the Imperative. 535–538.
    1. Circumlocutions. 535, 1.
    2. Imperative supplied. 535, 3; 487; 488, II.
    3. Imperative in Prohibitions. 538, 1 and 2.

331. Models.

I. Devote yourselves to study.
    I. *In studium incumbĭte.*

II. If I have committed any offence against you, pardon me.
    II. *Si quid in te peccāvi, ignosce.*

III. You shall consider the subject.
    III. *Rem penditōte.*

IV. The safety of the people shall be the *supreme* law.
    IV. *Salus popŭli suprēma lex esto.*

V. Do not wish that which cannot be done.
    V. *Nolīte id velle quod fiĕri non potest.*

VI. Let them be happy.
    VI. *Sint beāti.*

VII. If anything shall happen, you will let me know it.
    VII. *Si quid accidĕrit, facies ut sciam.*

332. REMARKS.

1. MODEL V. — DO NOT WISH, *nolite velle*, lit. *be unwilling to wish.* G. 535, 1, 3).

2. MODEL VI. — LET THEM BE = may they be, *sint.* G. 487.

3. MODEL VII. — SHALL HAPPEN = shall have happened, i. e. before you let me know, *accidĕrit*, Fut. Perf. G. 473. YOU WILL LET ME KNOW, Latin idiom, *you will make* (cause) *that I may know.* G. 492, 1. *Facies*, Fut. Indic. for the Imperative. G. 535, 3, 2).

333. VOCABULARY.

Conspirators, *conjurāti*, *ŏrum*, m. pl.

Devote one's self to, *incumbo, ĕre, cubui, cubĭtum, in with acc.*

Highest public welfare, *summa res publĭca.*

Liberal, *liberālis, e.*

Neglect, *neglĭgo, ĕre, lexi, lectum.*

Nor, with imperatives, *neve,* adv.

Oppose, *obsto, āre, stĭti, stātum.* G. 386.

Peril, *pericŭlum, i,* n.

Personal, of one's self alone, gen. of *solus, a, um.* G. 149.

Philosophy, *philosophia, ae,* ..

Violate, *viŏlo, āre, āvi, ātum.*

334. EXERCISE.

1. Let us devote ourselves to liberal studies. 2. Know, Conscript Fathers, that Catiline has formed a conspiracy against the republic. 3. Do not think that the consul will neglect the highest public welfare. 4. Do not doubt that this can be done. 5. Do not hesitate to do this. 6. Let me know what the *conspirators* are doing. 7. Let us not violate the laws, nor oppose the decrees of the senate. 8. Remember that Cicero preserved the republic at his own personal peril. 9. Do you not think that these books on philosophy are worthy to be read a second time?

Lesson LXVIII.

INFINITIVE.[1]

335. Lesson from the Grammar.

I. Tenses of the Infinitive. 540–544.

II. Subject of the Infinitive. 545.

III. Predicate after the Infinitive. 546.
   1. Predicate attracted. 547; 547, I. and II.

IV. Infinitive as Subject. 549.
   1. Personal Construction for Impersonal. 549, 4.

336. Models.

I. I hope that *our* friendship does not need *witnesses.*

I. *Spero nostram amicitiam non egēre testĭbus.*

II. I desire both to be grateful and to be so regarded.

II. *Volo et esse et habēri gratus.*

III. No one can be *happy* without virtue.

III. *Beātus esse sine virtūte nemo potest.*

IV. To defraud is base.

IV. *Fraudāre turpe est.*

V. It is true that there is friendship among the good.

V. *Verum est, amicitiam inter bonos esse.*

VI. *True* praise is thought to be due to virtue alone.

VI. *Vera laus debēri virtūti uni putātur.*

---

[1] The remaining Exercises in this work, although based entirely upon Ciceronian models, may accompany the reading of any Latin author.

VII. Demosthenes is said to have heard *Plato*.

VII. *Platōnem audivisse Demosthĕnes dicĭtur.*

337. Remarks.

1. Model I. — Does not need, *non egĕre*. After verbs of *hoping,* the Infinitive is generally in the Future tense; but it is in the Present when the action itself belongs to Present time.

2. Model II. — Both to be grateful and to be so regarded. Latin idiom, *both to be and to be regarded grateful.*

3. Model VII. — Emphasis places *Platonem* at the beginning of the sentence; accordingly the subject is placed later in the sentence — here directly before its verb.

338. Synonymes.

In vain, to no purpose; *frustra, nequidquam.*

1. *Frustra;* in vain, with disappointment, — used with reference to the disappointment of the person rather than to the failure of the undertaking.

2. *Nequidquam;* in vain, to no purpose, — used with reference to the failure of the undertaking.

339. Vocabulary.

Bring, bear, *fero, ferre, tuli, latum.*

Purpose, desire, *sententia, ae,* f. According to one's desire, *ex sententia.*

Rejoice, *gaudeo, ēre, gavīsus sum.* G. 272, 3.

Sail, to sail, *navĭgo, āre, āvi, ātum.*

Voyage, to have a prosperous voyage, *ex sententia navigāre,* lit. *to sail according to one's opinion,* or *desire.*

340. EXERCISE.

1. Did you not say that philosophers often disagree?
2. I said that philosophers disagree upon the most important subjects. 3. They all say that virtue makes men happy. 4. It is certain that virtue can make us happy. 5. The consul is said to have written this book. 6. Do you not wish to be happy? 7. We wish to be not only happy, but also good and wise. 8. God does nothing in vain. 9. *We* do many things in vain. 10. They brought *us* aid to no purpose. 11. Cicero says that Cato was called *wise*. 12. It is permitted us to be wise. 13. They rejoice that the consul has had a prosperous voyage.

LESSON LXIX.

INFINITIVE — CONTINUED.

341. LESSON FROM THE GRAMMAR.

I. 'Infinitive as Object. 550.
  1. With Subject Accusative. 551; 551, I.–III.
  2. Without Subject Accusative. 552; 552, 1 and 2.

II. Infinitive in Special Constructions. 553; 553, I. and II.

342. MODELS.

I. Let us consider that the glory of *virtue* is eternal.

I. *Cogitēmus virtūtis gloriam esse sempiternam.*

II. *No* art can imitate the skill of nature.

II. *Nulla ars imitāri sollertiam natūrae potest.*

III. That which is good can be made better by *instruction.*

III. *Quae bona sunt, fĭĕri meliōra possunt doctrīna.*

IV. We desire to avoid these things.

IV. *Haec vitāre cupĭmus.*

V. The *first* step towards wisdom is to know one's self.

V. *Primus gradus ad sapientiam est se ipsum novisse.*

VI. The oracle that Athens would be victorious had been given.

VI. *Oracŭlum datum erat victrīces Athēnas fore.*

343. REMARKS.

1. MODEL III. — THAT WHICH IS GOOD, i. e. whatever is good, *quae bona sunt*, lit. *what things are good.* The Latin uses the plural because the statement is general, and is not confined to a single object. The antecedent, which is the subject of *possunt*, is omitted. G. 451, 1. Emphasis places *doctrīna* at the end of the sentence.

2. MODEL V. — TO KNOW ONE'S SELF, *se ipsum novisse*, Predicate after *est.* G. 553, I. *Novisse*, Perfect in form, but Present in sense. G. 297, I. 2.

3. MODEL VI. — THAT ATHENS WOULD BE VICTORIOUS, *victrīces Athēnas fore*, in apposition with *oracŭlum.* G. 553, II.

344. SYNONYMES.

Opponent, enemy; *adversarius, hostis, inimīcus.*

1. *Adversarius, ii*, m.; OPPONENT, ADVERSARY, — the generic word for an opponent of any kind, whether in war or in peace.

2. *Hostis, is,* m.; PUBLIC ENEMY; ENEMY, — in war.

3. *Inimīcus, i,* m.; PERSONAL or PRIVATE ENEMY, PERSONAL FOE.

• 345. VOCABULARY. •

Arrive, come, *venio, īre, veni, ventum.*

Be unwilling, *nolo, nolle, nolui.* G. 293.

By, through, *per,* prep. with acc.

Exceedingly, *vehementer,* adv.

Foe, *inimīcus, i,* m.

Force, *vis, vis,* f. G. 88, III. 3.

Impose upon, *impōno, ĕre, posui, posĭtum.*

Opponent, *adversarius, ii,* m.

Profess, *profiteor, ēri, fessus sum,* dep.

Refute, *refūto, āre, āvi, ātum.*

Rumor, *rumor, ōris,* m.

Visit, *viso, ĕre, i, um.*

Young man, *adolescens, entis,* m.

346. EXERCISE.

1. There are some who profess to be wise.   2. No one is an orator who is unwilling to be like Demosthenes.   3. The young men wished to hear Demosthenes.   4. We all can be useful.   5. The tyrant is said to have imposed laws upon the state by force.   6. I desire to visit Rome and Athens.   7. I rejoice exceedingly that you have arrived safe in Italy, and that you have had a prosperous voyage.   8. There were some who favored the enemies of their country.   9. We call them not foes, but enemies.   10. Opponents must be refuted.   11. The rumor was, that the enemy had been conquered by Caesar.   12. I wonder at this, that you have not yet come to Rome.

LESSON LXX.

SUBJECT AND OBJECT CLAUSES.

347. LESSON FROM THE GRAMMAR.

I. Four Forms distinguished. 554, I.–IV.
II. Forms of Subject Clauses. 555, 556.
III. Forms of Object Clauses. 557, 558.

348. MODELS.

I. It is asked why they disagree.

II. That you are of a cheerful spirit greatly delights me.

III. The result is, that every one is delighted.

IV. It is a fault that they bestow too much study upon obscure subjects.

V. I know not what is to be done.

VI. I wonder that you write nothing to me.

VII. The sun causes all things to bloom.

I. *Quaerĭtur cur dissentiant.*

II. *Te hilări anĭmo esse valde me juvat.*

III. *Fit ut quisque delectētur.*

IV. *Vitium est quod nimis magnum studium in res obscūras confĕrunt.*

V. *Quid agendum sit nescio.*

VI. *Miror te ad me nihil scribĕre.*

VII. *Sol effĭcit ut omnia floreant.*

VIII. I grieved that I had   VIII. *Dolēbam quod con-*
lost the companion   *sortem   labōris*
of my labor.   *amisĕram.*

349. REMARKS.

1. It will be observed that, in the first four models, the indirect question, the infinitive clause, and the clauses with *ut* and *quod*, are all used as *subjects*, while in the other models the corresponding clauses are all used as *objects*.

2. MODEL III. — THE RESULT IS = it is effected, it comes to pass, *fit*. For mood in *delectētur*, see G. 495, 2.

3. MODEL VII. — CAUSES ALL THINGS TO BLOOM, Latin idiom, *effects that all things may bloom*.

350. VOCABULARY.

Absurd, *absurdus, a, um.*

Also; I, he, she, &c., also, *idem, eădem, idem ;* lit. *the same.*

Apparel, *vestītus, us,* m.

As, after *tam, quam,* adv.

Be the slave of, *servio, īre, īvi, ītum.* G. 385.

Civil, *civīlis, e.*

Costly, *pretiōsus, a, um.*

Happen, *fio, fiĕri, factus sum.* G. 294.

Indeed, *enim,* conj.

Knowledge, *scientia, ae,* f.

Law, *jus, juris,* n.; civil law, *jus civīle.*

Of greater value, *pluris.* G. 402, III. 1.

Show, *ostendo, ĕre, i, tensum.*

So much, *tantopĕre,* adv.

Some — others, *alii — alii.* G. 459.

That, in that, *quod,* conj.

Whether, in double questions, *utrum ; ne,* enclitic. G. 526, II.

351. EXERCISE.

1. You will inquire of us why we are so much delighted with the study of philosophy. 2. What, indeed, is so absurd as to be delighted *with costly apparel ?* 3. Py-

thagoras says that some men are the slaves of glory, others of money. 4. He also says that philosophers are students of wisdom. 5. It is my duty to show what I think. 6. It is my duty both to show what I think and to defend what you have done. 7. The question is asked whether eloquence or a knowledge of the civil law is of the greater value. 8. He boasted that he had conquered the enemy in many battles. 9. It often happens that men are delighted with glory.

Lesson LXXI.

GERUNDS.

352. Lesson from the Grammar.

I. Gerunds and Gerundives. 559–562.

II. Genitive of Gerunds and Gerundives. 563.

III. Dative of Gerunds and Gerundives. 564.

IV. Accusative of Gerunds and Gerundives. 565.

353. Models.

I. The power of *speech* enables us to teach others those things which we know.

II. *There have been formed* plans for destroying the city.

III. The season is suitable for gathering fruits.

I. *Eloquendi vis efficit ut ea quae scimus alios docēre possīmus.*

II. *Inĭta sunt consilia urbis delendae.*

III. *Tempus demetendis fructĭbus accommodātum est.*

IV. The day will furnish something for meditation.

IV. *Dies aliquid ad cogitandum dabit.*

V. He *assigned* the citizens to *Gabinius* to put to death.

V. *Attribuit cives interficiendos Gabinio.*

354. REMARKS.

1. MODEL I. — THE POWER OF SPEECH, *eloquendi vis*, lit. *the power of speaking.* WE KNOW, *scimus*, not attracted into the Subjunctive. See G. 527, 2, 1).

2. MODEL II. — PLANS FOR DESTROYING THE CITY, *consilia urbis delendae*, lit. *plans of the city to be destroyed.* For *urbis delendae* we may use *urbem delendi*.

3. MODEL V. — TO PUT TO DEATH, or TO BE PUT TO DEATH, *interficiendos*, agreeing with *cives.* See G. 565, 3.

355. SYNONYMES.

Mind, soul, intellect, talent; *animus, mens, ingenium.*

1. *Animus, i,* m.; MIND, SOUL, — especially as the seat of the emotions.

2. *Mens, mentis,* f.; THE INTELLECT, THE UNDERSTANDING, THE REASONING FACULTY.

3. *Ingenium, ii,* n.; TALENT, MENTAL ENDOWMENT.

356. VOCABULARY.

Abandon, *relinquo, ĕre, lĭqui, lictum.*

Accumulate, trans., *augeo, ĕre, auxi, auctum.*

Assign, *tribuo, ĕre, i, ūtum.*

Bestow upon, *impertio, īre, īvi* or *ii, ītum.*

Desire, *libīdo, ĭnis,* f.

Endowed with, *praeditus, a, um.*

For, after *idoneus, ad,* prep. with acc.

Furnish, *orno, āre, āvi, ātum.*

Government, *regnum, i, n.*

Labor, *labor, ōris,* m.

Mind, soul, *animus, i, m.*

Nature, *natūra, ae,* f.

Object, thing, *res, rei,* f.

Perceive, *percipio, ĕre, cēpi, ceptum.*

Plunder, *diripio, ĕre, ripui, reptum.*

Rejoice, *laetor, āri, ātus sum.*

Secure, cause, conciliate, *concilio, āre, āvi, ātum.*

Sense, *sensus, us,* m.

Strengthen, nourish, *alo, ĕre, alui, altum.*

Suitable, *idoneus, a, um.*

Talent, *ingenium, ii,* n.

Torture, *crucio, āre, āvi, ātum.*

Understanding, *mens, mentis,* f.

Very much, *plurimum,* adv.

Well, *bene,* adv.

357. Exercise.

1. Wisdom is the art of living well and happily. 2. I rejoice that you are desirous *of securing peace among the citizens.* 3. *Avaricious* men are tortured, not only by the desire of accumulating, but also by the fear of losing. 4. Cicero bestowed his labor upon the work of saving the republic. 5. Nature has furnished the mind *with senses suitable for perceiving objects.* 6. There were some who abandoned their country itself to be plundered. 7. What is better than a soul endowed with virtue? 8. *Great* talent, even if it is not strengthened by learning, often avails *very much.* 9. Cicero says that the government of the whole mind has been assigned to the understanding.

Lesson LXXII.

GERUNDS AND SUPINES.

358. Lesson from the Grammar.

I. Ablative of Gerunds and Gerundives. 566.

II. Supine in *um*. 567–569.
   1. Its place supplied. 569, 4.

III. Supine in *u*. 570.
   1. Its place supplied. 570, 3.

359. Models.

I. The mind is nourished by learning.	I. *Mens discendo alĭtur.*
II. *No* art is able *by imitation* to attain the skill of nature.	II. *Nulla ars sollertiam natūrae consĕqui potest imitando.*
III. They spend *all* their time in learning.	III. *Omne tempus in discendo consūmunt.*
IV. I was then thinking of (concerning) sending the boys into Greece.	IV. *De puĕris in Graeciam transportandis tum cogitābam.*
V. Verres sends to ask for the *vessels*.	V. *Verres mittit rogātum vasa.*
VI. It seems difficult to say what the cause is.	VI. *Difficĭle dictu vidētur quae causa sit.*

360. Remarks.

1. Model III. — All their time, *omne tempus*. The possessive is unnecessary.

2. **Model IV.** — Of (about, concerning) sending the boys into Greece, *de puĕris in Graeciam transportandis*, lit. *concerning the boys to be transported into Greece.*

361. Vocabulary.

Commit, commit to memory, *edisco, ĕre, didĭci.*

Exercise, *exerceo, ĕre, ui, ĭtum.*

Gratitude, *gratia, ae,* f.

Hearer, *audiens, entis,* m. and f.

Leisure, *otium, ii,* n.

Memory, *memoria, ae,* f.

More, *magis,* adv. G. 170.

Necessary, *necessarius, a, um.*

Requite a favor, *gratiam refĕro, ferre, tŭli, lātum.*

Salute, *salūto, āre, āvi, ātum.*

Spend, *consūmo, ĕre, sumpsi, sumptum.*

Understand, *cognosco, ĕre, nōvi, nĭtum.*

Word for word, *ad verbum ;* lit. *to a word.*

362. Exercise.

1. We all have spent much time in reading. 2. Cicero spent much time in reading the orators and poets. 3. That day was spent in reading; there was no leisure for writing. 4. The orator spent his leisure in writing history. 5. Let the memory be exercised by committing word for word the orations of Cicero. 6. He is the best orator who by his speaking both informs and delights the minds of his hearers. 7. No duty is more necessary than that of requiting a favor. 8. The ambassadors have come to salute the king. 9. The orations of Cicero are easy to understand.

Lesson LXXIII.

PARTICIPLES.

363. Lesson from the Grammar.

I. Tenses of Participles. 571–574.
II. Use of Participles. 575–581.

364. Models.

I. *Every* evil is in the beginning easily suppressed.	I. *Omne malum nascens facĭle opprimĭtur.*
II. The sun by its rising causes the day.	II. *Sol oriens diem confĭcit.*
III. Aeschines, when condemned, betook himself to Rhodes.	III. *Aeschĭnes damnātus se Rhodum contŭlit.*
IV. I should think unpopularity incurred by virtue, not unpopularity, but glory.	IV. *Invidiam virtūte partam gloriam, non invidiam, putārem.*
V. The mind, though it does not see itself, discerns other things.	V. *Anĭmus se non videns alia cernit.*
VI. He *assigned* us to *Cethegus* to slaughter.	VI. *Attribuit nos trucidandos Cethēgo.*
VII. Homer lived before the *founding of Rome.*	VII. *Homērus fuit ante Romam condĭtam.*

365. Remarks.

1. Model I. — In the beginning, *nascens*, lit. *arising, beginning.*
2. Model II. — By its rising, *oriens*, lit. *rising.*

3. MODEL III. — WHEN CONDEMNED, *damnātus*, lit. *having been condemned*.

4. MODEL V. — THOUGH IT DOES NOT SEE, *non videns*, lit. *not seeing*.

5. MODEL VI. — TO SLAUGHTER, *trucidandos*, lit. *to be slaughtered*.

6. MODEL VII. — BEFORE THE FOUNDING OF ROME, *ante Romam conditam*, lit. *before Rome founded*.

366. VOCABULARY.

Be born, *nascor, i, natus sum*, dep.

Born for, *natus, a, um, ad* with acc.

Dated, *datus, a, um;* lit. *given.*

Deed, *factum, i,* n.; lit. *thing done;* good deed, *recte factum;* lit. *thing rightly done.*

Eternal, *sempiternus, a, um.*

Hand, *manus, us,* f.

Hero, *vir, viri,* m.

Influence, induce, *indūco, ĕre, duxi, ductum.*

Letter from me, you, &c., *epistŏla mea, tua,* etc.; lit. *my,* &c., *letter.* Also *epistŏla a me,* etc.

Myself, yourself, &c., intensive, *ipse, a, um.*

Reward, *praemium, ii,* n.

Save, *conservo, āre, āvi, ātum.*

Seek, pursue, *sequor, i, secūtus sum,* dep.

So, *tam,* adv.; not so much — as, *non tam — quam.*

Spend (of time), *ago, ĕre, egi, actum.*

Think, *arbĭtror, āri, ātus sum,* dep.

Truth, *verum, i,* n.

367. EXERCISE.

1. The recollection of a well-spent life is eternal. 2. This brave hero, born for glory, has saved the republic. 3. I have received from you two letters dated at Rome. 4. Let us believe them when they speak the truth. 5. I think that you have never before read a letter from me, unless written by my own hand. 6. *Wise* men do not seek the rewards of good deeds, so much as good deeds

themselves.   7. The Aeduans, having accomplished these things, began to favor Caesar.   8. The Belgians, influenced by the love of *glory*, and relying upon their valor, waged *many* wars with the Germans.

Lesson LXXIV.

PARTICLES.

368. Lesson from the Grammar.

I. Use of Adverbs. 582–585.

II. Use of Prepositions. 586; 432–437.

III. Use of Coördinate Conjunctions. 587.

369. Models.

I. Furius Philus spoke Latin extremely well.	I. *Furius Philus perbēne Latīne loquebātur.*
II. I eagerly await your letter.	II. *Littĕras tuas vehementer exspecto.*
III. I will most carefully perform what I promise you.	III. *Quae tibi promitto, diligentissĭme faciam.*
IV. I will write on this subject.	IV. *Hac super re scribam.*
V. These things have taken place within ten years.	V. *Haec intra decem annos facta sunt.*
VI. Understanding, reason, and counsel are found in old men.	VI. *Mens et ratio et consilium in senĭbus est.*

VII. Pardon me that I write to you *so much and so often.*	VII. *Mihi ignosce quod ad te scribo tam multa toties.*

370. REMARKS.

1. MODEL I. — LATIN, *Latīne,* lit. *in Latin.*

2. MODEL II. — YOUR LETTER, *littĕras tuas* or *epistŏlam tuam.* See Synonymes, 200.

3. MODEL VI. — ARE FOUND, *est.* In Latin the verb *sum* is much more freely used than the English verb *to be.* For the *number* of the verb *est,* see G. 463, I. For the use of *et — et,* see G. 587, I. 5.

4. MODEL VII. — SO MUCH AND SO OFTEN, *tam multa toties,* lit. *so many things so often.*

371. SYNONYMES.

Temple; *templum, fanum, ædes.*

1. *Templum, i,* n.; TEMPLE, — the generic word for temple with all its sacred environs, but applied especially to the temples of the principal gods.

2. *Fanum, i,* n.; TEMPLE, SANCTUARY, — regarded as a consecrated edifice — applied especially to the inferior gods.

3. *Aedes, is,* f.; TEMPLE, — regarded simply as an edifice.

372. VOCABULARY.

Above, *supra,* adv.	Build, make, *facio, ĕre, feci, factum.*
Anger, *iracundia, ae,* f.	
Be wont, *soleo, ĕre, solĭtus sum.* G. 272, 3.	Excellently, *excellenter,* adv.
	Honestly, *honeste,* adv.
Bear, *fero, ferre, tuli, latum.*	Impudence, *impudentia, ae,* f.

Obstinacy, *pertinacia, ae,* f.
Pompey, *Pompēius, ii,* m.
Refute, *refello, ēre, felli.*
Sacred, *sanctus, a, um.*

Temple, *templum, i,* n.; *aedes, is,*
    f.; *fanum, i,* n.
Without, *sine,* prep. with abl.
Worship, *venēror, āri, ātus sum,*
    dep.

373. EXERCISE.

1. There is no doubt that the good and wise live well and happily. 2. To live well and happily is to live honestly and rightly. 3. The Romans bore this calamity bravely and wisely. 4. All these things were done bravely and excellently. 5. Let us always be prepared to refute without obstinacy, and to be refuted without anger. 6. Pompey, Scipio, and Caesar conquered the enemy in many battles. 7. I have said above, that the senate had assembled in the temple of Jupiter Stator. 8. *In this most sacred temple* the Romans were wont to worship Jupiter. 9. The Athenians built a temple to Impudence.

LESSON LXXV.

PARTICLES — CONTINUED.

374. LESSON FROM THE GRAMMAR.

I. Subordinate Conjunctions. 588.
II. Interjections. 589, 590.

375. MODELS.

I. I did this while it was
    lawful.

I. *Hoc feci, dum li-*
    cuit.

II. It is as you desired.	II. *Ut optasti, ita est.*
III. He is a *great* orator, if not the *greatest*.	III. *Is magnus orātor est, si non maxĭmus.*
IV. I exhort you to read these books on philosophy.	IV. *Te hortor ut hos de philosophia libros legas.*
V. You had inquired whether I did not think that the truth had been found.	V. *Quaesiĕras nonne putārem verum inventum esse.*
VI. Lo, your letter!	VI. *Ecce tuae littĕrae!*
VII. O, deceptive hopes!	VII. *O spes fallāces!*
VIII. O, the very great power of error!	VIII. *O vim maxĭmam errōris!*

376. REMARKS.

1. MODEL IV. — THESE BOOKS ON PHILOSOPHY, *hos de philosophia libros.* The rule for the place of the Genitive, G. 598, 3, is applicable to the Acc. or Abl. with a Preposition, when similarly used.

2. MODEL VI. — LO, YOUR LETTER! *ecce tuae littĕrae!* For the Nominative, *littĕrae*, see G. 367, 3; 381, 3.

377. SYNONYMES.

Wall; *murus, paries, moenia.*

1. *Murus, i,* m.; WALL, — the generic term for a wall of any kind.

2. *Paries, pariĕtis,* m.; THE WALL OF A HOUSE; THE WALL OF ANY BUILDING.

3. *Moenia, ium,* n. pl.; THE WALLS OF A CITY, CITY WALLS.

378. Vocabulary.

As soon as, *quum primum*.

Because, *quia*, conj.

Cover, to clothe, adorn, *vestio*, *ire*, *ivi* or *ii*, *itum*.

First, *primum*, adv.

For = about, concerning, *de*, prep. with abl.

Inner, *interior*, *ius*. G. 166.

More, *plus*, *pluris*. G. 165, 1.

Paint, *pingo*, *ĕre*, *pinxi*, *pictum*.

Painting, *tabŭla picta*; lit. *painted tablet*.

Practical knowledge, experience, *usus*, *us*, m.

Surround, *cingo*, *ĕre*, *cinxi*, *cinctum*.

Tablet, *tabŭla*, *ae*, f.

The = that, emphatic, *ille*, *a*, *ud*.

Unhappy, *infēlix*, *icis*.

Wall, *murus*, *i*, m.; *moenia*, *ium*, n. pl., G. 131, 1, 4); *paries*, *ĕtis*, m. Walls of the city, city walls, *moenia*; walls of my, your, &c., own house, *mei*, etc., *parietes*; lit. *my walls*.

Wonderful, *mirus*, *a*, *um*.

379. Exercise.

1. Marcus Cato was called wise because he had a practical knowledge of many things. 2. I will write more, if I have more leisure. 3. As soon as I came to Rome, I wrote to your father. 4. I exhort you to read studiously, not only these orations, but also these books on philosophy. 5. *Within the walls of the city* we have nothing to fear. 6. *We* must defend the *city walls*. 7. Cicero feared for his life within the walls of his own house. 8. The enemy were surrounding this place with a wall. 9. O, *your wonderful* memory, Marcus! 10. O, that *unhappy* day on which Sulla was made consul! 11. The inner walls of the temple were covered *with paintings*.

Lesson LXXVI.

FORMS FOR EXPRESSING PURPOSE.

380. Lesson from the Grammar.

I. The Subjunctive with a Conjunction — *ut, ne,* etc. 489.

II. The Subjunctive with a Relative. 500.

III. The Accusative (especially of the Gerund) with *ad.*[1] 565, 3; 408, 4.

IV. The Genitive with *Causa, Gratia,* etc. 395; 414, 2, 3).

V. The Supine in *um.* 569.

VI. The Participle. 578, V.

381. Models.

I. I explained my opinion, that I might ascertain *your judgment.*

II. Nature gave reason to man that he might be ruled by it.

III. It has been set before me *for imitation.*

IV. We have written many things to you for the purpose of exhorting you.

I. *Explicāvi sententiam meam, tuum judicium ut cognoscĕrem.*

II. *Natūra homĭni ratiō-nem dedit, qua rege-rētur.*

III. *Ad imitandum mihi posĭtum est.*

IV. *Multa ad te cohor-tandi gratia scripsĭ-mus.*

---

[1] The use of the Gerund in any other construction to express purpose, as in 563, 5, and 564, 2, should not be imitated by the learner.

V. We have come. *to remind* you, not *to importune* you.

VI. Lentulus assigned the city to *Cassius* to burn.

V. *Admonĭtum venĭmus te, non flagitātum.*

VI. *Lentŭlus attribuit urbem inflammandam Cassio.*

382. REMARKS.

1. MODEL I. — YOUR JUDGMENT, *tuum judicium.* Emphasis places these words at the beginning of the clause, even before *ut.* See G. 602, III. 1.

2. MODEL II. — THAT HE MIGHT BE RULED BY IT, *qua regerĕtur,* Relative clause expressing *purpose,* lit. *by which he might be ruled.*

3. MODEL IV. — FOR THE PURPOSE OF EXHORTING YOU, *cohortandi gratia. Te* is omitted because expressed just before. The Genitive precedes *gratia.*

4. MODEL V. — To REMIND, *admonĭtum,* Supine. See G. 569. But *ut* with the Subjunctive might be used instead of the Supine.

383. VOCABULARY.

Achieve, perform, *ago, ĕre, egi, actum.*

Advantage, gain, *emolumentum, i,* n.

As — as possible, with adjectives, *quam,* adv., with superlat.; as soon as possible, *quam primum.*

Cause, *causa, ae,* f.

Deliver, give over, *trado, ĕre, dĭdi, dĭtum.*

Desire, *opto, āre, āvi, ātum.*

Example, *exemplum, i,* n.

For the sake of, *causa* with gen. G. 414, 2, 3).

Profit, usefulness, *utilĭtas, ātis,* f.

Set before, *propōno, ĕre, posui, posĭtum.*

Somebody, something, *alĭquis, qua, quid.*

384. Exercise.

1. We desire to see you as soon as possible in this city. 2. Cicero was striving to save the republic. 3. Young men, devote yourselves *to this study*, that you may be wise. 4. Devote yourselves *to study*, that you may be able to be both an honor to yourselves and an advantage to the republic. 5. Ambassadors were sent to Caesar to say that the town had been taken. 6. Scipio was born to achieve something worthy of a man. 7. Let us set before our sons examples for imitation. 8. He delivered the city to the soldiers to plunder. 9. Ambassadors came to Rome to ask for peace. 10. The consul did many things for the sake of defending himself.

Lesson LXXVII.

FORMS FOR EXPRESSING CONDITION.

385. Lesson from the Grammar.

I. Clauses with certain Conjunctions. 503.

II. Relative Clauses. 513.

III. Participles. 503, 2, 1) ; 578, III.

IV. Oblique Cases with Prepositions. 503, 2, 2).

V. Imperative Clauses.[1] 535, 2.

---

[1] To these five forms a sixth might be added, the conditional sentence with *Si* omitted. See 503, 1. This form, however, cannot be safely imitated by the learner.

8

386. MODELS.

I. Arms are *of little value* abroad, unless there is wisdom *at home.*	I. *Parvi sunt foris arma, nisi est consilium domi.*
II. If any one should see these things, he would be delighted.	II. *Haec qui videat, delectētur.*
III. We are not wont to believe a liar, even if he speaks the truth.	III. *Mendāci homĭni ne verum quidem dicenti credĕre solēmus.*
IV. What would the life of men have been without philosophy?	IV. *Quid vita homĭnum sine philosophia fuisset?*
V. Provoke him; you will at once see him *frantic.*	V. *Lacesse; jam vidēbis furentem.*

387. REMARKS.

1. MODEL II. — IF ANY ONE SHOULD SEE, *si quis videat,* or *qui videat,* lit. *whoever may see.* The former is the common form, but in illustrating the various expressions for *condition,* the latter is here admissible.

2. MODEL III. — IF HE SPEAKS, *dicenti,* lit. *speaking.*

388. VOCABULARY.

Associate, *socius, ii,* m.	Cultivate, *colo, ĕre, colui, cultum.*
At once, immediately, *jam,* adv.	Fail, *defĭcio, ĕre, fēci, fectum.*
Attempt, *conor, āri, ātus sum,* dep.	Leisure, *otium, ii,* n.
Crime, *scelus, ĕris,* n.	Punishment, *supplicium, ii,* n.

Remove, *tollo, ĕre, sustŭli, sublā-tum.*

Restrain, *arceo, ĕre, ui, arctum.*

Set forth, *exprŏmo, ĕre, prompsi, promptum.*

Wicked, *imprŏbus, a, um.*

389. EXERCISE.

1. I would write more to you if I had more leisure. 2. The day would fail me if I should attempt to set forth all that can be said in regard to philosophy. 3. If we wish to be both good and happy, we must cultivate virtue. 4. If any one should free the state from fear, he would be praised by all. 5. *Without associates* Catiline would never have attempted to form a conspiracy against the republic. 6. What would restrain the wicked from crime, if the fear of punishment were removed? 7. Soldiers, defend the city; you will be at once praised by all.

LESSON LXXVIII.

FORMS FOR EXPRESSING CONCESSION.

390. LESSON FROM THE GRAMMAR.

I. Clauses with certain Conjunctions. 515.

II. Relative Clauses. 515, II.

III. Participles.[1] 578, IV.

---

[1] To these three forms one or two others might be added, but they would not be safe models for the learner.

391. Models.

I. Though *all* excellence attracts us to itself, yet liberality does this in the highest degree.	I. *Quamquam omnis virtus nos ad se allĭcit, tamen liberalĭtas id maxĭme effĭcit.*
II. Who is there who does not praise Socrates, though he never saw him?	II. *Quis est, qui Socrătem non laudet, quem nunquam vidĕrit?*
III. The eye, though it does not see itself, discerns other things.	III. *Ocŭlus, se non videns, alia cernit.*

392. Remarks.

1. Model II. — Praise, *laudet.* See G. 501, I. Though he never saw him, *quem nunquam vidĕrit,* lit. *whom he never saw.*

2. Model III. — Other things, *alia.* See G. 441.

393. Synonymes.

Happy, prosperous, fortunate; *beātus, felix, fortunātus.*

1. *Beātus, a, um;* happy.

2. *Felix, ĭcis;* (1) happy, prosperous, — happy because successful and prosperous; (2) transitively, giving joy and happiness.

3. *Fortunātus, a, um;* fortunate, successful, favored by fortune.

394. VOCABULARY.

Acquit, *absolvo, ĕre, i, solūtum.*

Death, *mors, mortis,* f.

Excel, *excello, ĕre, cellui, celsum.*

Fear, to fear greatly, *pertimesco, ĕre, timui.*

Friends, my, your, &c., friends, *mei, tui,* etc. G. 441, 1.

High, ample, *amplus, a, um.*

However much, *quantumvis,* adv.

Mucius, *Mucius, ii,* m.

Prosperous, *felix, ĭcis.*

Raise, conduct, *perdūco, ĕre, duxi, ductum.*

Rescue, *erĭpio, ĕre, rĭpui, reptum.*

Slay, *interfĭcio, ĕre, fĕci, fectum.*

395. EXERCISE.

1. Although they do not dare to praise Catiline, they are yet to be feared. 2. You would not be able, however much you may excel, to raise all your friends to the highest honors. 3. They dare to defend Catiline, though he is endeavoring to destroy the republic. 4. We know that the conspirators, though acquitted, cannot be rescued from the hands of the Roman people. 5. Caius Mucius attempted to slay king Porsena, though death was set before him (as the penalty). 6. We cannot be happy without virtue. 7. We all desire that you should be happy. 8. All desire that we should be prosperous. 9. There are some who seem to be always fortunate.

LESSON LXXIX.

FORMS FOR EXPRESSING TIME.

396. LESSON FROM THE GRAMMAR.

I. Accusative of Time. 378 ; 427.

II. Ablative of Time. 426.

III. Clauses with Conjunctions. 521–523 ; 588, I.

IV. Participles. 578, I.

V. Appositive. 363, 3.

397. MODELS.

I. Pericles presided over Athens forty years.

I. *Perĭcles quadraginta annos praefuit Athēnis.*

II. He lived three hundred years since.

II. *Abhinc annos trecentos fuit.*

III. Socrates on the last day of his life discoursed much on the immortality of souls.

III. *Socrătes suprēmo vitae die multa de immortalitāte animōrum disseruit.*

IV. He obeyed when it was necessary.

IV. *Paruit quum necesse erat.*

V. While they are quiet, they approve.

V. *Quum quiescunt, probant.*

VI. The grape, when it has ripened, becomes sweet.

VI. *Uva maturāta dulcescit.*

VII. Cicero learned many things when a boy.

VII. *Cicĕro puer multa didĭcit.*

398. REMARKS.

1. MODEL II. — LIVED, *fuit*, lit. *was*. The verb *sum* is often thus used.

2. MODEL VI. — WHEN IT HAS RIPENED, *maturāta*, lit. *having ripened*.

3. MODEL VII. — CICERO WHEN A BOY, *Cicĕro puer*, lit. *Cicero a boy*.

399. SYNONYMES.

Daily, day by day; *quotidie, in dies, in singŭlos dies.*

1. *Quotidie;* DAILY, DAY BY DAY, — the usual adverb for *daily*, whether with or without increase.

2. *In dies*, or *in singŭlos dies;* DAILY, DAY BY DAY, — used with comparatives and with words which involve increase or decrease.

400. VOCABULARY.

Arganthonius, *Arganthonius, ii*, m.

At the age of, *natus, a, um*, with the acc. of time. At the age of twenty, *viginti annos natus*, lit. *having been born twenty years*.

Daily, *quotidie*, adv.

Die, *morior, mori, mortuus sum*, dep.

Eighty, *octoginta*, indecl.

Entitle, *inscrĭbo, ĕre, scripsi, scriptum*.

Expect, *exspecto, āre, āvi, ātum*.

From day to day, *in dies*.

Govern, *guberno, āre, āvi, ātum*.

House, one's house, *domus, i*, f. G. 117, 1.

Hundred, *centum*, indecl.

Isocrates, *Isocrătes, is*, m.

Marius, *Marius, ii*, m.

Panathenaicus, *Panathenaĭcus, i*, m.

Plato, *Plato, ōnis*, m.

Seventh time, *septĭmum*, adv.

The = that, not emphatic, *is, ea,* | Vice, *vitium, ii,* n.
   id. | Weep at, *illacrĭmor, āri, ātus sum,*
Twenty, *viginti,* indecl. | dep. G. 386.

401. Exercise.

1. When virtue governs the republic, the citizens are happy.   2. Having come to Athens, I devoted myself to the study of philosophy.   3. Arganthonius is said to have reigned eighty years.   4. Cicero says that this king lived one hundred and twenty years.   5. Cato died at the age of eighty-five.   6. Isocrates is said to have written a book in his ninety-fourth year.   7. This book is entitled Panathenaicus. 8. Cicero, while reading Plato, wept at the death of Socrates.   9. Marius, while consul for the seventh time, died in his own house.   10. I will send a letter to you *daily.*   11. We are daily expecting your brother.   12. There are some who say that vice increases from day to day.

Lesson LXXX.

FORMS FOR EXPRESSING CAUSE.

402. Lesson from the Grammar.

I. Ablative of Cause.   414.
   1. A Preposition with its Case.   414, 2, 3), (1).
   2. A Perfect Participle with an Ablative. 414, 2, 3), (2).

II. Clauses with Conjunctions.   517–523.

III. Relative Clauses.   519.

IV. Participles.   578, II.

403. MODELS.

I. The father exults with joy.	I. *Pater exsultat laetitia.*
II. Death, because of the shortness of life, is never far distant.	II. *Mors propter brevitātem vitae nunquam longe abest.*
III. They seek *friendship*, led by the hope of a reward.	III. *Amicitiam spe mercēdis adducti expĕtunt.*
IV. Since a thanksgiving has been decreed, celebrate *those days.*	IV. *Quoniam supplicatio decrēta est, celebratōte illos dies.*
V. O fortunate youth, since you have obtained Homer as the herald of *your valor.*	V. *O fortunāte adolescens, qui tuae virtūtis Homērum praecōnem invenĕris.*
VI. I affirm nothing, since I am in doubt and distrust myself.	VI. *Nihil affirmo, dubĭtans et mihi diffĭdens.*

404. REMARKS.

1. MODEL V. — SINCE YOU HAVE OBTAINED, *qui invenĕris*, lit. *who have found.* For the mood, see G. 519.

2. MODEL VI. — SINCE I AM IN DOUBT, *dubĭtans*, lit. *doubting.*

405. SYNONYMES.

The right, law ; *fas, jus, lex.*

1. *Fas*, indecl. n.; THE RIGHT, — that which accords with the divine law.

2. *Jus, juris,* n.; THE RIGHT, JUSTICE, LEGAL RIGHT, — that which accords with law in general.

3. *Lex, legis,* f.; LAW, ENACTMENT, — human law.

406. VOCABULARY.

Ahala, *Ahăla, ae,* m.

Annoyance, *molestia, ae,* f.

Clodius, *Clodius, ii,* m.

Consult for, *consŭlo, ĕre, sului, sultum,* with dat. G. 385, 3.

Enact, *sancio, īre, sanxi, sanctum.*

Fabricius, *Fabricius, ii,* m.

For my, your, &c., sake, *mea causa, tua causa,* etc. G. 414, 2, 3).

Influence, to influence, *addūco, ĕre, duxi, ductum.*

Maelius, *Maelius, ii,* m.

Nation, *gens, gentis,* f. The law of nations, *jus gentium.*

Regal power, *regnum, i,* n.

Right, *fas,* n. indecl.

Seek, *appĕto, ĕre, petīvi, petītum.*

Slay, *occĭdo, ĕre, i, cīsum.*

Spurius, *Spurius, ii,* m.

407. EXERCISE.

1. We do many things *for the sake of our friends* which we would never do for our own sake. 2. I thank you because you have freed me from all annoyance. 3. Cicero praises Fabricius because he was just. 4. There are some who obey the laws on account of fear. 5. The commander, influenced by the hope of peace, sent ambassadors to the king. 6. Cicero is especially to be praised, because he consulted for the safety of the citizens. 7. Nothing which is right delights *Clodius.* 8. This was done in accordance with the law of nations. 9. The senate enacted many laws. 10. Servilius Ahala slew Spurius Maelius because he was seeking regal power.

PART THIRD.

ELEMENTS OF LATIN STYLE.

CHAPTER I.

CHOICE OF WORDS AND CONSTRUCTIONS.

LESSON LXXXI.

ABSTRACT NOUNS. NUMBER.

408. Abstract nouns designating the periods of life, as *boyhood, youth, old age*, are generally best rendered into Latin, not by *pueritia, juventus,* and *senectus,* but by *puer, juvĕnis,* and *senex.* See Part II. 165, IV.

409. Names of offices, as *consulship, generalship, leadership*, when used to designate time, should be rendered into Latin by the corresponding names of officers, as *consul, imperātor, dux.* See Model I.

410. Verbal nouns, designating the action in the abstract, may often be rendered into Latin by Participles:

The violation of the laws, *violātae leges.* For (concerning) the recovery of the captives, *de captivis recuperandis.* See Model II.

411. Substantives which are singular in English are sometimes rendered by those which are plural in Latin. Thus, —

1. Many names of cities are plural :

Athens, *Athēnae;* Thebes, *Thebae;* Syracuse, *Syracūsae.* See G. 131, 1.

2. Many nouns, which are singular in English, are plural in Latin, because they are so used as really to involve that number :

To have in hand,[1] *in manĭbus habēre.* To go on foot,[1] *pedĭbus ire.* To urge night and day, *noctes atque dies urgēre.*

412. The force of the English expressions, *kinds of, instances of, examples of,* is often denoted in Latin by simply putting the following noun in the plural, especially if it be an abstract noun :

All instances of avarice, *omnes avaritiae.* There are two kinds of memory, *sunt duae memoriae.* Examples of glorious death, *clarae mortes.*

413. MODELS.

I. Piso proposed this law in the consulship of Censorinus and Manilius.	I. *Piso hanc legem Censorīno et Manilio consulĭbus tulit.*
II. Precepts are given for the observance of duty.	II. *Officii conservandi praecepta tradantur.*
III. I have a great work in hand.	III. *Opus ˙ magnum in manĭbus habeo.*

414. REMARKS.

1. MODEL I. — IN THE CONSULSHIP OF, etc., lit. *Censorinus and Manilius being consuls.*

---

[1] The words *hand* and *foot,* as here used, involve the plural, as the action is by no means confined to *one* hand or *one* foot. The plural is also involved in the expression *night and day,* meaning night after night and day after day. Hence the Latin uses the plural in such instances.

2. MODEL II. — FOR THE OBSERVANCE OF DUTY, lit. *of duty to be observed.*

415. VOCABULARY.

Adorn, *exorno, āre, āvi, ātum.*

Africanus, *Africānus, i,* m.

Appius, *Appius, ii,* m.

Arise, *exsisto, ĕre, stĭti, stĭtum.*

Attain, *consĕquor, i, secūtus sum,* dep.

Attendant, *comes, ĭtis,* m. and f.

Censor, *censor, ōris,* m.

Claudius, *Claudius, ii,* m.

Complain, *queror, i, questus sum,* dep.

Desire, *cupidĭtas, ātis,* f.

Find, *repĕrio, ĭre, pĕri, pertum.*

Guide, *dux, ducis,* m. and f.

Highest results, highest things, *summa, ōrum,* n. adj. used as substant.

Just, with numbers, *ipse, a, um.* G. 452, 3.

Manilius, *Manīlius, ii,* m.

Manius, *Manius, ii,* m.

Monument, *monumentum, i,* n.

Plautus, *Plautus, i,* m.

Power, *potentia, ae,* f.

Statue, *signum, i,* n.

Tarentum, *Tarentum, i,* n.

416. EXERCISE.

1. I find that Plato came to Tarentum in the consulship of Lucius Camillus and Appius Claudius. 2. Plautus died during the censorship of Cato. 3. Cato the censor died in the consulship of Lucius Marcius and Manius Manilius, just eighty-three years before the consulship of Cicero. 4. You have attained the highest results under the guidance of virtue, with the attendance of fortune. 5. They were complaining of the loss of liberty. 6. Scipio Africanus *always* had Xenophon in hand. 7. Pericles adorned Athens with the most beautiful statues and monuments. 8. There are some who devote themselves day and night to study. 9. You have from boyhood devoted yourself to study. 10. *In the greatest minds* there often arises the *desire* for honor, power, and glory.

Lesson LXXXII.

SUBSTANTIVES UNITED BY PREPOSITIONS.

417. In English, substantives are often brought into immediate relation to each other by the simple use of prepositions, as *the march into Italy, the army in Macedonia, the temples around the forum.* In Latin, the same construction is admissible, but is used much more cautiously in the best writers.

418. This construction may be used in Latin with certain Prepositions and in certain senses. Thus, —

1. With *cum* and *sine*.

Cupid with a lamp, *Cupīdo cum lampăde.* A man without hope, *homo sine spe.*

2. With *in, erga, adversus, contra,* and *pro,* before the name of the object with reference to which the feeling is exercised or the action performed:

Hatred of the human race, *odium in* (towards) *homĭnum genus* (the race of men). Love to you, *erga te amor.* See G. 398, 4.

3. With *de, ex, inter,* in a partitive sense:

A plebeian, *homo de plebe* (a man of the people). One of the heroes, *unus ex viris.* See G. 398, 4.

4. With *de* in the sense of concerning, from, out of, *ex,* from, out of, *inter* with *se* or *ipsos,* and with *ad* and *apud* in expressions of place:

A book on civil law, *liber de jure civīli.* The marble tables, *mensae e marmŏre* (tables made from or of marble). The naval battle near Tenedos, *apud Tenĕdum pugna navālis.*

419. This combination of substantives, by means of prepositions, may be somewhat more freely used when the preposition with its case is placed between the leading noun and its modifier:

The most disgraceful flight from the city, *fuga ab urbe turpissĭma.*

420. When good authority cannot be furnished for this construction, it will be advisable either to insert a Relative Clause or a Participle before the preposition, or to give the sentence such a form as to bring the preposition with its case into relation to the verb:

In the temple near the city, *in fano, quod est propter urbem* (which is near the city).

421. MODELS.

I. Behold the silver Cupid with a lamp.	I. *Vide argenteum Cupidĭnem cum lampăde.*
II. Aristotle, in his third book on philosophy, does not dissent from Plato.	II. *Aristotĕles in tertio de philosophia libro a Platōne non dissentit.*
III. They admire the necklace of gold and gems.	III. *Monīle ex auro et gemmis admirantur.*
IV. In most things the mean between too much and too little is the best.	IV. *In plerisque rebus mediocrĭtas quae est inter nimium et parum optĭmum est.*

422. REMARKS.

1. MODEL III. — OF GOLD, *ex auro*, lit. *from gold.*

2. MODEL IV. — THE MEAN BETWEEN TOO MUCH, etc., *mediocrĭtas quae est inter*, etc.

423. SYNONYMES.

Teacher, preceptor; *doctor, praeceptor, magister.*

1. *Doctor, ōris,* m.; TEACHER, — regarded simply as one who imparts knowledge.

2. *Praeceptor, ōris,* m.; PRECEPTOR, INSTRUCTOR, TEACHER, — regarded as one who moulds the character of his pupils.

3. *Magister, tri,* m.; MASTER, TEACHER, — with reference to his superiority and power.

424. VOCABULARY.

Abundance, *copia, ae,* f.

Around, *circum,* prep. with acc.

Attention, study, zeal, *studium, ii,* n.

Bestow, *confĕro, ferre, tŭli, collātum.*

Credit, *fides, ĕi,* f.

Edifice, *aedes, is,* f. G. 132.

Elegance, *elegantia, ae,* f.

Epicurus, *Epicūrus, i,* m.

Forum, *forum, i,* n.

In = situated in, placed in, *posĭtus, a, um, in* with abl.

Instruct, teach, *doceo, ĕre, docui, doctum.*

Means, property, *res, rei,* f.

Occult, *occultus, a, um.*

On = concerning, *de,* prep. with abl.

Present one's self, *se praebēre; praebeo, ēre, ui, ĭtum.*

Refinements, culture, *cultus, us,* m.

Sedition, *seditio, ōnis,* f.

Select, selected, *exquisĭtus, a, um.*

Set fire to, burn, *incendo, ĕre, cendi, censum.*

Station, to place, *collŏco, āre, āvi, ātum.*

Sure, *certus, a, um.*

Teacher, *doctor, ōris,* m.; as master, *magister, tri,* m.

Too, *nimis,* adv.

Upon, *in,* prep. with acc. and abl. G. 435, 1.

425. EXERCISE.

1. Your letter on friendship was most acceptable to me. 2. The refinements of life, with elegance and abundance, delight us. 3. All the philosophers before Socrates bestowed too great attention upon occult subjects. 4. This man, without means, without credit, without hope, the leader of sedition, set fire, with his own hands, to the sacred edifices. 5. *True* wisdom presents itself to us as the surest guide *to happiness.* 6. Valor even in an

enemy delights brave men. 7. The army was stationed in the forum and in all the temples around the forum. 8. This preceptor will instruct us in regard to philosophy. 9. We send our sons to the teachers of wisdom. 10. Epicurus boasted that he had had *no* teacher (master). 11. Tiberius Gracchus always had select teachers (masters) from Greece.

Lesson LXXXIII.

SPECIAL WORDS AND EXPRESSIONS.

426. Such words as *property, duty, business, mark, characteristic,* after the verb *to be,* are generally omitted in rendering into Latin, as their force is fully expressed in the Predicate Genitive:

It is the duty of a judge, *judĭcis est.* It is the mark of a narrow mind, *angusti anĭmi est.*

427. Substantives after *as, when, for, of,* are often rendered by Appositives, the particles *as, when,* etc., being omitted. See Model II.

428. But in such cases, *as* is sometimes rendered by *ut,* and then the appositive shows in what capacity or light the person or thing denoted by the leading substantive is viewed. See Model III.

429. While the relation denoted by the preposition *of* is generally rendered by the Genitive, that denoted by some other prepositions, as *to, for, from, in, on account of,* is sometimes so rendered:

Gratitude for a favor, *benefĭcii gratia.* Escape from labors, *labŏrum fuga.* See above, 413, Model II.

430. Models.

I. It is the part of barbari-
ans to live for the day
only.

II. Philip procured Aristotle as a teacher for
Alexander his son.

III. I have often praised
Cato as a citizen.

I. *Barbarōrum est in
diem vivĕre.*

II. *Philippus Aristotĕlem
Alexandro filio doc-
tōrem accīvit.*

III. *Catōnem ut civem
saepe laudāvi.*

431. Synonymes.

Pride, arrogance, insolence; *superbia, arrogantia, insolentia.*

1. *Superbia, ae,* f.; PRIDE, HAUGHTINESS, SELF-SUFFI-
CIENCY.

2. *Arrogantia, ae,* f.; ARROGANCE, HAUGHTINESS, — as
shown in great pretensions and assumptions.

3. *Insolentia, ae,* f.; INSOLENCE, — an offensive display of
superiority in an insulting manner.

432. Vocabulary.

Achilles, *Achilles, is,* m.

Antiochus, *Antiŏchus, i,* m.

Antony, *Antonius, ii,* m.

Arrogance, *arrogantia, ae,* f.

As, *ut,* adv.

But, *vero,* etc., conj. G. 587,
III. 2.

Caius, *Caius, Caii,* m.

Consider, *cogĭto, āre, āvi, ātum.*

Contrary to, *contra,* prep. with acc.

Excite, *concĭto, āre, āvi, ātum.*

Hatred, *odium, ii,* n.

Insolence, *insolentia, ae,* f.

Narrow, *angustus, a, um.*

Obtain, find, *invĕnio, īre, vēni,
ventum.*

Perceive, *perspĭcio, ĕre, spexi,
spectum.*

Perfect, *perfectus, a, um.*

Popilius, *Popilius, ii,* m.

Pride, *superbia, ae,* f.

Prudence, *prudentia, ae,* f.

Regard, *habeo, ĕre, ui, ĭtum*, lit. to have, hold.

Require, compel, *cogo, ĕre, coēgi, coactum.*

Riches, *divitiae, ārum*, f. pl. G. 131, 1, 4).

Senator, *senātor, ōris*, m.

Wickedness, *scelus, ĕris*, n.

433. EXERCISE.

1. To love riches is the mark of a *narrow mind*. 2. It is the part of a wise man to do nothing contrary to the laws. 3. It is the duty of a good man to cultivate all the virtues. 4. Caius Popilius was sent as an ambassador to Antiochus the king. 5. Achilles obtained Homer as the herald of *his valor*. 6. Jupiter was regarded both as the king and as the father of all the gods. 7. It is the duty of a judge to consider, not what he himself wishes, but what the law requires. 8. To defend that which is right, I have ever thought a characteristic both of brave heroes and of great men. 9. To think this, is a mark of prudence; to do it, of fortitude; but both to think and to do it, of perfect virtue. 10. Great hatred is often excited *against pride and arrogance*. 11. We have perceived, not only the audacity and wickedness of *Antony*, but also his insolence and pride. 12. All greatly praise your Cato, as a senator, as a commander, and as a man.

LESSON LXXXIV.

RENDERING OF CERTAIN NOUNS AND ADJECTIVES.

434. In English, Adjectives are used substantively only in the Plural, but in Latin they are occasionally so used even in the Singular, especially in the Neuter with an abstract sense:

The truth, *verum* (a true thing). No sincerity, *nihil sinceri* (nothing of the sincere).

435. Proper names of places, when used with *of* or *from* to designate *nativity* or *origin*, are usually rendered by Latin Adjectives:

Archytas of Tarentum, *Archytas Tarentinus.* Gorgias of Leontini, *Gorgias Leontinus.* See G. 441, 5.

436. Proper names with prepositions, as *of*, *in*, are often rendered by Latin Adjectives:

Ulysses in Homer, *Homericus Ulixes.* Hercules in Xenophon, *Hercules Xenophonteus.* The battle of Pharsalia, *proelium Pharsali-oum.* The battle of Cannae, *Cannensis pugna.* See G. 441, 5.

437. The English expressions, *the first part of, the middle* (part) *of, the last part of, the highest part of, the lowest part of*, and the like, are generally rendered by Latin Adjectives:

The first part of the province, *prima provincia.* The middle of summer, *media aestas.* See G. 441, 6.

438. Substantives, which designate persons as the agents of actions, may often be best rendered into Latin by Relative Clauses:

Hearers, *ii qui audiunt* (those who hear). Statesmen, *ii qui rei publicae praesunt* (those who preside over the republic). Lawgivers, *ii qui leges scribunt* (those who write laws).

439. Participial nouns and verbal nouns with *of*, should generally be rendered into Latin by a Passive Participle or a Gerund:

In liberating the country, *in liberanda patria.* Desirous of hearing you, *cupidus te audiendi.* See G. 580; 559–566.

440. Many adjectives are best rendered into Latin by the Genitive of nouns.

Thus, —

1. SPIRITUAL, MENTAL, must be rendered by *animi, mentis,* or *ingenii ;* BODILY, by *corporis :*

By mental diseases, *anĭmi morbis.*   Bodily pain, *dolor corpŏris.* Mental culture, *cultūra anĭmi.*

2. LITERARY may be rendered by *litterārum;* LEARNED, sometimes by *doctrīnae, doctrinārum; artis, artium;* PHILOSOPHICAL, by *philosophiae,* or *de philosophia:*

Literary pursuits, *litterārum studia.*   Learned studies, *doctrīnae studia.*

441. Adjectives with adverbial modifiers may often be best rendered into Latin by the Genitive or Ablative of Characteristic.   See Model III.

442. MODELS.

I. The temple of Diana of Ephesus was burned.	I. *Templum Ephesiae Diānae deflagrāvit.*
II. Many are careless in selecting friends.	II. *Multi in amīcis eligendis negligentes sunt.*
III. *How blameless* ought *commanders* to be.	III. *Quanta innocentia debent esse imperatōres.*

443. REMARKS.

1. MODEL II. — IN SELECTING FRIENDS.   See G. 580.

2. MODEL III. — HOW BLAMELESS, *quanta innocentia,* lit. *with* (of) *how great innocence.*

444. VOCABULARY.

Advantage, *utilĭtas, ātis,* f.
Atticus, *Attĭcus, i,* m.
Battle, fight, *pugna, ae,* f.
Between, *inter,* prep. with acc.
Ceus, of Ceus or Cea, *Ceus, a, um.*
Crotona, *Croto, ōnis,* m. and f.
Delight, *oblecto, āre, āvi, ātum.*

Difference, there is a difference, *intĕrest, fuit.*
Enact, write, *scribo, ĕre, scripsi, scriptum.*
Epaminondas, *Epaminondas, ae,* m.
Gorgias, *Gorgias, ae,* m.

Lawgiver, be a lawgiver, *leges scri-běre*, lit. *to enact laws.*

Learned = of learning, *doctrīnae*, f. sing. gen.

Leontine, of Leontini, *Leontīnus, a, um.*

Less, *minor, us,* comp. of *parvus.* G. 165.

Leuctrian, of Leuctra, *Leuctrĭcus, a, um.*

Lighten, *levo, āre, āvi, ātum.*

Literary = of letters, *litterārum*, f. pl. gen.

No, *non,* adv.

Of = out of, *e, ex,* prep. with abl.

Old age, *senectus, ūtis,* f.

Pharsalian, of Pharsalus, or Pharsalia, *Pharsalius, a, um.*

Prodicus, *Prodĭcus, i,* m.

Propose to one's self no other aim, *nihil sibi aliud nisi proponěre; propōno, ěre, posui, posĭtum ;* lit. *to propose to one's self nothing else except.*

So, sometimes rendered by *is, ea, id;* so virtuous, *ea virtūte,* lit. *of that virtue;* so wise, *ea sapientia,* lit. *of that wisdom.* G. 428.

Statesman, be a statesman, *rei publĭcae praesum, esse, fui;* lit. *to superintend the republic.*

Suffering, pain, *dolor, ōris,* m.

Superbus, *Superbus, i,* m.

Tarquinius, *Tarquinius, ii,* m.

Useful, be useful, *utilitātem affěro, ferre, attŭli, allātum,* lit. *impart advantage.*

Warrior, be a warrior, *bellum gero, ěre, gessi, gestum,* lit. *to wage war.*

While, when, *quum,* conj.

Wrong, *pravus, a, um.*

445. Exercise.

1. As there is a difference between the right and the wrong, so is there between the true and the false. 2. Gorgias of Leontini, the teacher of Isocrates, lived one hundred and seven years. 3. Prodicus of Ceus was in great honor. 4. After the battle of Pharsalia, Cicero wrote to Atticus. 5. After the battle of Leuctra, Epaminondas was in great honor. 6. Solon the lawgiver was regarded as wise, one of the Seven. 7. Statesmen are no less useful than warriors. 8. Pythagoras came to

Crotona in the fourth year of the reign of Tarquinius Superbus. 9. Literary studies delight old age. 10. Many while in exile have lightened their suffering by learned studies. 11. Our forefathers were *so virtuous and wise*, that, in enacting laws, they proposed to themselves no other aim than the safety and advantage of the republic.

Lesson LXXXV.

ADJECTIVES — Continued.

446. When two or more Adjectives belong to the same substantive, as attributives, —

1. They may be separate and independent modifiers of that substantive, and must then be connected by conjunctions.

2. One of them may modify the substantive directly, while the others modify the complex idea formed by the substantive and adjective united. The connective is then omitted:

Obscure and difficult subjects, *res obscŭras atque difficĭles.* All Latin words, *omnia verba Latĭna.*

447. By a difference of idiom, the Latin generally uses the connective after *multi, permulti, plurĭmi,* etc., though the English omits it in similar cases:

Many large states, *multae et magnae civitātes.*

448. The Positive with *too, somewhat, unusually,* may be rendered by the Latin Comparative, and the Positive with *very, exceedingly,* by the Superlative:

Too short, *brevior.* Very short, *brevissĭmus.*

But instead of the Latin Comparative in the sense of *too,* the Positive with *nimis* may be used, and instead of the Superlative in the sense of *very,* the Positive with *valde:*

Too great, *nimis magnus.* Very great, *valde magnus.*

Here the emphasis rests upon *too* and *very*, rather than upon the adjective itself.

449. The Positive with *as — as possible* is rendered by the Superlative with *quam* or *quantus*, with or without *possum :*

As great as possible, *quam maxĭmus*, with or without *possum*. See Model II.

450. When in English two comparatives occur with *the — the*, or with *the — so much the*, they are generally best rendered into Latin by Comparatives with *quanto — tanto*, *quo — eo* or *quo — hoc.* See Model III.

451. Models.

I. This state has been relieved of the whole debt.

I. *Haec civĭtas omni aere aliēno liberāta est.*

II. He led the army to Rome with as rapid marches as possible.

II. *Quam potuit maxĭmis itinerĭbus Romam exercĭtum duxit.*

III. The more difficult it is, the more honorable.

III. *Quo est difficilius, eo praeclarius.*

452. Remarks.

1. Model I. — Debt, *aes aliēnum*, lit. *copper* or *money belonging to another.*

2. Model III. — The — the, *quo — eo*, lit. *by what* or *how much — by this* or *so much.*

453. Synonymes.

Good, upright, honorable ; *bonus, probus, honestus.*

1. *Bonus, a, um ;* good, — the generic word for this quality, applicable both to persons and to things.

2. *Probus, a, um ;* UPRIGHT, BLAMELESS, — a negative quality, free from blame rather than worthy of praise.

3. *Honestus, a, um ;* HONORABLE, VIRTUOUS, NOBLE-MINDED, — involving a delicate sense of honor and duty.

454. VOCABULARY.

Another's, belonging to another, *aliĕnus, a, um.*

Armenian, *Armenius, ii,* m.

Contract, *contraho, ĕre, traxi, tractum.*

Debt, *aes aliĕnum,* lit. *another's money.*

Drive, *pello, ĕre, pepŭli, pulsum.*

Equity, *aequĭtas, ātis,* f.

Heavy, weighty, great, severe, *gravis, e.*

Long-continued, very long, *perdiuturnus, a, um.*

Loud, great, *magnus, a, um.*

Many of the, *multi, ae, a,* pl., in agreement with noun.

Money, *aes, aeris,* n., lit. *copper.*

Noble-minded, *honestus, a, um.*

Occupy the mind, *in anĭmo versor, āri, ātus,* lit. *to move about in the mind.*

Princely, *regālis, e.*

Pursuit, exertion, *studium, ii,* n.

Release, *libĕro, āre, āvi, ātum.*

Seem, *videor, ēri, visus sum.*

Since, ago, *abhinc,* adv.

Syllable, *syllăba, ae,* f.

The — the, with comparatives, *quo — eo.* G. 418. Lit. *by how much — by so much.*

Thought, *cogitatio, ōnis,* f.

Tigranes, *Tigrānes, is,* m.

Till, *colo, ĕre, colui, cultum.*

Upright, *probus, a, um.*

Verse, *versus, us,* m.

Voice, *vox, vocis,* f.

455. EXERCISE.

1. Cicero says that the good are always happy. 2. Nothing seems to Xenophon so princely as the pursuit of tilling the field. 3. The Romans waged a severe and long-continued war with Tigranes the *king of the Armenians.* 4. Cicero released the state from a false debt. 5. The consuls contracted no new debt for the state. 6.

9

This large and heavy debt was contracted many years since. 7. Many weighty thoughts occupied the mind of the commander. 8. This verse is too long by one sylla- ble. 9. No one can be too honorable. 10. ·The orator spoke with as loud a voice as possible. 11. The greater the fault is, the greater the pain. 12. Nothing is more worthy of a great and good man than virtue. 13. All upright men love equity itself. 14. Many of the best citizens and most noble-minded men were driven into exile.

Lesson LXXXVI.

PRONOUNS. — PERSONAL. REFLEXIVE.

456. The Nominatives *I, you, we,* when not emphatic, are omitted in rendering into Latin. See Model I.

457. *He, she, it, they, him, her, them,* when not emphatic, are usually omitted in rendering, if they can be omitted with- out ambiguity. See Model II.

458. When necessary, these Pronouns are rendered (1) generally by *is ;* but (2) if more demonstrative in force, in the sense of *this one, that one,* by *hic* or *ille ;* and (3) if em- phatic, but not reflexive (G. 448), *he himself, himself,* by *ipsē.* See Models I. and III.

459. But these Pronouns must sometimes be rendered by the Reflexive *se.*

Thus, —

1. The Objectives *himself, herself, itself, themselves,* must be rendered by *se.* See Model IV.

2. In a Subordinate Clause expressing the sentiment of the Principal Subject, the Objectives *him, her, it, them,* must be rendered by *se* when they refer to the Principal Subject. See Model V.

3. In a Subordinate Clause which must be rendered by the Accusative with the Infinitive and which expresses the sentiment of the Principal Subject, *he, she, it, they,* must be rendered by *se* when they refer to the Principal Subject. See Model VI.

460. The Objectives *myself, ourselves, yourselves,* are rendered by the Personal Pronouns *ego* and *tu.* See Model VII.

461. But when special emphasis rests upon the Objectives *myself, ourselves, yourselves,* IPSE is added to, the Personal Pronoun. See Model VIII.

462. Personal Pronouns with prepositions are sometimes rendered by Possessives, especially with such words as *epistŏla, littĕrae,* etc. See Model IX.

463. MODELS.

I. You know how highly I prize them.	I. *Eos quanti faciam scis.*
II. It is necessary that you should praise this plan, for it cannot be changed.	II. *Hoc consilium laudes necesse est; mutāri enim non potest.*
III. It is fitting that he should himself be a good man.	III. *Oportet ipsum esse virum bonum.*
IV. The boys conduct themselves very prudently.	IV. *Puĕri valde prudenter se gerunt.*
V. Caesar asks me to come to him.	V. *Caesar ut veniam ad se rogat.*
VI. The consul thinks that he has friends.	VI. *Consul se amīcos habēre arbitrātur.*
VII. We console ourselves.	VII. *Nos consolāmur.*
VIII. See that you guard yourself.	VIII. *Fac ut te ipsum custodias.*

IX. I have received three letters from you.

IX. *Accēpi tuas tres epistŏlas.*

464. REMARKS.

1. MODEL I. — How HIGHLY, *quanti.* See G. 402, III.

2. MODEL II. — THAT YOU SHOULD PRAISE, *laudes.* See G. 496, 1.

3. MODEL V. — To COME, *ut veniam,* lit. *that I may come.* See G. 492, 2.

4. MODEL VIII. — SEE THAT YOU GUARD, *fac ut custodias,* lit. *do or make that you guard.* See G. 492, 1.

5. MODEL IX. — FROM YOU, *a te,* or *tuas* agreeing with *epistŏlas.*

465. VOCABULARY.

Admit, confess, *confiteor, ēri, fessus sum,* dep.

Again and again, *etiam atque etiam,* adv.

Allow, *concēdo, ĕre, cessi, cessum.*

As, for, *pro,* prep. with abl.

As much, *quantus, a, um,* relative to *tantus.*

Await, *exspecto, āre, āvi, ātum.*

Be ignorant of, *ignōro, āre, āvi, ātum.*

Born, be born, *nascor, i, natus sum.*

British, of or from Great Britain, *Britannĭcus, a, um.*

Dutiful affection, *piĕtas, ātis,* f.

I, emphatic, *egŏmet.* G. 184, 3.

Indeed, *quidem,* adv.

Joy, *laetitia, ae,* f.

Move, affect, *afficio, ĕre, fēci, fectum.*

Myself, reflexive, not intensive, *ego, mei.* G. 448.

Others, the others, the rest, *cetĕri, ae, a,* pl.

Satisfy, *satisfacio, ĕre, feci, factum.* G. 26, 2, 3), (b); 385, 2.

So much, *tantus, a, um,* antecedent to *quantus.*

State, say, *dico, ĕre, dixi, dictum.*

Take, appropriate, *sumo, ĕre, sumpsi, sumptum.*

Thyself, yourself, reflexive, not intensive, *tu, tui.* G. 448.

To, towards, of friendly feelings and conduct towards a person, *erga,* prep. with acc.

466. Exercise.

1. You, Cato, were born not for me, not for yourself, but for your country. 2. You will not deny that you are very desirous of *glory.* 3. I have never denied that *they* (these) are very desirous of glory. 4. There were some who called themselves wise. 5. I was moved with the *greatest* joy, when I heard that you had been made consul. 6. Philosophers admit that they are ignorant of *many things,* and that they have to learn many things again and again. 7. *As much time* as is allowed them for pleasures, *I* shall take for myself for my studies. 8. There is nothing new, which, indeed, either you would wish to hear, or which I should dare to state as certain. 9. I satisfy *all* the others by my dutiful affection to you; myself I never satisfy. 10. I am awaiting your letter from Great Britain.

Lesson LXXXVII.

PRONOUNS. — POSSESSIVE.

467. The Possessive Pronouns, *my, your, his,* etc., when not emphatic, should be omitted in rendering into Latin, if they can be supplied from the context. See Model I.

468. When necessary, the Possessives of the Third Person, *his, her, its, their,* are rendered, —

1. By *suus.* This occurs (1) when they refer to the subject of the clause in which they stand, and (2) when in a Subordinate Clause expressing the sentiment of the Principal Subject, they refer to that subject. See Models II. and III.

2. By the Genitive of a Demonstrative or Relative. This occurs when *suus* is not admissible. See Model IV.

469. The Latin Possessive belonging to two or more nouns is generally expressed but once. See Model V.

470. The Possessive with *own* — *my own, your own,* etc. — is generally rendered by the simple Possessive; but if *own* is emphatic, it must be rendered by the Genitive of *ipse.* See Model VI.

471. MODELS.

I. Socrates already held in his hand the deadly cup.

II. He instructed his brother.

III. They know what their fellow-citizens think.

IV. Socrates and all his disciples were delighted with the study of philosophy.

V. I impart a share of my *burden* to no one, of my glory to all the good.

VI. He is moved by his own power.

I. *Socrătes in manu jam mortifĕrum illud tenēbat pocŭlum.*

II. *Fratrem suum erudĭvit.*

III. *Sciunt quid sui cives cogĭtent.*

IV. *Socrătes atque omnes ejus discipŭli studio philosophiae delectāti sunt.*

V. *Onĕris mei partem nemĭni impertio, gloriae bonis omnĭbus.*

VI. *Sua vi* (or *sua ipsīus vi*) *movētur.*

472. REMARKS.

1. MODEL I. — THE DEADLY CUP, *mortifĕrum illud pocŭlum,* lit. *that deadly cup.* See G. 450, 4.

2. MODEL IV. — ALL HIS, *omnes ejus.* Here *his* is not reflexive, and is accordingly rendered by *ejus,* not by *suus.*

473. SYNONYMES.

City, town, state, republic; *urbs, oppĭdum, civĭtas, res publĭca.*

1. *Urbs, urbis,* f.; CITY, — the usual word for city.

2. *Oppĭdum, i,* n.; FORTIFIED TOWN or CITY.

3. *Civĭtas, ātis,* f.; STATE, — as a political organization, with its laws and institutions.

4. *Res publĭca, rei publĭcae,* f.; COMMONWEALTH, REPUBLIC.

474. VOCABULARY.

Achievement, *res gesta, rei gestae,* lit. *thing performed.*

Admire, *admĭror, āri, ātus sum,* dep.

Approach, *accēdo, ĕre, cessi, cessum.*

Catulus, *Catŭlus, i,* m.

Cimbrian, *Cimbrĭcus, a, um.* A victory over the Cimbrians, *Cimbrĭca victoria.*

Colleague, *collēga, ae,* m.

Consider, judge, *existĭmo, āre, āvi, ātum.*

Dignity, *dignĭtas, ātis,* f.

Discourse, *oratio, ōnis,* f.

Esteem, *facio, ĕre, feci, factum,* lit. *to make.*

Except, *praeter,* prep. with acc.

Exhort, *cohortor, āri, ātus sum,* dep.

Genius, *ingenium, ii,* n.

How highly, with verbs of valuing, *quanti.* G. 402, III. 1.

Life, period of life, *aetas, ātis,* f.

Milesian, of Miletus, *Milesius, a, um.*

Most exalted, *summus, a, um,* superlat. of *supĕrus.* G. 163, 3.

Rest upon, be situated in, *esse posĭtus, a, um, in* with abl.

Share, *communĭco, āre, āvi, ātum.*

Thales, *Thales, is,* m.; acc. *em* or *en.*

Worth, moral worth, *virtus, ātis,* f.

475. EXERCISE.

1. The orator spent his life in the study of eloquence. 2. Marius shared with his colleague Catulus the glory of his victory over the Cimbrians. 3. All the seven wise men, except Thales of Miletus, presided over their states. 4. It is a characteristic of your wisdom to consider that

all your dignity rests upon your worth and achievements.
5. Socrates said that he knew nothing. 6. His whole
discourse was spent in praising virtue, and in exhorting
all men to the pursuit of virtue. 7. There is no doubt
that Rome was a most beautiful city. 8. All the states
are compelled to await *your* aid. 9. You all know how
highly I esteem the republic. 10. Our forces were approaching the town of Antioch. 11. Many admired
Plato on account of his most exalted genius.

Lesson LXXXVIII.

PRONOUNS. — DEMONSTRATIVE. RELATIVE.

476. The Demonstratives, *this, that, these, those,* are rendered into Latin, —

1. Literally by *hic, ille, iste.* For the difference in the use
of these forms, see G. 450. See Models IV. and VI.

2. By the Relative, to mark a close connection with the
preceding sentence or clause. See Model I.

3. The expressions, *and that too, and that indeed,* are rendered by *is* with a conjunction. See Model II.

4. Before an objective with OF, *this, that, these,* or *those,*
referring to a noun already expressed before a preceding *of,*
is generally omitted in rendering. See Model III.

477. The Relative is generally rendered by the Latin
Relative, but certain differences of idiom require attention.

1. As the Relative clause in Latin often precedes the Antecedent clause, the Antecedent itself is often introduced
into the Relative clause. It is then usually represented in
its own clause by a demonstrative, *is, idem, hic,* etc. See
Model IV.

2. When the real Antecedent is an Appositive, it must in Latin be introduced into the Relative clause. See Model V.

3. Adjectives belonging in sense to the antecedent sometimes stand in the Relative clause, in agreement with the relative, especially comparatives, superlatives, and numerals. See Model VI.

478. Models.

I. The fact itself speaks, and this always has *very great* weight.	I. *Res loquĭtur ipsa ; quae semper valet plurĭmum.*
II. You have a memory, and that too an unbounded one.	II. *Habes memoriam, et eam infinītam.*
III. Whose eloquence was more conspicuous than that of Pisistratus?	III. *Cujus eloquentia praestabilior fuit quam Pisistrăti?*
IV. Let every one occupy himself in the art with which he is acquainted.	IV. *Quam quisque norit artem, in hac se exerceat.*
V. Thence I hastened to Amanus, a mountain which separates Syria from Cilicia.	V. *Inde ad Amānum contendi, qui mons Syriam a Cilicia divĭdit.*
VI. Agamemnon vowed to Diana the most beautiful thing which had been born *that year* in his kingdom.	VI. *Agamemnon devōvit Diānae quod in suo regno pulcherrĭmum natum esset illo anno.*

479. Remarks.

1. Model III. — Whose, *cujus*, lit. *of whom.*

2. Model IV. — *Norit,* Potential Subj., lit. *whatever art each one may know.*

3. Model V. — A mountain which, *qui mons*, lit. *which mountain.*

4. Model VI. — The most beautiful thing which, *quod pul-cherrĭmum*, lit. *which the most beautiful.*

480. Vocabulary.

And that too, *et is, ea, id ; et is quidem.*

As to, after so, *ut,* conj. with subj.

Astyages, *Astyăges, is,* m.

Be held = to be, *sum, esse, fui.*

Compare, *confĕro, ferre, tŭli, col-lătum.*

Conduct one's self, *se gerĕre ; gero, ĕre, gessi, gestum.*

During, in, *in,* prep. with abl.

Eclipse, *defectio, ŏnis,* f.

Entertain, hold, *teneo, ĕre, ui, tentum.*

Expose one's self, *se opponĕre ; oppōno, ĕre, posui, posĭtum.*

Famous, *clarus, a, um.* The famous, sometimes rendered by *ille, a, ud.*

Foolish, *demens, entis.*

He, she, etc. = the same one, *idem, eădem, idem.*

Joyful, *laetus, a, um.*

Of after superlatives = among, *inter,* prep. with acc.

Predict, *praedīco, ĕre, dixi, dic-tum.*

Rhetorician, *rhetor, ŏris,* m.

Say, relate, *fero, ferre, tuli, la-tum.*

Small, contracted, *angustus, a, um.*

Sufficiently, *satis,* adv.

Suitably = worthily enough, *satis digne,* adv.

Surpass the folly = be more fool-ish, *esse dementior, ius.*

Take place, happen, *fio, fĭĕri, fac-tus sum.* G. 294.

Unpopularity, *invidia, ae,* f.

Well-known, sometimes rendered by *ille, a, ud.* G. 450, 4.

Worthily, *digne,* adv.

481. Exercise.

1. Gorgias of Leontini, the well-known ancient rhetori-cian, was held in great honor. 2. At Rome there were some who exposed themselves to *unpopularity* for the safety of their country. 3. Cicero was in Athens just ten days.

4. Nothing can surpass the folly of those who, in a free state, so conduct themselves as to be feared. 5. That which is base is never useful. 6. Thales of Miletus, who is said to have been the wisest of the Seven, has never been suitably praised. 7. He is said to have predicted the eclipse of the sun which took place in the reign of Astyages. 8. Epicurus, in one house, and that too a small one, entertained *many friends*. 9. Of the many most joyful days which Scipio had seen during his life, that day was the most famous. 10. Let us compare the life of Demosthenes with that of Cicero.

Lesson LXXXIX.

PRONOUNS. — INTERROGATIVE. INDEFINITE.

482. Why? how is it that? may be rendered by *quid?* Why then? what indeed? by *quid enim?* What of the fact that? by *quid quod?* See Model I.

483. The article *a*, or *an*, is generally omitted in rendering, unless it has the force of *a certain, some, any*, in which case it may be rendered by *aliquis*, sometimes even by *quidam* or *quispiam*. See Model II.

484. The article *the* is generally omitted in rendering; but when it has the force of *that*, especially before a relative clause, it is rendered by the pronoun *is*, and sometimes by *ille*. See Model III.

485. *Every* with an ordinal, and, in most instances, *all* with a superlative or ordinal, should be rendered by *quisque*. See Models I. and IV.

486. *One another, each other*, may be rendered by *inter* *se,* or *inter ipsos,* and *one, one — another, another,* by *alius — alium.* See Model V.; also above, 270, Model VIII.

487. MODELS.

I. What shall we say of the fact that the best men ever die with the greatest equanimity?	I. *Quid, quod optĭmus quisque aequissĭmo anĭmo morĭtur ?*
II. Cicero did not discuss a part of the case, but spoke upon the whole subject.	II. *Cicĕro non partem egit causae, sed de tota re dixit.*
III. Xenophon, the pupil of Socrates, wrote history.	III. *Xenŏphon, Socratĭcus ille, scripsit historiam.*
IV. At every third word of his oration, he threatened me.	IV. *Tertio quoque verbo oratiōnis suae mihi minabātur.*
V. They were unlike each other.	V. *Dissimĭles inter se fuērunt.*

488. REMARKS.

1. MODEL I. — WHAT SHALL WE SAY OF THE FACT THAT, *quid, quod,* lit. *what, that,* i. e. what of the fact that, or what shall we say? &c.

2. MODEL II. — THE PUPIL OF SOCRATES, *Socratĭcus ille,* THE — emphatic rendered by *ille.*

489. SYNONYMES.

I. Who, which, what; *quis, uter, qui ?*

1. *Quis, quae, quid ;* WHO, WHICH ONE, WHICH ? — who, which, of any number.

2. *Uter, utra, utrum ;* WHO, WHICH ONE ? — which of two.

3. *Qui, quae, quod ;* WHAT, OF WHAT CHARACTER OR

KIND, — inquires after some distinguishing characteristic of the object, while *quis* and *uter* inquire after the object itself.

II. All, every; *omnis, quisque, unus quisque.*

1. *Omnis, e ;* ALL, EVERY, EVERY ONE, EVERY PART, — with the idea of including the whole.

2. *Quisque, quaeque, quidque* or *quodque ;* EVERY, EVERY ONE, EACH ONE, — giving prominence to the individual, rather than to the whole of which he is a part.

3. *Unus quisque (unus, a, um) ;* EVERY ONE, EVERY SINGLE ONE, EVERY INDIVIDUAL OBJECT, — stronger than *quisque,* as it admits no exception.

490. VOCABULARY.

Age, period of life, *aetas, ătis,* f.

All, each, every, *quisque, quaeque, quodque* and *quidque* or *quicque ;* G. 191, 1, 1) ; *omnis, e.* Each topic, *quidque.* All the good, *optĭmus quisque,* lit. *each best man.*

Commend, make acceptable, *probo, āre, āvi, ātum.*

Commit to writing, *littĕris mando, āre, āvi, ātum.*

Condition, state, *status, us,* m.

Constantly, *assiduus, a, um.* G. 443.

Conversation, *sermo, ōnis,* m.

Desirable, *optabĭlis, e.*

Fifth, *quintus, a, um.*

For the reason that, *propterea quod,* conj.

Friend of the people, *populāris, e.*

Individual, one, *unus, a, um.* G. 176, 1.

Is doing, is done, *agĭtur, actum est,* pass. of *ago.*

Lightly, *levĭter,* adv.

On the subject of, concerning, *de,* prep. with abl.

Once, formerly, *quondam,* adv.

Praetor, *praetor, ōris,* m.

Roscius, *Roscius, ii,* m.

Seek, *expĕto, ĕre, petīvi, petītum.*

Sextus, *Sextus, i,* m.

Take the census of, *censeo, ĕre, ui, censum.* The census of Sicily is taken, *Sicilia censētur.*

Touch, *tango, ĕre, tetĭgi, tactum.*

Which, which one, of two, *uter, utra, utrum.* G. 149.

With each other, *inter se.* G. 448, 1.

491. EXERCISE.

1. Who saluted him?   2. Which one of us is the friend of the people, you or I?   3. What is the condition of the republic?   4. I have committed to *writing* the conversation which Crassus and Antony once (formerly) held with each other on the subject of eloquence.   5. The census of Sicily was taken every fifth year; it was taken in the praetorship of Verres.   6. What is more desirable than wisdom? what more worthy of a man?   7. Those who seek *this* are called philosophers.   8. Death is common to every age.   9. Each of your friends will write to you.   10. I will touch *lightly* each individual topic.   11. The consuls so conducted themselves that they commended their plans to all the good.   12. Sextus Roscius not only was not at Rome, but did not know at all what was doing at Rome, for the reason that he was constantly in the country.

LESSON XC.

VERBS. — ACTIVE. PASSIVE. TRANSITIVE. INTRANSITIVE.

492. With transitive verbs a thought may in general, at the pleasure of the writer, be expressed either actively or passively; but if the subject of the active construction would be an abstract noun with a genitive of the real agent, the passive construction is preferred. See Models I. and II.

493. Those verbs which in English are used both transitively and intransitively must be rendered into Latin with special care, as we often find in such cases that the transitive sense must be rendered by one verb and the intransitive by another. Thus the verb *to increase*, when used transitively, must be rendered by *augeo*, but when used intransitively by *cresco*.

494. The English Impersonal Construction in the passive voice is often rendered personally in Latin. This is especially common with verbs of *perceiving, declaring, saying, thinking, finding, seeming*, and the like. See Model III.

1. But in the Compound tenses of verbs of *saying* and *thinking*, the Latin prefers the Impersonal Construction: *tradĭtum est, dictum est, dicendum est, credendum est*, etc. See Model IV.

495. But the English Personal Construction may sometimes be rendered into Latin by the Impersonal. Thus, —

1. The Second Periphrastic Conjugation is often Impersonal. See Model V.

2. Latin verbs which are intransitive in the active — i. e. do not govern the accusative — in the passive can be used only impersonally. See Model VI.

496. MODELS.

I. All things were ordained by God.

I. *A Deo omnia constitūta sunt.*

II. *The prudence of Cicero* liberated the republic from the greatest dangers.

II. *Cicerōnis prudentia res publĭca maxĭmis perĭcŭlis est liberāta.*

III. It is related that Aristides was the most just of all.

III. *Aristīdes omnium justissĭmus fuisse tradĭtur.*

IV. It has been said that the law is a silent magistrate.

IV. *Dictum est legem esse mutum magistrātum.*

V. The plans of *audacious*

V. *Audacium civium con-*

citizens must often be resisted.	*siliis saepe est resistendum.*
VI. An unsuccessful battle was fought by the consuls.	VI. *A consulĭbus male pugnātum est.*

497. REMARKS.

1. MODEL II. — In this sentence, though the Active construction is used in the English, the Passive is preferable in the Latin.

2. MODEL III. — Observe the Personal construction.

3. MODEL V. — The Impersonal construction is necessary in the Passive, because *resisto* does not admit the Accusative.

4. MODEL VI. — AN UNSUCCESSFUL BATTLE WAS FOUGHT, *male pugnātum est*, lit. *it was fought badly.*

498. VOCABULARY.

Acquire, *paro, āre, āvi, ātum.*

Act, do, *facio, ĕre, feci, factum.*

Admire, wonder at, *miror, āri, ātus sum*, dep.

Be eminent, *unus, a, um, emĭneo, ĕre, ui,* or *emĭneo* alone.

Commonwealth, *res publĭca, rei publĭcae,* f.

Desert, *desĕro, ĕre, serui, sertum.*

Diminish, *minuo, ĕre, ui, ūtum.*

Eminent, excelling, *excellens, entis.*

Esteem lightly, despise, *contemno, ĕre, tempsi, temptum.*

Great, illustrious, *amplus, a, um.*

Increase, trans., *augeo, ĕre, auxi, auctum.*

Kind, every kind, *omne genus ; genus, ĕris,* n.

My, your, etc., own productions, *mea, tua,* etc. G. 441, 1.

Old, *senex, senis ;* as substant., *an old person.*

Oratory, *dicendi, o, um, o,* ger. of *dico,* lit. *of, for,* etc., *speaking.*

Resources, means, *opes, opum,* f. pl. G. 133, 1.

Scaevola. *Scaevŏla, ae,* f.

So far, *tantum,* adv. So far am I from, *tantum abest ut* with subj., the clause with *ut* being the subject of *abest.*

Spirit, courage, *anĭmus, i,* m.

Withdraw, *decĕdo, ĕre, cessi, cessum.*

499. Exercise.

1. Money has always been lightly esteemed by all the greatest and most distinguished men. 2. He *defended* the commonwealth when he was a *young man;* he will not *desert* it now that he is *old.* 3. I have always praised Cato as a commander. 4. Cato, as a man eminent (excelling) in every virtue, has been praised by *all.* 5. It seems to me that Crassus acted more wisely than Scaevola. 6. So far are we from admiring our own productions, that Demosthenes himself, who is eminent among all *in every kind of oratory* (speaking), does not satisfy us. 7. Your plans will not *diminish,* but *increase,* the calamity. 8. There is no doubt that the resources and spirits of the enemy are increasing from day to day. 9. The *valor of Scipio* compelled Hannibal to withdraw from Italy. 10. We must not only acquire wisdom, but also use it.

Lesson XCI.

VERBS. — GENERAL STATEMENTS.

500. In general statements the second person singular, or the first and third persons plural, are often used in Latin to denote an indefinite subject, as people, persons in general. Thus, —

I. The second person singular is used when the remark is conceived of as addressed to *any one* who may chance to hear or read it; *you, any one.* The second person of the subjunctive is frequently so used. See Model III.

II. The first person plural is used when the speaker wishes to include himself in the general statement; *we ought, every one ought.* The third person plural is used in such general expressions as *they say, they report, they think,* etc. See Models I. and II.

III. But in such general statements, the third person singular of the passive voice is often used in Latin. See Model III.

501. MODELS.

I. We envy those who have the things which we long to have.

II. They say that Solon was the wisest of the Athenians.

III. Having obtained a victory, you should consult for those whom you have subdued by force.

I. *Iis aemulāmur qui ea habent, quae nos habēre cupĭmus.*

II. *Solōnem dicunt Atheniensium sapientissĭmum fuisse.*

III. *Parta victoria, iis quos vi devicĕris consulendum est.*

502. REMARKS.

1. MODEL II. — For the position of *dicunt,* see Remarks 304, 1.

2. MODEL III. — YOU SHOULD CONSULT FOR = one should consult for, *consulendum est.*

503. SYNONYMES.

Knowledge, foresight, wisdom; *scientia, prudentia, sapientia.*

1. *Scientia, ae,* f.; KNOWLEDGE, SKILL, — knowledge both theoretical and practical.

2. *Prudentia, ae,* f.; FORESIGHT, PRUDENCE, SAGACITY, SOUND JUDGMENT.

3. *Sapientia, ae,* f.; WISDOM, — involving both discernment and culture.

504. VOCABULARY.

Adversary, *adversarius, ii,* masc. adj. used as substant.

Author, adviser, *auctor, ōris,* m. and f.

Avoid, *vito, āre, āvi, ātum.*

Be on one's guard, *caveo, ēre, cavi, cautum.*

Confidence, *fides, ĕi,* f. Have confidence in, *fidem habeo* with dat.

Contend, *decerto, āre, āvi, ātum.*

Easily, *facile,* adv.

Injury, harm, *injuria, ae,* f.

Instance, thing, *res, rei,* f.

Know, understand, *intelligo, ĕre, lexi, lectum.*

Live, one lives, men live, *vivĭtur,* lit. *it is lived.*

Magian, pl. the Magi, *Magus, i,* m.

Mother, *mater, tris,* f.

Muse, *Musa, ae,* f.

Openly, *palam,* adv. An open adversary, *palam adversarius.*

Possess, have, *habeo, ēre, ui, ĭtum.*

Quickly, *celerĭter,* adv.

Set fire to, *inflammo, āre, āvi, ātum.*

Suggestion, at the suggestion of, *auctor* in the abl. abs. At the suggestion of the Magi, *Magis auctorĭbus,* lit. *the Magi being advisers.*

Think, *arbĭtror, āri, ātus sum,* dep.

Towards, *adversus,* prep. with acc.

Undertake, *suscĭpio, ĕre, cĕpi, ceptum.*

Unharmed, *sine injuria,* lit. *without harm,* according to connection, without *doing* or without *suffering* wrong.

Xerxes, *Xerxes, is,* m.

505. EXERCISE.

1. They say that he is the wisest who most quickly perceives in each instance what is true. 2. We have confidence in those whom we think to know (understand)

more than ourselves. 3. By being on your guard, you would easily avoid him who is an open adversary. 4. It is said that Xerxes, at the suggestion of the Magi, set fire to the temples of Greece. 5. There are certain duties to be observed even towards those from whom you have received an injury. 6. Wars must be undertaken that men may live in peace unharmed (without injury). 7. Although the results of war are uncertain, yet one should contend for liberty at the peril of life. 8. While we sleep the Muses will not give us the knowledge of writing, reading, and the other arts. 9. Cicero says that wisdom is the mother of all good arts. 10. The knowledge of the liberal arts is more useful than money. 11. All statesmen ought to possess the highest prudence.

LESSON XCII.

VERBS. — TENSES.

506. In English the Present tense is sometimes used of an action which is really future, and must therefore be rendered into Latin by the Future tense. See Model I.

507. In English, the Present, the Future, or the Perfect, is sometimes used of a future action which must be completed before some specified event. In such cases it must be rendered into Latin by the Future Perfect. See Model II.

508. When the English Imperfect or Past tense simply states an historical fact, without any reference to the continuance of the action, it must be rendered into Latin by the Perfect; but when it pictures a scene, or represents the action as continuing, it must be rendered by the Imperfect. See Models III. and IV.

509. The Imperfect with *while* is often best rendered by *dum* with the Present. See Model IV.

510. The Perfect with *have*, when used of an action which has been going on for some time, is best rendered by the Present, generally with *jamdiu. jamdūdum*, etc. See Model V.

511. MODELS.

I. If we follow *nature*, we shall not go astray.	I. *Natūram si sequēmur, non aberrabĭmus.*
II. When I reach Rome, I will write to you.	II. *Romam quum venĕro, scribam ad te.*
III. They saw the gleaming swords.	III. *Fulgentes gladios vidēbant.*
IV. While our soldiers were collecting these things, the king himself escaped *from their hands.*	IV. *Haec dum nostri collĭgunt, rex ipse effŭgit e manĭbus.*
V. I have not known for a long time what you are doing.	V. *Jamdiu ignōro quid agas.*

512. REMARKS.

1. MODEL I. — IF WE FOLLOW, Latin idiom, *if we shall follow.* The action really belongs to the future.

2. MODEL II. — WHEN I REACH, Latin idiom, *when I shall have reached,* — a future action to be completed before the time of writing.

3. MODEL IV. — WHILE OUR SOLDIERS WERE COLLECTING, Latin idiom, *while our* (soldiers) *collect.*

4. MODEL V. — I HAVE NOT KNOWN FOR A LONG TIME, Latin idiom, *for a long time I do not know.*

513. Synonymes.

Innocence, honesty, integrity, virtue; *innocentia, honestas, integrĭtas, virtus.*

1. *Innocentia, ae,* f.; INNOCENCE, BLAMELESSNESS, — freedom from guilt.

2. *Honestas, ātis,* f.; HONESTY, MORAL WORTH, — especially as shown in character and intention.

3. *Integrĭtas, ātis,* f.; INTEGRITY, UPRIGHTNESS, — involving the idea of *soundness* and *completeness* of moral character.

4. *Virtus, ūtis,* f.; VIRTUE, MORAL WORTH, — as shown both in life and in character, more comprehensive than either of the other three words.

514. Vocabulary.

Accommodate one's self to, yield to, *obsĕquor, i, secūtus sum,* dep.

Assiduously, *studiōse,* adv.

Consider, consider as, *arbĭtror, āri, ātus sum.*

Defendant, *reus, rei,* m.

Eagerly, *cupĭde,* adv.

For a long time, *jamdūdum,* adv.

Good will, *benevolentia, ae,* f.

Happen, befall, *accĭdo, ĕre, cĭdi.*

If any, *si quis, quae* or *qua, quid.* G. 190, 2.

Indeed, I, thou, etc.: a personal pronoun with a conj. is often best rendered by the relat. *qui, quae, quod.* G. 453.

Inhabitant, *incŏla, ae,* m. and f.

Innocence, *innocentia, ae,* f.

Less, *minus,* adv.

Let = cause that, *facio, ĕre, fēci, factum, ut* with subj.

Means, by no means, *nulla re,* lit. *by no thing.*

Moral worth, honor, *honestas, ātis,* f.

More fully, *plurĭbus verbis,* lit. *with more words.*

Obtain, *nanciscor, i, nactus sum,* dep.

Occasion, there is occasion, need, *opus est, fuit.*

One's, one's own, *suus, a, um.*

Others', of others, another's, *aliēnus, a, um.*

Preceptress, *praeceptrix, icis,* f.

Proof, *testimonium, ii,* n.

World, *mundus, i,* m.

Yesterday's, of yesterday, *hesternus, a, um.* Yesterday, *hesterno die.* G. 426.

515. EXERCISE.

1. Socrates considered himself an inhabitant and citizen of the whole world. 2. If anything *new* shall happen, we will let you know. 3. If there shall be any occasion, you will let us know. 4. I will write to you more fully when I obtain more leisure. 5. Our forefathers assiduously cultivated their own fields; they did not eagerly seek those of others. 6. I never pleased myself less than yesterday; indeed, while I accommodated myself to the young men, I forgot that I was old. 7. The defendant has given me the proof of his innocence. 8. I have often admired the moral worth of *Socrates.* 9. With wisdom as a preceptress, one can live in tranquillity. 10. Statesmen can by no means more easily secure the good will of the multitude than by integrity and virtue. 11. I have *for a long time* desired to visit Athens. 12. We had for a long time desired to visit Rome.

Lesson XCIII.

VERBS. — INDICATIVE.

516. The English Indicative must often be rendered by the Latin Subjunctive. Thus, —

1. Often in clauses denoting Cause, or Time and Cause. See Model I.

2. In Indirect Questions. See Model II.

3. In the Subordinate Clauses of Indirect Discourse. See Model III.

4. In Relative Clauses defining indefinite antecedents. See Model IV.

5. In Clauses denoting Result, and sometimes in Conditional and in Concessive Clauses. See Model V.

517. The Indicative with *that*, in a clause which is used either as the subject or the object of a verb, is generally best rendered into Latin by the Infinitive with a Subject Accusative. See Model VI.

518. Models.

I. Panaetius praises Scipio Africanus, because he was temperate.

I. *Panaetius Scipiōnem Africānum laudat, quod fuĕrit abstĭnens.*

II. It is asked whether one duty is greater than another.

II. *Quaerĭtur numquod officium aliud alio majus sit.*

III. Ennius does not think that one should mourn over death which immortality follows.

III. *Ennius non censet lugendam esse mortem quam immortalĭtas consequātur.*

IV. There is no one who is not able to attain to virtue.

V. I would not decline the labor, if I had any leisure time.

VI. We hear that Catiline spoke of the republic with some in one way and with others in another.

V. *Nemo est qui ad virtūtem pervenīre non possit.*

V. *Labōrem non recusārem, si mihi ullum esset vacuum tempus.*

VI. *Catilīnam alīter cum aliis de re publīca locūtum audīmus.*

519. Remarks.

1. Model III. — That one should mourn over death, *lugendam esse mortem*, lit. *that death should be mourned.*

2. Model VI. — With some in one way and with others in another, *alīter cum aliis*, lit. *in another way with others.*

520. Vocabulary.

Alone, *solus, a, um.* G. 149.

Aristotle, *Aristotĕles, is,* m.

Delightful, charming, *dulcis, e.*

Destitute of, *expers, ertis.* G. 399.

Do, act, *ago, ĕre, egi, actum.*

Entirely, *omnīno,* adv.

Evening, *vesper, ĕris,* m. At evening, *vespĕri.*

For the sake of, *gratia* or *causa* with gen. G. 414, 2, 3).

Justice, *justitia, ae,* f.

Justly, *juste,* adv.

Learning, erudition, *eruditio, ōnis,* f.

Offer, *affĕro, ferre, attŭli, allātum.*

Opinion, *opinio, ōnis,* f.

Prince, *princeps, ĭpis,* m.

Recall, call to mind, *commemŏro, āre, āvi, ātum.*

Say — not, deny, *nego, āre, āvi, ātum.* Say that no one = deny that any one, *nego,* etc.

Wont, be wont, *soleo, ĕre, solĭtus sum.* G. 272, 3.

521. Exercise.

1. Brutus has written to me; but what he wishes I do not know; for what counsel can I offer him, since I need *counsel* myself? 2. For the sake of exercising my memory, I recall at *evening* what each day I have said, heard, and done. 3. *When boys, we* had the opinion that Socrates, the prince of philosophers, was entirely destitute of all learning. 4. Epicurus says that one cannot live happily, unless one lives wisely, honestly, and justly. 5. Cicero says that no one, who does not live honestly, can live happily. 6. Publius Scipio was wont to say, that he was never less at leisure than when at leisure, nor less alone than when alone. 7. The poets are so delightful that they are not only read, but also committed to memory.

Lesson XCIV.

VERBS. — POTENTIAL MOOD.

522. The English Potential Mood, with the signs, *may, can, might, could, would, should,* is generally best rendered by the Latin Subjunctive. See Model I.

523. But the Potential may sometimes be rendered by the Indicative, and sometimes even by the Infinitive. Thus, —

1. By the Indicative of the Periphrastic Conjugations in the historical tenses, especially in conditional sentences. See Model II.

2. The Potential may be rendered by the Indicative in

expressions of *duty, necessity, ability*, and the like, and in such expressions as, *it would be fair, proper, just, tedious, difficult, better, more useful*, etc. See Model III.

3. The Potential after *that* may sometimes be rendered by the Infinitive. See Model IV.

524. In English, after the conjunctions, *if, unless, except, though, although, that, lest, in order that*, etc., the verb takes the *form* sometimes of the Indicative, sometimes of the Potential, and sometimes of the Subjunctive. But the verb after these conjunctions must generally be rendered into Latin either by the Indicative or by the Subjunctive, and in choosing between these two moods, the learner must be guided by the directions given him in his Grammar. See G. 489–523; also Model V.

525. MODELS.

I. What can seem *great* to him to whom all eternity is known?

I. *Quid videātur ei magnum, cui aeternĭtas omnis nota sit?*

II. This condition should not have been accepted.

II. *Haec conditio non accipienda fuit.*

III. It would be tedious to reply to all that has been said by you.

III. *Longum est ad omnia respondēre quae a te dicta sunt.*

IV. It is of great interest to us that you should come as soon as possible.

IV. *Magni nostra intĕrest te quam primum venīre.*

V. If I ask you anything, will you not reply?

V. *Si te rogavĕro alĭquid, nonne respondēbis?*

526. Remarks.

1. Model II. — Should not have been accepted, Latin idiom, *was not to be accepted*, or *did not deserve to be accepted*.

2. Model III. — It would be tedious, Latin idiom, *it is long*, i. e. a long task.

3. Model V. — If I ask, *si rogavĕro*, lit. *if I shall have asked*.

527. Vocabulary.

Appropriate to, apply to, *confĕro, ferre, tŭli, collātum, in* with acc.

As much — as, *tantus — quantus :* each, of course, to be in its proper construction in its own clause.

Asia, *Asia, ae,* f.

Beneficence, *beneficentia, ae,* f.

Better, preferable, *satius,* properly neut. comp. from *satis;* lit. *more satisfactory.*

Certainly, *certe,* adv.

Depart from, *exeo, ire, ii, ĭtum.*

Differently, *alĭter,* adv.

Either — or, *vel — vel,* etc.   G, 587, II., 2.

Flaccus, *Flaccus, i,* m.

Follow, *sequor, i, secūtus sum,* dep. To follow this course, that course, &c., *hoc, illud,* etc., *sequor.*

Govern, rule, *rego, ĕre, rexi, rectum.*

Impel, *impello, ĕre, pŭli, pulsum.*

Important, is important to, *intĕrest, fuit.* G. 408.

Inform, *certiŏrem facio, ĕre, feci, factum ;* lit. *make more certain.*

Liberality, *liberalĭtas, ātis,* f.

Mention, *commemŏro, āre, āvi, ātum.*

Noble, honorable, *honestus, a, um.*

Object of interest, *quod visendum est ;* lit. *what should be visited.*

Silent, *mutus, a, um.*

Sufficient, be sufficient, be able, *possum, posse, potui.*

Think little of, despise, *contemno, ĕre, tempsi, temptum.*

Understand, *intellĭgo, ĕre, lexi, lectum.*

Unnecessary, not necessary, *non necessarius, a, um.*

Vender, *vendĭtor, ŏris,* m.

Whole, the whole of, *totus, a, um,* adj.   G. 149.

528. EXERCISE.

1. It would be tedious and unnecessary to mention all the objects of interest in the *whole of Asia*. 2. Flaccus thinks that it is important to him that I should write you as often as possible. 3. If I thought differently, certainly your admonition would be sufficient to impel me to follow the course which you think best. 4. I wish that you would write to me on what day you think that you will depart from Rôme, that I may inform you in what place I shall be. 5. Would it not be better to be silent, than to speak that which no one understands? 6. The republic should have been wisely governed. 7. Nothing is more noble than to think little of money, if you do not have it; and if you have it, to appropriate it to beneficence and liberality. 8. What is there which cannot be purchased, if you give as much as the *vender* wishes?

LESSON XCV.

VERBS. — IMPERATIVE.

529. The Imperative with *let* is generally best rendered by the First and Third Persons of the Latin Subjunctive, while other Imperatives are generally best rendered by the Latin Present Imperative. See Models I. and II.

530. Remember that the Imperative with a negative is best rendered by *noli* and *nolīte* with the Infinitive. See Model III.

531. Models.

I. See that you come as soon as possible.	I. *Cura ut quam primum venias.*
II. Since life without friends is full of fear, let us secure friendships.	II. *Quum vita sine amīcis metus plena sit, amicitias comparēmus.*
III. Do not think that the consul did this without great pain.	III. *Noli putāre consŭlem hoc sine magno dolōre fecisse.*

532. Remarks.

1. Model I. — See that, *cura ut*, lit. *take care that*.

2. Model III. — Do not think, *noli putāre*, lit. *do not wish to think*. See G. 538, 2.

533. Synonymes.

To approve, to praise, to extol; *probo, laudo, extollo laudĭbus* or *laudando*.

1. *Probo, āre, āvi, ātum ;* to approve.

2. *Laudo, āre, āvi, ātum ;* to praise, to commend.

3. *Extollo, ĕre, laudĭbus* or *laudando ;* to laud, extol.

534. Vocabulary.

Action, deed, *factum, i,* n.

Arrange with reference to, *refĕro, ferre, tŭli, lātum, ad* with acc.; lit. *refer to.*

Care for, *curo, āre, āvi, ātum.*

Desire, *volo, velle, volui,* G. 293; *opto, āre, āvi, ātum.* See Syn. 618.

Eagerly, *vehementer*, adv.

Engaged, be engaged in, *sum, esse, fui, in* with abl.; lit. *to be in.*

Extol, *extollo, ĕre*, with *laudĭbus* or *laudando.*

Guard, defend, *tueor, ēri, tuĭtus sum*, dep.

Heaven, *coelum, i*, n. See G. 143, 1.

Immortal, *immortālis, e.*

Interests, profit, *utĭlĭtas, ātis*, f.

Observe, retain, *teneo, ēre, ui, tentum.*

Other, the other, the second of two, *alter, ĕra, ĕrum.* G. 149; 149, 2.

Proceed, *pergo, ĕre, perrexi, perrectum.*

Such — as, in quality, *talis — qualis ;* in character, *is — qui ;* lit. *the one who* or *which.* See G. 186, 4, and 451, 4.

That, not strongly demonstrative, especially as antecedent of relative, *is, ea, id.*

Toil, labor, *labor, ŏris*, m.

535. Exercise.

1. Do not doubt that there were *poets* before Homer. 2. Proceed, young men, and devote yourselves to the study in which you are now engaged, that you may be both an honor to yourselves and an advantage to your friends. 3. Let us imitate those who, by their counsels and toils, have attained immortal glory. 4. Let us think that the most useful, which will be the best. 5. Let us be such as we wish to be regarded. 6. I am eagerly awaiting a letter from you, and indeed such a one as I especially desire. 7. Let us arrange all our plans and actions with reference to virtue. 8. We not only approve, but also praise, your plans. 9. There are some who, with their praises, extol Marcus Cato to heaven. 10. Let those who are to be statesmen observe two precepts of Plato, one that they should guard the interests of the citizens, the other that they should care for the whole state.

Lesson XCVI.

VERBS. — INFINITIVE.

536. When the English Infinitive is simply the subject or the object of a verb, it should be rendered by the Latin Infinitive. See Model I.

537. When the English Infinitive either expresses purpose or result, or is dependent upon a noun or adjective, it can seldom be rendered by the Latin Infinitive. When thus used, it should generally be rendered by one of the following constructions:

1. By the Subjunctive of Purpose or Result. See Model II.; also G. 489–501.

2. By the Genitive of the Gerund or Gerundive with *causa* or *gratia*. See Model III.

3. By the Accusative of the Gerund or Gerundive with *ad*. See Model IV.

4. By a Relative Clause. See Model V.; also G. 501, III.

5. By the Supine in *u*. See Model VI.

538. Models.

I. All wished to hear Cicero.	I. *Omnes Cicerōnem audīre voluērunt.*
II. I exhort you to read this oration.	II. *Te hortor ut hanc oratiōnem legas.*
III. He came to Rome *to visit me.*	III. *Romam venit mei visendi causa.*
IV. Cicero arose to reply.	IV. *Cicĕro ad respondendum surrexit.*

V. The consul was worthy to command.

V. *Consul dignus fuit qui imperāret.*

VI. Let us inquire what it is best to do.

VI. *Quaerāmus quid optĭmum factu sit.*

539. REMARKS.

1. MODEL III. — TO VISIT ME, *mei visendi causa,* lit. *for the sake of visiting me.*

2. MODEL V. — WORTHY TO COMMAND, Latin idiom, *worthy who should command,* i. e. worthy that he should command.

540. VOCABULARY.

Advantage, *commŏdum, i,* n.

Archytas, *Archy̆tas, ae,* m.

Assembly, *concio, ōnis,* f.

Attention, exertion, *opĕra, ae,* f.

Connected, *contĭnens, entis.*

Curio, *Curio, ōnis,* m.

Deserve, *mereo, ĕrĕ, ui, ĭtum ; mereor, ĕri, ĭtus sum,* dep.

Devise, *invĕnio, ĭre, vēni, ventum.*

Dion, *Dio* or *Dion, ōnis,* m.

Discourse, *oratio, ōnis,* f.

Early in the morning, *mane,* adv.

Evident, be evident, *consto, āre, stĭti, stātum.*

Give heed, *opĕram do, dare, dedi, datum.*

Injure, *noceo, ĕre, ui, ĭtum.* G. 385.

Interrupt, *interpello, āre, āvi, ātum.*

Know, know how, *scio, scire, scivi, scitum.*

Lawful, it is lawful, *licet, licuit* or *licĭtum est.* G. 299.

Not, not at all, *nihil.* G. 380, 2.

Pay one's respects to, *salūto, āre, āvi, ātum.*

Perhaps, *forsĭtan,* adv.

Reply, *respondeo, ĕre, spondi, sponsum.*

Syracusan, of Syracuse, *Syracusĭus, a, um.*

Urge, *impello, ĕre, pŭli, pulsum.*

Wonderful, *mirabĭlis, e.*

541. Exercise.

1. If we wish to be both wise and happy, we must give heed to virtue.   2. Plato wrote to *Archytas* to remember that he was born, not for himself only, but for his country. 3. We are prepared to hear.   4. It is not lawful to injure *another* for the sake of one's own advantage.   5. It is evident that *laws* were devised for the safety of citizens. 6. I will not interrupt you at all; I prefer to hear a connected discourse.   7. Plato urged Dion of Syracuse to liberate his country.   8. Perhaps this which I am about to say may be wonderful to hear, but I will certainly say that which I think.   9. Pompey is a suitable person to command the Roman army.   10. Know that Curio came to me *to pay his respects*.   11. Early in the morning men come into the assembly; they inquire what it is best to do.   12. Socrates replied to his judges that he had deserved to be presented with the highest honors.   13. All things are easily learned, if you know how to learn.

Lesson XCVII.

VERBS. — PARTICIPLES.

542. The English Participle may generally be rendered by the Latin Participle.   See Model I.

543. The English Perfect Active Participle may be rendered by one of the following constructions:

1. By the Perfect Participle of a Deponent verb.   See Model II.

2. By the Perfect Passive Participle in the Ablative Absolute. See Model III.

3. By *Quum* with the Subjunctive. See Model IV.

4. By *Postquam* with the Indicative. See Model V.

544. The English expressions, *so called, the so called, what they* or *you call*, are rendered by Relative Clauses, *qui dicĭtur, qui vocātur, qui appellātur, quem dicunt* or *dicis, quem vocant* or *vocas*, etc. See Model VI.

545. The English Participle in *ing*, when used substantively, must be rendered by the Gerund or Gerundive. See Model VII.

546. Models.

I. I *have received* your carefully written letter.

I. *Accēpi tuam diligenter scriptam epistŏlam.*

II. Having tarried a few days at Corinth, he came to Athens.

II. *Corinthi paucos dies commorātus, Athēnas venit.*

III. The commanders, having conquered the enemy, presented their secretaries with gold rings.

III. *Imperatōres, hoste superāto, scribas suos annŭlis aureis donavērunt.*

IV. Mithridates, having betaken himself into his own kingdom, made an attack upon the Roman army.

IV. *Mithridātes, quum se in regnum recepisset suum, in exercĭtum Romānum impĕtum fecit.*

V. The actor, having been hissed from the stage, fled to you for protection.

V. *Histrio, postquam e scena sibĭlis explodebātur, ad te confūgit.*

VI. That law, as you call it, is not a law.	VI. *Lex ista quam vocas non est lex.*
VII. We are animated with the desire of living happily.	VII. *Beāte vivendi cupiditāte incensi sumus.*

547. REMARKS.

1. MODEL III. — HAVING CONQUERED THE ENEMY, *hoste superāto,* lit. *the enemy having been overcome.*

2. MODEL IV. — HAVING BETAKEN HIMSELF, *quum se recepisset,* lit. *when he had betaken himself.*

3. MODEL VI. — AS YOU CALL IT, *quam vocas,* lit. *which you call.*

548. SYNONYMES.

To be grateful, to thank, to reciprocate a favor; *gratiam (gratias) habeo, gratias ago, gratiam refĕro.*

1. *Gratiam (gratias) habeo, ēre, ui, ĭtum;* TO BE GRATEFUL, — to have or feel gratitude.

2. *Gratias ago, ĕre, egi, actum;* TO THANK, TO RETURN THANKS, — to express gratitude.

3. *Gratiam refĕro, ferre, tŭli, lātum;* TO RECIPROCATE A FAVOR, TO RETURN OR REQUITE A FAVOR, — to show gratitude by deeds.

549. VOCABULARY.

Carefully, *diligenter,* adv.	Maiden, *virgo, ĭnis,* f.
Deed, thing, *res, rei,* f.	Mantinea, *Mantinēa, ae,* f.
Entertain gratitude, be grateful, *gratiam habeo, ēre, ui, ĭtum.*	Novel, *novus, a, um.*
	Olympus, *Olympus, i,* m.
Establish, *firmo, āre, āvi, ātum.*	Part, *pars, partis,* f.
Express thanks, *gratias ago, ĕre, egi, actum.*	Poor, with limited means, *inops, ŏpis.*

Robber, *praedo, ŏnis,* m.

Sabine, *Sabīnus, a, um.*

Seize, *rapio, ĕre, rapui, raptum.*

Servilius, *Servilius, ii,* m.

Some time = at some time, *ali-*
   quando, adv.

Start, set out, *proficiscor, i, profec-*
   tus sum, dep.

Surely, *certe,* adv.

Tarry, *commŏror, āri, ātus sum,*
   dep.

Towards, *versus,* adv., usually after
   the word denoting place.

550. Exercise.

1. Having been asked my opinion, I said many things in regard to the *republic.* 2. Cicero, having been asked his opinion, said that which was most worthy of the republic. 3. I received *many* letters from you on the *same day,* all carefully written. 4. We see all parts of Italy adorned with the most beautiful monuments. 5. Publius Servilius, the commander of the Roman army, having achieved the greatest deeds, took the ancient city of Olympus. 6. Epaminondas, having conquered the Lacedaemonians at Mantinea, died in joy and victory. 7. The robbers, having tarried one night at Capua, started towards Rome. 8. I entertain the greatest gratitude to you for your favor. 9. O that we some time may be able to requite *your* favor; we shall indeed *ever* be grateful. 10. A poor man, if he cannot requite a favor, can surely be grateful. 11. We desire to express our thanks to you in the strongest terms. 12. Romulus pursued a novel plan *for establishing a state,* when he ordered the Sabine maidens to be seized.

Lesson XCVIII.

DISTINCTION IN THE USE OF PARTICIPLES, RELATIVE CLAUSES, AND CLAUSES WITH CONJUNCTIONS.

551. Participles, Relative Clauses, and Clauses with Conjunctions, are in Latin kindred constructions, and must, accordingly, be used with care and discrimination. Thus, —

I. The Relative Clause is generally used when we wish to *identify* a person or thing by specifying some characteristic, or *to call attention* to some *permanent* and *essential* quality or habit. See Models I. and II.

II. A Clause with a Conjunction is generally used when we wish to make the relation of *time, cause, condition, concession,* etc., particularly prominent. See Model III.

III. The Participle may be used, —

1. Instead of the Relative Clause, when we wish to indicate only an *accidental* or *temporary* connection between a quality or an action and the noun to which it is referred; and, —

2. Instead of a Clause with a Conjunction, when the relation of *time, cause, condition, concession,* etc., is not particularly prominent. See Models IV. and V.

552. Models.

I. In the book entitled Laelius, Cicero wrote on the subject of friendship.

I. *In eo libro qui inscribĭtur Laelius, Cicĕro de amicitia scripsit.*

II. The virtue which boldly meets coming evils is called fortitude.

II. *Virtus quae venientĭbus malis obstat fortitūdo nominātur.*

III. I seem to be in *Rome* when I read your letters.

III. *Romae videor esse quum tuas epistŏlas lego.*

IV. I have sent *you* a letter written in Greek.

IV. *Epistŏlam Graece compositam misi ad te.*

V. Not knowing the true path of glory, he prefers to be feared by the citizens rather than loved.

V. *Ignōrans verum iter gloriae, metui a civĭbus quam dilĭgi mavult.*

553. REMARKS.

1. MODEL I. — ENTITLED LAELIUS. This identifies the book thus entitled, and must therefore be expressed by the Relative Clause.

2. MODEL II. — COMING. This does not identify the evils, and may therefore be rendered by the Participle.

554. SYNONYMES.

To remember, to recollect, to recall to mind; *memĭni, reminiscor, recordor.*

1. *Memĭni;* TO REMEMBER, — to retain in memory. See G. 297.

2. *Reminiscor, i;* TO REMEMBER, TO RECOLLECT, TO RECALL TO MIND, — to recall by an effort of the memory.

3. *Recordor, āri, ātus sum;* TO RECALL TO MIND, TO CHERISH THE MEMORY OF, — to recall to mind and to dwell upon the recollection, generally with pleasure.

555. VOCABULARY.

Advice, give advice, advise, *suadeo, ēre, suasi, suasum.*	All, all together, *cunctus, a, um.*
	Any, *ullus, a, um.* G. 149.

Civil, belonging to the city, *ur-bānus, a, um.*

Excellent, good, *bonus, a, um.* G. 165.

For the first time, *primum,* adv.

Hearing, in the hearing of, pres. part. of *audio* in the abl. absol. ; e. g., in the hearing of Greece, *audiente Graecia,* lit. *Greece hearing.*

Hippias, *Hippias, ae,* m.

Hortensius, *Hortensius, ii,* m.

I myself, you yourself, he himself, &c., *ipse, a, um.* G. 452, 1.

Inscribe, *inscrĭbo, ĕre, scripsi, scriptum.*

Military, pertaining to war, *bellĭcus, a, um.*

Nearly, *paene,* adv.

Nineteen, *undeviginti,* indecl.

Olympia, *Olympia, ae,* f.

Recall to mind, *recordor, āri, ātus sum,* dep.

Trust, hope, *spero, āre, āvi, ātum.*

Very, with nouns, *ipse, a, um.* G. 452, 2.

556. EXERCISE.

1. Do not philosophers inscribe their names in these very books which they write on the subject of despising glory? 2. Hippias, having come to Olympia, boasted, in the hearing of nearly all Greece, that there was nothing, in any art, which he did not himself know. 3. In the conversation held with Cato, Cicero said many things on the subject of virtue. 4. Isocrates wrote, in his ninety-fourth year, the book entitled Panathenaicus. 5. In the consulship of Lucius Crassus and Quintus Scaevola, Quintus Hortensius the orator spoke for the first time in the forum at the age of nineteen. 6. I remember what advice you then gave me. 7. I trust that you, who are wont to forget nothing except injuries, recall to mind many things in regard to this most excellent man, Marcus Cato. 8. Recall to mind those things which you learned when a boy. 9. Pericles, excelling in learning, in coun-

sel, and in eloquence, presided for forty years over *Athens, both in civil and in military affairs.*

LESSON XCIX.

EXPRESSIONS OF DUTY, NECESSITY.

557. The general meaning conveyed by the English word *must* is expressed in Latin in five different ways. These, however, must be carefully distinguished from each other. Thus, —

I. *Debeo,* I ought, denotes a moral obligation, I ought, or I must, because I ought:

What ought we to do? *Quid facĕre debēmus?* What ought we to have done? *Quid facĕre debuĭmus?* See Model I.

II. *Oportet,* it behooves, also denotes moral obligation, but with the accessory notion of propriety. It also differs from *debeo* in expressing the obligation *impersonally* and *abstractly,* as a duty in itself considered:

This ought to be said, *Hoc dici oportet.* See Model II.

III. The Second Periphrastic Conjugation and the Participle in *dus,* denote (1) a necessity growing out of the circumstances of the case, and (2) propriety or desert:

That plan must be commended, *Illud consilium laudandum est.* See Model III.

IV. *Necesse est,* it is necessary, is the strongest and most unqualified expression of stern necessity:

This must be done, *Hoc fiĕri necesse est.* See Model IV.

V. *Opus est,* it is needful, there is need, denotes only a qualified necessity, and has reference to the attainment of an object:

It is needful that this should be done, *Hoc fiĕri opus est.* See Model V.

558. Models.

I. We ought to have aided you.	I. *Te juvāre debuĭmus.*
II. This ought long since to have been done.	II. *Hoc jamprīdem factum esse oportuit.*
III. We *ought* to consider what we have to fear.	III. *Debēmus cogitāre quid nobis sit metuendum.*
IV. Why was it necessary for you to write that letter?	IV. *Quid tibi necesse fuit illam epistŏlam scribĕre?*
V. You will defend us, if it shall seem to be needful.	V. *Nos, si opus esse vidēbĭtur, defendes.*

559. Remarks.

1. MODEL I. — OUGHT TO HAVE AIDED, Latin idiom, *were under obligation* (owed) *to aid.* See G. 541, 3.

2. MODEL II. — *Factum esse* is here used, instead of *fĭĕri*, to emphasize the completion of the action.

560. Vocabulary.

Accomplish, *effĭcio, ĕre, fēci, fectum.*

Admiration, a feeling of admiration, *admiratio, ōnis,* f.

Admit, concede, *concēdo, ĕre, cessi, cessum.*

Amount, quantity, *vis, vis,* f. G. 88, III. 3.

Attempt, *tento, āre, āvi, ātum.*

Change, to alter, *muto, āre, āvi, ātum.*

Choose, select, *elĭgo, ĕre, lēgi, lectum.*

Depend upon, *posĭtus, a, um, esse, in* with abl.; lit. *be placed in.*

Evil, *malum, i,* n.

Exist, *sum, esse, fui.*

Frequently, *saepe*, adv.; comp. *saepius*, superlat. *saepissime*.

Good, *bonum*, *i*, n.

Learn, observe, *accǐpio*, *ěre*, *cěpi*, *ceptum*.

Least, *minǐmus*, *a*, *um*, superlat. of *parvus*, G. 165; adv., *minǐme*.

Magistrate, *magistrātus*, *us*, m.

Minister, servant, *minister*, *tri*, m., *ministra*, *ae*, f. To minister to, *minister* or *ministra esse* with gen.; lit. *to be the minister of*.

More highly, with verbs of valuing, *pluris*, adv.

Necessary, it is necessary, *necesse est*, *fuit*.

Perhaps, *fortasse*, adv.

Possession, *possessio*, *ōnis*, f.

Pray, I pray, parenthetical, *quaeso*.

Prize, *aestǐmo*, *āre*, *āvi*, *ātum*.

Prompt, affect, *commǒveo*, *ěre*, *mǒvi*, *mōtum*.

Prove, *probo*, *āre*, *āvi*, *ātum*.

Silver, *argentum*, *i*, n.

561. Exercise.

1. That which ought to be accomplished by worth is often attempted by means of *money*. 2. We have learned from *good men*, that of evils it behooves one to choose the least. 3. It must be admitted that an honorable life is a happy life. 4. No possession, no amount of gold and silver, must be more highly prized than virtue. 5. The arts which minister to pleasures are *least* to be commended. 6. It must be admitted that a *happy life* depends upon *virtue*. 7. Consider, I pray, what we ought to do. 8. All things should be arranged with reference to the *highest good*. 9. There is need of magistrates, without whose prudence and diligence a state cannot exist. 10. Prompted by a feeling of admiration, I praise *Plato* more frequently, perhaps, than is necessary. 11. I will not prove to these judges that the praetor took money contrary to the laws.

LESSON C. .

USE OF SPECIAL VERBS.

562. *Permission* may be expressed in Latin, —

1. By *licet*, it is lawful, permitted by human law. See Model I.

2. By *fas est*, it is right, permitted by divine law. See Model II.

3. By *concedĭtur, concessum est*, it is allowed, permitted by all law. See Model I.

563. *Power, ability*, is expressed by *possum*, I am able, I can. See Model III.

564. *Possibility, uncertainty*, may be expressed, —

1. By *fiĕri potest ut*, with the Subjunctive, it can happen that, it may be that. See Model IV.

2. By the Potential Subjunctive. See Model V.

565. The Latin has three principal ways of expressing possession :

I. *Sum* with the Ablative is used of necessary and permanent possession. This is used especially when the thing possessed is a part, a quality, or a characteristic of the possessor. See Model VI.

II. *Habeo* is the most common equivalent for the English verb *to have*, but is used especially to denote external possession. See Models VII. and VIII.

III. *Sum* with the Dative has the same general force as · *habeo*, but calls attention to the thing possessed by making it the subject of the verb. See Models IX. and X.[1]

---

[1] In expressions of naming, as in Model IX., *sum with the Dative* is the regular construction. It is also the usual construction when the

566. MODELS.

I. We say that is lawful which is permitted by the laws.	I. *Licēre id dicĭmus quod legĭbus concedĭtur.*
II. The consul defended you, as far as he was able, as far as was right, and as far as was lawful.	II. *Consul, quoad posset, quoad fas esset, quoad licēret, vos defendit.*
III. They might have aided you very much.	III. *Te plurĭmum juvāre potuērunt.*
IV. It may be that I am mistaken.	IV. *Fiĕri potest ut fallar.*
V. Who would hesitate to defend his country?	V. *Quis dubĭtet patriam defendĕre?*
VI. Africanus was possessed of the greatest eloquence.	VI. *Erat in Africāno summa eloquentia.*
VII. He has an ancestral estate in Italy.	VII. *Fundum in Italia paternum habet.*
VIII. Demosthenes possessed wisdom united with eloquence.	VIII. *Demosthĕnes sapientiam cum eloquentia junctam habuit.*
IX. At Syracuse there is a fountain whose name is Arethusa.	IX. *Syracūsis est fons cui nomen Arethūsa est.*
X. I have no dealings with him.	X. *Nihil mihi est cum illo.*

subject stands connected with an oblique case with or without a preposition, as in Model X., *nihil cum illo*, no dealings with him.

567. REMARKS.

1. MODEL IV. — IT MAY BE THAT, Latin idiom, *it can take place* (be done) *that.*

2. MODELS VI. — VIII. — Observe the different ways of expressing possession.

3. MODEL IX. — WHOSE NAME IS, Latin idiom, *to which there is the name.*

568. VOCABULARY.

Acquaintance, experience, *usus, us,* m. A very intimate acquaintance, *summus usus.*

Administer, *gero, ĕre, gessi, gestum.*

And yet = and, *et,* conj.

Aware, be aware, know, *scio, scire, scivi, scitum.*

By myself, by yourself, &c., *mecum, tecum,* etc.; lit. *with myself,* &c.

Correctly, *recte,* adv.

Elegantly, *polite,* adv.

Ever, *unquam,* adv.

Express, utter, *elŏquor, i, locŭtus sum,* dep.

Fabius, *Fabius, ii,* m.

Innumerable, *innumerabĭlis, e.*

Know, be acquainted with, *cognosco, ĕre, nŏvi, nĭtum.*

May be, it may be that, *fiĕri potest ut* with subj.

Negligent, *neglĭgens, entis.*

No one, nobody, *nemo, ĭnis ; nullus, a, um.* See G. 457, 2.

Not, followed by either — or, = neither — nor, *neque* or *nec — neque* or *nec.*

One, any one, any thing, *quis, quae, quid.*

Repeat, *reddo, ĕre, dĭdi, dĭtum.*

So that, *ut,* conj.

Strongly, *valde,* adv.

Such — as = so great, or so much — as, *tantus — quantus.*

Talent, mental ability, *mens, mentis,* f.

Think, ponder, *cogĭto, āre, āvi, ātum.*

Think out, *commentor, āri, ātus sum.*

Whoever, whatever, *quisquis, quaequae, quodquod* and *quicquid* or *quidquid.* He — who, that — which, *is — qui.*

Writing, *scriptum, i,* n.

Wrong, *nefas,* n. indecl.

569. Exercise.

1. Whatever is not lawful we ought to regard as wrong. 2. It may be that one may think correctly, and yet not be able to express elegantly that which one thinks. 3. You would not be able to praise Plato either too strongly or too frequently. 4. I do not think that Verres will deny that he has innumerable pictures. 5. O that there had been in Tiberius Gracchus such talent for administering the republic well, as there was genius for speaking well! 6. It is not permitted me to be negligent in this thing. 7. I have, as I think you are aware, a very intimate acquaintance with Marcus Fabius. 8. *Hortensius* had such a memory as I think I have known in no one (else), so that, whatever he had thought out by himself, he could, without writing, repeat in the same words in which he had thought it.

Lesson CI.

PREPOSITIONS.

570. In many instances where the English idiom uses prepositions, the Latin adopts some different construction.

571. The preposition *without* may be variously rendered into Latin, but most frequently (1) by the preposition *sine*, (2) by a participle with *non* or some other negative word, and (3) by *ut non, qui non*, or *quin*, with the Subjunctive. See Models I.—III.

572. The preposition *for* may generally be rendered (1) by the Dative of the Indirect Object, (2) by *pro* with the

Ablative, and (3) by other prepositions; *ad, ob, propter* with the Accusative, or *de* with the Ablative. See Models IV. —VI.

573. The preposition *to* may be rendered, (1) by the Dative of the Indirect Object, (2) by *ad* with the Accusative, and (3) by the Accusative of Limit. See Models VII. — IX.

574. MODELS.

I. I *shall say* without hesitation that which I think.	I. *Dicam sine cunctatiōne quod sentio.*
II. It is sad to be troubled without accomplishing anything.	II. *Misĕrum est nihil proficientem angi.*
III. I allowed *no* day to pass without writing something to you.	III. *Nullum intermīsi diem quin alĭquid ad te scribĕrem.*
IV. We were born, not only for ourselves, but also for our country.	IV. *Non nobis solum, sed etiam patriae, nati sumus.*
V. The soldiers fought for liberty.	V. *Milĭtes pro libertāte pugnavērunt.*
VI. Publius Scipio seems to have been born for glory.	VI. *Publius Scipio ad gloriam natus esse vidētur.*
VII. The commander will yield to the laws.	VII. *Imperātor legĭbus cedet.*
VIII. I write to those who write to me.	VIII. *Scribo ad eos qui ad me scribunt.*
IX. Archias came to Rome *in the consulship of Marius and Catulus.*	IX. *Archias Romam venit Mario et Catŭlo consulĭbus.*

575. REMARKS.

1. MODEL II. — WITHOUT ACCOMPLISHING ANYTHING, *nihil profici-entem*, lit. *accomplishing nothing.*

2. MODEL III. — WITHOUT WRITING, *quin scrib̆erem*, lit. *but that I wrote.*

3. MODELS IV. AND VI. — FOR OURSELVES, *nobis*, Indirect Object. FOR GLORY, *ad gloriam*, the Object or End for which.

576. SYNONYMES.

To think, to have an opinion; *opīnor, puto, arbĭtror, sentio, censeo.*

1. *Opīnor, āri, ātus sum,* dep.; TO THINK, TO HAVE AN IMPRESSION, — used especially of mere impression, as opposed to well-founded opinion.

2. *Puto, āre, āvi, ātum;* TO THINK, TO SUPPOSE, — implying a more decided opinion than *opīnor.*

3. *Arbĭtror, āri, ātus sum,* dep.; TO THINK, TO HAVE A CONVICTION, — used especially (1) of opinions which rest upon one's own personal convictions, and (2) of opinions which have authority, as those of an arbitrator.

4. *Sentio, īre, sensi, sensum;* TO THINK, TO PERCEIVE, TO FEEL, — used especially of one's sentiments, as dependent upon one's own experience, upon what one has perceived and felt.

5. *Censeo, ēre, ui, censum;* TO THINK, TO DECIDE, — to express one's opinion authoritatively and officially, as a senator may do by vote or otherwise.

11

577. VOCABULARY.

Allow to pass, *intermitto, ĕre, mĭsi, missum.*

Appear, seem, *videor, ēri, visus sum,* pass. of *video ;* lit. *to be looked upon as.*

Attain, *adipiscor, i, adeptus sum,* dep.

Conduce to, be conducive to, *condūco, ĕre, duxi, ductum.* G. 385.

Consult, consult for, consult for the interest of, *consŭlo, ĕre, sului, sultum.* G. 385, 3.

Discord, *discordia, ae,* f.

Encounter, go to meet, *oppĕto, ĕre, ĭvi* and *ii, ĭtum.*

Express opinion, think, *censeo, ēre, ui, censum.*

Give, deliver, *trado, ĕre, dĭdi, dĭtum.*

Glorious, *gloriōsus, a, um.*

Have reference to, *refĕror, ferri, lātus sum, ad* with acc. ; lit. *be referred to.*

In regard to, sometimes rendered by gen. ; e. g. a precept in regard to duty, *officii praeceptum,* lit. *a precept of duty.*

Introduce, bring in, *indūco, ĕre, duxi, ductum.*

Not even, *ne quidem,* with the emphatic word after *ne.* Not even when, *ne tum quidem, quum;* lit. *not then even, when.*

Point, thing, *res, rei,* f.

Sacrifice, spend, *profundo, ĕre, fūdi, fūsum.*

Suppose, think, *arbĭtror, āri, ātus sum,* dep. ; *pŭto, āre, āvi, ātum.*

Tear, *lacrĭma, ae,* f.

Think, be of opinion, *opĭnor, āri, ātus sum,* dep.

Thus far, *adhuc,* adv.

Without, variously rendered. See 571.

Witness, *testis, is,* m. and f.

578. EXERCISE.

1. Death encountered for one's country is wont to appear, not only glorious, but also happy.   2. Senators who consult for the interests of a part of the citizens, and neglect a part, introduce sedition and discord into the

state.   3. I was writing to you those things which I supposed to be conducive to your safety.   4. All laws ought
to have reference to the welfare of the state.   5. There
were many in Rome who were prepared to sacrifice for
their country, not only money, but also life.   6. We are
not able to *state* these things without tears.   7. Who is
there, indeed, who would dare to call himself a *philosopher* without giving some precepts in regard to duty.   8.
The witness says that he does not think this, but knows
it; that he has not heard it, but seen it.   9. I think that
you have heard what opinion I expressed *on the other
points*.   10. The Athenians thought that whatever was
not honorable was not even useful.   11. That which is
base is never useful, not even when you attain that which
you suppose to be useful.   12. He has thus far allowed
no day to pass without consulting for the safety of the
citizens.

Lesson CII.

ADVERBS AND CONJUNCTIONS.

579. The English Adverbs may sometimes be rendered
literally by corresponding Latin Adverbs, and sometimes by
other parts of speech.   Thus adverbs and adverbial expressions may sometimes be rendered, —

1. By Adjectives.   See Model I.

2. By Pronouns.   Thus *also* may sometimes be rendered
by *idem ;* *always* sometimes by *quisque.*   See Model II.;
also G. 451, 3, and 458, 1.

580. *Not very,* before adjectives and adverbs, may be

rendered by *non ita ;* and *not very much*, before verbs, by *non ita valde.* See Models III. and IV.

581. In negative sentences, the negative is commonly joined with the conjunction:

And not, *neque*, or *et non ;* for not, *neque enim*, or *non enim ;* yet not, *neque tamen*, or *non tamen.* See Model V.

582. In a clause expressing purpose, *that*, with a negative adjective, pronoun, or adverb, should be rendered by *ne* with the corresponding affirmative adjective, pronoun, or adverb:

That no one, nobody, *nequis*, not *ut nemo ;* that no, *ne ullus*, not *ut nullus ;* that nothing, *nequid*, not *ut nihil ;* that never, *ne unquam*, not *ut nunquam.* See Model VI.

583. MODELS.

I. *At that time* Cicero was *constantly* at Rome.

I. *Eo tempŏre Cicĕro Romae fuit assiduus.*

II. There is nothing wrong which is not also disgraceful.

II. *Est nihil pravum, quod idem non turpe.*

III. These statues are very beautiful, but not very ancient.

III. *Haec signa sunt pulcherrĭma, sed non ita antīqua.*

IV. We are not very much moved by these things.

IV. *His rebus non ita valde movēmur.*

V. I came to Athens, said Democritus, and no one recognized me.

V. *Veni Athēnas, inquit Democrĭtus, neque me quisquam agnōvit.*

VI. Who does not know, that it is the first law of history, that nothing false should be said ?

VI. *Quis nescit, primam esse historiae legem, nequid falsi dicātur ?*

584. REMARKS.

1. MODEL I. — WAS CONSTANTLY, *fuit assiduus*, lit. *was constant.*

2. MODEL II. — WHICH IS ALSO, *quod idem*, lit. *which the same.* *Est* is omitted because it can be so readily supplied.

3. MODEL III. — NOT VERY ANCIENT, *non ita antiqua*, lit. *not so ancient.*

585. SYNONYMES.

To teach, to instruct, to cultivate, to educate; *doceo, erudio, praecipio, instituo.*

1. *Doceo, ēre, ui, tum;* TO TEACH, — with the simple idea of imparting instruction or knowledge.

2. *Erudio, īre, īvi, ītum;* TO INSTRUCT, TO CULTIVATE, TO REFINE, — with special reference to the *effect* of the instruction in refining the character.

3. *Praecipio, ĕre, cēpi, ceptum;* TO INSTRUCT, TO FURNISH WITH PRECEPTS, — with special reference to the maxims and precepts imparted for the guidance of the pupil.

4. *Instituo, ĕre, ui, ūtum;* TO INSTRUCT, TO TRAIN UP, TO EDUCATE, — more comprehensive than either of the above terms.

586. VOCABULARY.

Branch of learning, *doctrīna, ae,* f.

But not, and not, *neque,* conj.

By no means, *minĭme,* adv.; lit. *least.*

Desirous, *studiōsus, a, um.* See 222.

Devote one's self to, apply one's self to, *se conferre ad* with acc.; *confĕro, ferre, tŭli, collātum.*

Do, perform, *gero, ĕre, gessi, gestum.*

Dream, *somnium, ii,* n.

Fear, *vereor, ēri, ĭtus sum,* dep.

Give precepts, *praecĭpio, ĕre, cēpi, ceptum.*

Gravity, *gravĭtas, ātis,* f.

Hostile, unfriendly, *inimĭcus, a, um.*

Lysis, *Lysis, ĭdis,* m.

Much, exceedingly, *valde,* adv.

No one, that no one, in clauses denoting purpose, *ne quis.* G. 190, 2.

Not very, *non ita,* adv.

Perhaps, sometimes rendered by *haud scio an;* lit. *I know not whether.*

Perishable, *cadūcus, a, um.*

Pythagorean, *Pythagorēus, a, um.*

Teach, *doceo, ēre, ui, doctum;* train up, *instituo, ēre, ui, ūtum.*

Troublesome, *molestus, a, um.*

Unwillingly, unwilling, *invĭtus, a, um.* G. 443.

Well known, sometimes rendered by *ille, a, ud.* G. 450, 4.

Wholly, whole, *totus, a, um.* G. 149; 443.

587. EXERCISE.

1. There were some who devoted themselves wholly to learned studies. 2. You will perceive from these letters, both what I have done and what I have said. 3. Those things which seem to be useful, but are not so, are hostile to virtue. 4. Wealth, power, honors, and pleasures, are perishable and uncertain. 5. The consuls devoted themselves wholly to the safety of the republic. 6. There were many who admired the gravity, justice, and wisdom of Caesar. 7. We did this most unwillingly. 8. These things are not, indeed, very troublesome to me. 9. Men are not very much moved by *dreams.* 10. The well-known Pythagorean Lysis taught the Theban Epaminondas, perhaps, without exception, the greatest hero of all Greece. 11. To give precepts *on the subject of eloquence* is by no means easy. 12. Let us teach those who are desirous of learning. 13. Plato instructed Dion of Syracuse in all branches of learning. 14. We all fear that no one may approve your plan.

CHAPTER II.

ARRANGEMENT OF WORDS AND CLAUSES.

LESSON CIII.

ARRANGEMENT OF WORDS.

588. General Rules for the Arrangement of Words. See G. 593–597.

  1. Effect of Emphasis and Euphony. G. 594.
  2. Contrasted Groups. G. 595.
  3. Kindred Words. G. 596.
  4. Words with a Common Relation. G. 597.

589. Special Rules for the Arrangement of Words. See G. 598–602.

  1. Modifiers of Nouns. G. 598.
  2. Modifiers of Adjectives. G. 599.
  3. Modifiers of Verbs. G. 600.
  4. Modifiers of Adverbs. G. 601.
  5. Position of Special Words. G. 602.

590. MODELS.

I. We were occupied at that time day and night in the study of all the branches of knowledge.

I. *Nos eo tempŏre noctes et dies in omnium doctrinārum meditatiōne versabāmur.*

II. We have heard that *Plato* traversed the most *distant* lands.	II. *Ultĭmas terras lustrasse Platōnem accepĭmus.*
III. New names must be assigned to new things.	III. *Rebus novis nova sunt ponenda nomĭna.*
IV. We admire the justice and wisdom of *Caesar*.	IV. *Caesăris justitiam et sapientiam admirāmur.*

591. Remarks.

1. Model II. — We have heard, *accepĭmus*, lit. *we have received,* i. e. *we have received* or *learned by report.*

2. Model III. — Must be assigned, *ponenda sunt,* lit. *must be placed.* For the order of words, see G. 595, observing that *nomĭna,* which might stand directly before *sunt,* is made still more emphatic by its present position.

592. Synonymes.

To see, perceive, behold, visit; *video, cerno, specto, viso.*

1. *Video, ēre, vidi, visum;* TO SEE, — the usual word in this sense.

2. *Cerno, ĕre;*[1] TO PERCEIVE, TO SEE CLEARLY, TO DISCERN, — involving the idea of discriminating, as well as that of seeing.

3. *Specto, āre, āvi, ātum;* TO BEHOLD, TO LOOK UPON, — with attention or interest.

4. *Viso, ĕre, visi, visum;* TO DESIRE TO SEE, TO GO TO SEE, TO VISIT.

---

[1] In the best prose, the Perfect and Supine do not occur in this sense.

593. Vocabulary.

Affluent, copious, *uber, ĕris.*

Aged, old, *senex, senis.*

Beauty, *pulchritūdo, ĭnis,* f.

Deserve, often expressed by the Pass. Periphrastic Conj. See G. 231.

Ear, *auris, is,* f.

Eye, *ocŭlus, i,* m.

For a long time, *jamprĭdem,* adv. G. 467, 2.

Game, *ludus, i,* m.

Invention, *inventum, i,* n.

Lost, engaged, busy, *impedītus, a, um.*

Necessity, *necessĭtas, ātis,* f.

Open, *apertus, a, um.*

Perceive, discern, *cerno, ĕre.*

Pursuit, study, *studium, ii,* n.

Remove, take away, *tollo, ĕre, sustŭli, sublātum.*

Thought, *cogitatio, ōnis,* f.

Thus, *sic,* adv.

Tyranny, *tyrannis, ĭdis,* f.

Unimpaired, *intĕger, gra, grum.*

Witness, *specto, āre, āvi, ātum.*

594. Exercise.

1. Young men are led by the precepts of the *aged* to the pursuits of *virtue.* 2. Who would not admire the *beauty of virtue ?* 3. We have been taught by our forefathers to arrange all our plans and actions with reference to virtue. 4. Who is more affluent in speaking than Plato? 5. There were some who said that Jupiter would speak thus, if he should speak Greek. 6. If these things deserve to be seen, you have often seen them. 7. We, who have witnessed these games, have seen nothing new. 8. Often, when lost in thought, with eyes and ears open and unimpaired, we neither see nor hear. 9. Many things, which cannot be seen with the eyes, can yet be perceived with the mind. 10. I have been for a long time desiring

to visit you.   11. We cannot sufficiently praise Brutus and Cassius, whom you defend.   12. We see that tyranny remained, though the tyrant was removed.   13. Those things which moved me would also have moved *you*.   14. The inventions of *necessity* are more ancient than those of *pleasure*.

Lesson CIV.

EUPHONY AND RHYTHM.

595. In arranging a Latin sentence, attention must be paid to Euphony and Rhythm. But here the best results can be secured only by the aid of a cultivated ear. A few practical directions, however, may aid the learner in avoiding obvious errors.

I. Avoid the monotonous effect produced by a series of words of the same length, especially of monosyllables; as, *et fons et pons.*

II. Avoid the frequent repetition of the same letters in corresponding parts of successive words, especially in the endings; as, *Graeciam quondam magnam vocātam.*

III. Avoid the genitive plural of future active participles, on account of the harshness of its sound; as, *moniturōrum, recturārum.* But the genitive plural of *futūrus* is sometimes necessary.

IV. Avoid placing a word which ends in two or more consonants before one which begins with two or more consonants; as, *ingens stridor.*

V. Aim at variety in the length, sound, and ending of successive words, and in the ending of successive clauses. See Models I. and II.

VI. Special attention should be given to the end of the sentence. A word of two or more syllables with a round and full sound should be selected for this place when the sense permits. A monosyllable should not be so used, unless it be the copula *sum, es, est,* etc., or some other word which blends readily, in sound and in sense, with what precedes. See Models I. and II.

596. MODELS.

I. Publius Africanus, having destroyed Carthage, adorned the cities of the Sicilians with the most beautiful statues and monuments.

II. I demand from you *no* reward of virtue, *no* badge of honor.

I. *Publius Africānus, Carthagĭne delēta, Siculōrum urbes signis monumentisque pulcherrĭmis exornāvit.*

II. *Nullum ego a vobis praemium · virtūtis, nullum insigne honōris postŭlo.*

597. SYNONYMES.

To surpass, conquer, overcome; *supĕro, vinco, devinco.*

1. *Supĕro, āre, āvi, ātum;* TO SURPASS, TO OVERCOME, TO SURMOUNT.

2. *Vinco, ĕre, vici, victum;* TO CONQUER, — the usual word in this sense.

3. *Devĭnco, ĕre, vīci, victum;* TO CONQUER COMPLETELY, TO OVERCOME, TO SUBDUE, — stronger than *vinco.*

598. Vocabulary.

By = from, in accordance with, e, ex, prep. with abl.

Clear, *clarus, a, um.*

Communicate, relate, *trado, ĕre, dĭdi, dĭtum.*

Conquer completely, *devinco, ĕre, vĭci, victum.*

Contend, *contendo, ĕre, i, tentum.*

Dionysius, *Dionysius, ii,* m.

Duillius, *Duillius, ii,* m.

Fitting, it is fitting, *oportet, uit,* impers.

How, *quam,* adv.

Invite, *invīto, āre, āvi, ātum.*

Mention, say, *dico, ĕre, dixi, dictum.*

Opulent, *opulentus, a, um.*

Preserve, *conservo, āre, āvi, ātum.*

Prosperous, happy, *beātus, a, um.*

Reason, *ratio, ōnis,* f.

Short, brief, *brevis, e.*

Some, any, *alĭqui, qua, quod.*

    Some time, at some time, *alĭquo tempŏre.*

Thirty-eight, *duodequadraginta.*

Young man, youth, *juvĕnis, is,* m.

599. Exercise.

1. Reason invites young men to justice, equity, and fidelity. 2. How many things do we do *for the sake of our friends*, which we would never do for the sake of our foes! 3. Dionysius was *for thirty-eight years* the tyrant of a most opulent and prosperous state. 4. I did not suppose even those things which I have mentioned above, to be new to you. 5. It is fitting that he who obeys should hope that he will some time rule, and that he who rules should consider that he must in a short time obey. 6. Those things which you have said are clearer than the sun itself. 7. Epaminondas, the commander of the Thebans, did not deliver the army to him who by law had succeeded him as praetor, but, having himself retained it a few days contrary to law, he conquered the Lacedaemonians. 8. Even if many should contend with you in *valor*, you would yet easily surpass them all. 9. Caius Duillius

completely conquered the Carthaginians in a very great battle. 10. Cicero, whose orations we read when boys, preserved the republic. 11. It is not easy to find one who does not communicate to another what he himself knows.

Lesson CV.

ARRANGEMENT OF CLAUSES.

600. Rules for the Arrangement of Clauses. See G. 603–606.

601. A verb which has an Infinitive Clause as its object, may either precede or follow such clause, or may be inserted within it; and, in the latter case, it usually stands directly after the Subject Accusative, or directly before it. See Model II.

602. A subject or object which is common to both the principal and the subordinate clauses, generally stands at the beginning of the sentence, and is followed by the subordinate clause. See Model III.

603. Models.

I. Let us defend that which we think; for our judgments *are free.*

I. *Defendāmus quod sentīmus; sunt enim judicia libĕra.*

II. Thales said that water was the first principle of all things.

II. *Thales aqŭam dixit esse initium omnium rerum.*

III. Cato, though born at Tusculum, was admitted to the rights of Roman citizenship.

III. *Cato, quum esset Tuscŭli natus, in popŭli Romāni civitātem susceptus est.*

604. REMARKS.

1. MODEL II. — *Dixit* might have been placed before *aquam*, or even at the end of the sentence.

2. MODEL III. — TO THE RIGHTS OF ROMAN CITIZENSHIP, *in popŭli Romāni civitātem*, lit. *into the citizenship of the Roman people.*

605. SYNONYMES.

To feign, invent, pretend, disguise ; *fingo, simŭlo, dissimŭlo.*

1. *Fingo, ĕre, finxi, fictum ;* TO FEIGN, TO INVENT, TO DE-VISE, — with the leading idea of forming or devising something, whether true or false.

2. *Simŭlo, āre, āvi, ātum ;* TO PRETEND, TO FEIGN, — to represent as true that which is known to be false.

3. *Dissimŭlo, āre, āvi, ātum ;* TO DISGUISE, TO CONCEAL.

606. VOCABULARY.

Accomplish, attaĭn, *assĕquor, i, secŭtus sum,* dep.

Accusation, *crimen, ĭnis,* n.

After, *post,* prep. with acc.

Alexander, *Alexander, dri,* m.

Bear, suffer, *patior, i, passus sum,* dep.

Censure, *reprehendo, ĕre, di, sum.*

Disguise, *dissimŭlo, āre, āvi, ātum.*

Displease, *displĭceo, ĕre, ui, ĭtum.*

For the purpose, *causa* with gen. G. 414, 2, 3).

Frequently, *crebro,* adv.

How long? *quousque ?* adv.

Indeed, then, *tandem,* adv.; lit. *at length.*

Invent, devise, *fingo, ĕre, finxi, fictum.*

Macedon, of Macedon, a Macedonian, *Macĕdo, ŏnis,* m.

Mad, be mad, *furo, ĕre, ui.*

Multitudes assemble, *concursus fit ;* lit. *a concourse is made.*

Olive tree, *olea, ae,* f.

Pretend, *simŭlo, āre, āvi, ātum.*

Produce, bear, *fero, ferre, tuli, latum.*

Render service, *prosum, prodesse,*

profui. G. 290; 385. To render a greater service, *plus prodesse.*

Some time, at some time, *aliquando,* adv.

State, commonwealth, *res publica, rei publicae,* f.

Teach, *doceo, ĕre, docui, doctum ;*

instruct, *erŭdio, ĭre, ĭvi* or *ĭi, ĭtum.*

That, expressing purpose, when the dependent clause contains a comparative, *quo,* conj.

Without, be without, *careo, ĕre, ui, ĭtum.* G. 425.

Work, memorial, monument, *monumentum, i,* n.

607. EXERCISE.

1. When Demosthenes was expected to speak, multitudes assembled from the whole of Greece for the purpose of hearing him. 2. Men do not wonder at what they frequently see, even if they do not know why it happens. 3. When I was praised by Cato, I could easily bear even to be censured by the others. 4. Philosophers have taught many to be better citizens and more useful to their states, as Lysis taught Epaminondas of Thebes; Plato, Dion of Syracuse; Aristotle, Alexander of Macedon. 5. And not only while alive do they instruct and teach those who are desirous of learning, but they also accomplish this same thing by their literary works even after death. 6. How long, indeed, shall he who has surpassed all enemies in crime be without the name of an enemy? 7. I shall not be able to disguise the fact that those things which have been done thus far displease me. 8. Solon pretended to be mad, both that his life might be more secure, and that he might render a greater service to the republic. 9. They have invented many accusations against the consul. 10. The Athenians were wont to say that every land which produced the olive tree was theirs.

CHAPTER III.

STRUCTURE OF LATIN SENTENCES.

LESSON CVI.

COMPACTNESS OF STRUCTURE.

608. The Latin in the form and structure of sentences differs widely from the English. Accordingly, in translating from the vernacular into that language, it is often necessary to reconstruct the sentence to adapt it to the Latin idiom.

609. But the true type of the Latin sentence, with its compactness, symmetry, and beauty, cannot be learned from rules. It can be acquired only by a careful study of the best models. On this point, therefore, the learner must turn for instruction and guidance to the pages of Caesar and Cicero, those great masters of Latin style. It is only necessary, therefore, in this chapter, to call his attention to the leading characteristics of the Latin sentence, and to guard him against certain errors into which he is liable to fall.

610. Compactness of structure is a prominent characteristic of the Latin idiom. Accordingly an English sentence which is to be translated into Latin, if not already concisely expressed, must first be thrown into a compact form, preparatory to a literal rendering. Thus, —

I. English sentences beginning with the impersonal forms, *it is said that he, they,* etc., *it is reported that,* etc., *it is thought that, it seems that, the order is given that,* and the like, may be more compactly expressed in the personal form, and must, accordingly, be so changed to adapt them to the Latin idiom. The corresponding personal forms are, *he is said, he is reported, he is thought, he seems, he is ordered.* See Model I.

II. English sentences beginning with *it is, it was,* before a predicate noun and a relative clause, must be so reconstructed that the thought contained in the two clauses, the antecedent and the relative, may be expressed in one. Thus: *It was he who did it,* becomes, *He did it.* See Model II.

III. In English, with verbs of *thinking, saying, knowing,* and the like, the subject of discourse is sometimes introduced with a preposition, as, *concerning, in regard to, in respect to, of,* and then repeated in the form of a pronoun in a clause with *that ;* as, *In regard to Socrates, we know that he was wise.* This construction, though admissible in Latin when the subject of discourse is especially emphatic, should in general be avoided. The above sentence when adapted to the Latin idiom becomes, *We know that Socrates was wise.* See Model III.

611. Models.

I. It is said that Epaminondas played upon the lyre excellently.

II. It was Pisistratus who first arranged the books of Homer as we now have them.

III. It is related of Romulus that he most successfully waged many wars with his neighbors.

I. *Epaminondas fidǐbus praeclāre cecinisse dicǐtur.*

II. *Pisistrătus primus Homēri libros sic disposuit ut nunc habēmus.*

III. *Romǔlus bella cum finitǐmis multa felicissǐme gessisse tradǐtur.*

612. REMARKS.

1. MODEL I. — IT IS SAID THAT EPAMINONDAS, Latin idiom, *Epaminondas is said.*

2. MODEL II. — IT WAS PISISTRATUS WHO FIRST, Latin idiom, *Pisistratus first.*

3. MODEL III. — IT IS RELATED OF ROMULUS THAT, Latin idiom, *Romulus is related.*

613. VOCABULARY.

Achievements are accomplished, *res geruntur.*

Admitted, it is admitted, *constat, constitit.*

Apollo, *Apollo, inis,* m.

As = that which, a thing which, *id quod.* G. 445, 7.

Authority, *auctoritas, atis,* f.

Banish, expel, *expello, ere, puli, pulsum.*

Bear, support, *sustineo, ere, ui, tentum.*

Become acquainted with, *cognosco, ere, novi, nitum.*

Bring to, *adduco, ere, duxi, ductum, ad* with acc.

Confirm, *confirmo, are, avi, atum.*

Cypselus, *Cypselus, i,* m.

Delphic, *Delphicus, a, um.*

Demaratus, *Demaratus, i,* m.

Endure, *fero, ferre, tuli, latum.*

Etruria, *Etruria, ae,* f.

Flourishing, *florens, entis.*

Live, alive, living, *vivus, a, um.*

Milo, *Milo* and *Milon, onis,* m.

Money, sum of money, *pecunia, ae,* f.

Open, *aperio, ire, ui, pertum.*

Ox, *bos, bovis,* m. G. 90, 2.

Relate, *trado, ere, didi, ditum.*

Say, " they say," subject indefinite, *ferunt.* It is said, *fertur,* etc.

Shoulder, *humerus, i,* m.

Stadium, *stadium, ii,* n.

Syracuse, *Syracusae, arum,* f. pl.

Tarquinii, *Tarquinii, orum,* m. pl.

Through, *per,* prep. with acc.

Unable, to be unable = not to be able, *non possum, posse, potui.*

Walk, go along, *ingredior, i, gressus sum,* dep.

Withdraw, call off, *avoco, are, avi, atum.*

Without a nomination from the people, *injussu populi.* G. 414, 2, 3).

614. Exercise.

1. It is related of Servius Tullius that he was the first who reigned without a nomination from the people. 2. It is said that Demaratus, the father of king Tarquin, having been unable to endure the tyrant Cypselus, fled with a large sum of money, and betook himself to Tarquinii, a very flourishing city of Etruria. 3. It is not by force, but by wisdom, that great achievements are accomplished. 4. It is not with the eyes, but with the mind, that we perceive those things which we see. 5. It was Lycurgus who confirmed his laws by the authority of the Delphic Apollo. 6. It is said that Milo walked through the stadium at *Olympia*, bearing upon his shoulders a *live ox*. 7. It was Socrates who first brought philosophy to common life. 8. It seems to me, as is admitted among all, that Socrates was the first to withdraw philosophy from occult subjects, and to bring it to common life. 9. They say that Plato came into Italy to become acquainted with the Pythagoreans. 10. It is said that Dionysius the tyrant, having been banished from Syracuse, *opened a school* at Corinth.

Lesson CVII.

UNITY OF THE LATIN SENTENCE.

615. Unity, though important in the English sentence, is still more so in the Latin. All the various parts of the sentence should be nicely adapted to each other, and made to unite harmoniously in one complete organic whole. Thus, —

I. When a Latin sentence consists of two or more clauses, it is usually so constructed, if possible, that these clauses have the same subject.　See Model I.

II. When the subjects of successive clauses are not the same, they should, if possible, be of the same form.　Thus they may all be nouns, or all infinitives, or all indirect questions.　See Model II.

III. The objects of successive clauses should also, when practicable, be of the same form.　See Model III.

· IV. The predicates of successive clauses should also, when practicable, be of the same form.　Thus they may all be verbs, or all predicate nouns with the copula *sum*, or all predicate adjectives with the copula.　See Model IV.

V. The same general law also applies, though not with the same force, to the other elements of the sentence.　See Model I.

616. MODELS.

I. We see that the blessings which we enjoy and the air which we breathe are given us by God.

I. *Commŏda quibus fruĭmur spiritumque quem ducĭmus a Deo nobis dari vidēmus.*

II. If hope is the expectation of good, fear is the expectation of evil.

II. *Si spes est exspectatio boni, metus est exspectatio mali.*

III. I shall consider, not only what it becomes you to hear, but also what it becomes me to say.

III. *Non solum, quid te audīre, verum etiam quid me deceat dicĕre, considerābo.*

IV. *Can* that which is useless to the republic be useful to any citizen?

IV. *Num potest, quod inutĭle rei publĭcae sit, id cuiquam civi esse utĭle?*

617. Remarks.

1. MODEL I. — Air = breath, *spirĭtum*.

2. MODEL IV. — Observe the position of *id* after the Relative clause. See G. 604, II.

618. Synonymes.

To wish, desire ; *volo, opto, cupio.*

1. *Volo, velle, volui ;* TO WISH, — used of the calm exercise of the will, but involving the purpose to realize the wish.

2. *Opto, āre, āvi, ātum ;* TO WISH, TO DESIRE, — used of the simple exercise of the will, without involving the purpose to act.

3. *Cupio, ĕre, īvi, ītum ;* TO DESIRE, TO DESIRE EAGERLY, — used especially of passionate and eager desire.

619. Vocabulary.

Adversity, *res adversae*, f. pl.   G. 441, 4.

Apply one's self to, *se applicāre ad* with acc.; *applĭco, āre, āvi* and *ui, ātum* and *ĭtum.*

Arouse, *erĭgo, ĕre, rexi, rectum.*

Attentive, *attentus, a, um.*

Blessing, good, *bonum, i, n.*

Day before, *pridie*, adv.

Fortunate, *fortunātus, a, um.*

From that place, thence, *inde*, adv.

Future, yet to come, *futūrus, a, um.*

Greatest (in rank), highest, *summus, a, um.*   G. 163, 3.

Hearer, *audĭtor, ōris*, m.

July, of July, *Quintĭlis, e.*

Look forward to, *exspecto, āre, āvi, ātum.*

Nones, usually the *fifth* day of the month, but the *seventh* in March, May, July, and Oct., *nonae, ārum*, f. pl.   G. 708, I. 2.

Overthrow, *everto, ĕre, verti, versum.*

Past, *praeterĭtus, a, um.*

Pertain to, *pertĭneo, ĕre, ui, ad* with acc.

Pleased, be pleased, rejoice, *laetor, ări, ātus sum*, dep.

Present, *praesens, entis.*

Promise, *polliceor, ēri, ĭtus sum,* dep.

Prosperity, *res secundae*, f. pl. G. 441, 4.

Recall to mind, *recordor, ări, ātus sum*, dep.

Regard as, believe, *statuo, ĕre, ui, ūtum.*

Show, *demonstro, āre, āvi, ātum.*

Sixth of July, *pridie Nonas Quintiles,* lit. *the day before the Nones of July.* G. 708, I.— III.; 437, 1.

So, in such a manner, *sic*, adv.

Temperate, *tempĕrans, antis.*

Unusual, *inusitātus, a, um.*

620. Exercise.

1. As we are aroused by those blessings which we expect, so we are pleased by those which we recall to mind. 2. Some apply themselves to philosophy, some to the civil law, and others to eloquence. 3. The wise remember the blessings which are past, enjoy those which are present, and look forward to those which are future. 4. It seemed to me that Caius Marius was one of the most fortunate of men in prosperity, and one of the greatest of heroes in adversity. 5. After the overthrow of the republic, Cicero wrote more in a short time than in many years while the republic was standing. 6. Cicero, having been in Athens just ten days, set out from that place on the 6th of July. 7. You cannot be *brave* while judging pain the greatest evil, or *temperate* while regarding pleasure as the highest good. 8. They desire to know what can be done. 9. We wish to be both wise and happy. 10. We shall have *attentive* hearers, if we promise to speak of great, new, and unusual subjects. 11. We shall make them attentive, if we show that those things, which we are about to state, pertain to the highest public welfare.

Lesson CVIII.

PERSPICUITY.

621. Perspicuity is another most important quality of Latin style. The best Latin writers express their thoughts with great fulness, clearness, and exactness. In the choice of words, they prefer the specific to the general, the concrete to the abstract. Thus, —

I. Instead of pronouns or other general words, more specific terms, referring not so much to the entire person as to some particular part of his nature, are often used. Thus *animus* may be so used when the action relates especially to the mind; *corpus* when it relates to the body; *ingenium* when it relates to natural endowments; *tempus* when it relates to time and opportunity; *ocŭlus, auris*, etc., when it relates to the senses. See Models I. and II.

II. When a single word is insufficient to express the idea with the requisite fulness and clearness, two or more words are often employed. See Model II.

III. The Latin has certain favorite circumlocutions. Thus, —

1. *Facio ut*, with the Subjunctive, is often used to represent the action as *intentional;* though, in English, one verb would be sufficient, and that, too, generally in the Indicative. See Model III.; also G. 489, 1.

2. *Accĭdit ut, contingit ut*, or *evĕnit ut*, with the Subjunctive, is often used to represent the action as *accidental.* See Model IV.

3. *Fĭĕri potest ut*, with the Subjunctive, is often used to represent the action as *possible.* See Model IV., under 566.

4. Here may be mentioned also the free use of *res, genus,*

modus, and a few other words : *res secundae*, prosperity, *res adversae*, adversity ; *res gestae*, exploits, achievements, deeds ; *res publĭca*, republic ; *in hoc genĕre*, in this respect ; *quo in genĕre*, in which respect ; *in omni genĕre*, in every respect ; *omni genĕre virtūtis*, in every kind of virtue ; *omni modo*, in every way ; *mirum in modum*, wonderfully. See Model V.

622. Models.

I. I devoted all my time to the exigencies of my friends.

II. The eyes of *many* will observe and watch you.

III. I thought that I ought briefly to reply to your communication.

IV. It was Cicero's good fortune to be very dear to the senate.

V. It is difficult to bear adversity with equanimity.

I. *Omne meum tempus amicōrum temporĭbus transmīsi.*

II. *Multōrum te ocŭli speculabuntur atque custodient.*

III. *Faciendum mihi putāvi ut tuis littĕris brevĭter respondērem.*

IV. *Cicerōni contĭgit ut esset senatui carissĭmus.*

V. *Adversas res aequo anĭmo ferre diffĭcĭle est.*

623. Remarks.

1. Model III. — I ought to reply, *faciendum mihi, ut respondērem*, lit. *it was to be done by me that I should reply*.

2. Model IV. — To be, *ut esset*, lit. *that he should be (was)*.

624. Synonymes.

To happen, to come to pass, to result; *accĭdo, contingo, evenio.*

1. *Accĭdo, ĕre, accĭdi;* TO HAPPEN, — the most common word for this general meaning, used of unexpected occurrences, whether favorable or unfavorable, but especially of those which are unfavorable.

2. *Contingo, ĕre, contĭgi, contactum ;* TO HAPPEN, TO BE ONE'S GOOD FORTUNE, — used chiefly of fortunate occurrences.

3. *Evenio, īre, evēni, eventum ;* TO HAPPEN, TO RESULT, TO TURN OUT, — used chiefly of events which are regarded as the results of antecedent causes.

625. Vocabulary.

Aid, *adjumentum, i,* n.; often in pl.

Bring, *affĕro, ferre, attŭli, allā-tum.*

By letter, *per littĕras.*

Communicate, converse, *collŏquor, i, locūtus sum,* dep.

Contrary to, *praeter,* prep. with acc.

Design, *consilium, ii,* n.

Distrusting, *diffĭsus, a, um,* part. from *diffĭdo.* G. 385.

Empire, *imperium, ii,* n.

Event, issue, *eventus, us,* m.; thing, *res, rei,* f.

Expectation, opinion, *opinio, ōnis,* f.

For, after *parātus, ad,* prep. with acc. For = during, *per,* prep. with acc.

Happen, of desirable occurrences (be one's good fortune), *contingo, ĕre, tĭgi, tactum ;* of undesirable occurrences, *accĭdo, ĕre, i.*

Harmony, *concordia, ae,* f.

Lasting, *sempiternus, a, um.*

Military science, *res militāris,* f.

More, of more value, *pluris.* G. 402, III. 1.

Native talent, *ingenium, ii,* n.

12

Now, *nunc*, adv.

Offend, *offendo, ĕre, i, sum.*   G. 385, 1.

Possess, *possĭdeo, ĕre, sēdi, sessum.*

Possessed of, *praedĭtus, a, um.* G. 419, III.

Profitable, *fructuōsus, a, um.*

Quiet, *otium, ii,* n.

Rather, more, *magis,* adv.

Result, be the result, *evĕnio, ĭre, vēni, ventum.*

Since, because, *quoniam,* conj.

So many, *tot,* indecl.

Then, *tum,* adv.

This = that, *is, ea, id.*

Treasures, possessions, things, *res, rerum,* f. pl.

Wealthy, *dives, ĭtis.*

Willingly, *libenter,* adv.

Would that, I would that, *utĭnam,* adv. G. 488, 1.

626. Exercise.

1. I shall willingly communicate with you by letter as often as possible.   2. Since it was not my good fortune to be with you, I would that I had been informed of your design.   3. It may be that the consul will offend the senate.   4. I will admit, Cato, that, distrusting myself (my native talents), I sought the aid of learning.   5. May this event bring to you and to all the citizens, peace, tranquillity, quiet, and harmony.   6. Those who are possessed of *virtue* are alone wealthy; for they alone possess treasures both profitable and lasting, and alone are content with their possessions.   7. A leader skilled in military science is often of more value in battle than all the other soldiers.   8. Nothing could have happened so contrary to my expectation.   9. I, who then feared that the things which have happened would be the result, now fear nothing, and am prepared for every event.   10. Who of the Carthaginians surpassed in counsel, valor, and achievements, that very Hannibal who, for so many years, con-

tended with the Romans for empire and glory? 11. I ought to expect letters from you, rather than you from me; for there is nothing doing at Rome which I think you *would care to know.*

Lesson CIX.

LOGICAL QUALITIES OF THE SENTENCE.

627. The logical relations which subsist between the different parts of the Latin sentence should be expressed with great exactness and care. Thus,—

I. If the actions are coördinate, they must be expressed in coördinate clauses or sentences. See Model I.

II. If one action is subordinate to the other, its clause must also be made subordinate. See Model II.

III. The relations of actions to each other in point of time must be indicated with great exactness by the Latin tenses. See Model III.

IV. Correlative clauses, indirect questions, and clauses with conjunctions, are favorite constructions in the Latin. See Model III., under 616.

628. Models.

I. A *brief* life has been given us by God; but the recollection of a well-spent life is eternal.

II. Even if I had anything to say, I should yet

I. *Brevis a Deo nobis vita data est; at memoria bene redditae vitae sempiterna.*

II. *Etiamsi habērem aliquid, quod dicĕ-*

| wish to hear you, be-
cause I have myself
spoken so much. | *rem, tamen te au-
dīre vellem, quod
ipse tam multa dix-
issem.* |
| III.　You will assign to these
volumes as much time
as you wish. | III.　*Tribues his voluminī-
bus tempŏris quan-
tum voles.* |

629. REMARKS.

1. MODEL I. — Is ETERNAL, *sempiterna*. *Est* is omitted. See G. 367, 3.

2. MODEL II. — *Dixissem.* The pluperfect is here used to denote an action completed at the time of *vellem.*

3. MODEL III. — AS YOU WISH, *quantum voles*, lit. *as you will wish.* The action is really future.

630. SYNONYMES.

To shun, to flee, to escape; *vito, fugio, effugio.*

1. *Vito, āre, āvi, ātum ;* TO SHUN, TO AVOID.

2. *Fugio, ĕre, fugi, fugĭtum ;* TO FLEE, — to attempt to escape by flight.

3. *Effugio, ĕre, effūgi ;* TO FLEE FROM, TO ESCAPE.

331. VOCABULARY.

Academy, *Academĭa, ae,* f.

Beginning, *initium, ii,* n.

Busy, be busy, *occupatĭōne disti-
nēri ;* lit. *be distracted by busi-
ness* or *occupation.* How very busy one is, *quanta occupati-
ōne, etc.*

Celestial, *coelestis, e.* Celestial bodies, *coelestia, ium,* n. pl.

Clear, *perspicuus, a, um.*

Commit one's self, *se tradĕre ; tra-
do, ĕre, dĭdi, dĭtum.*

Contemplate, *contemplor, ari, ātus sum,* dep.

Dictate, *dicto, are, avi, atum.*

Distract, *distineo, ere, ui, tentum.*

Entirely, *totus, a, um.* G. 149; 443.

Escape, *effugio, ere, fugi.*

Especially, *praesertim,* adv.

Flee, escape, *profugio, ere, fugi.*

Flight, *fuga, ae,* f.

For, *nam,* conj.

Heavens, *coelum, i,* n.

Impel, incite, *concito, are, avi, atum.*

Infer, *colligo, ere, legi, lectum.*

Leisure, unoccupied, *vacuus, a, um.*

Look upon, *suspicio, ere, spexi, spectum.*

Manifest, *apertus, a, um.*

Occupation, *occupatio, onis,* f.

Only, *modo,* adv.

Owe, *debeo, ere, ui, itum.*

Part, is the part of, often rendered by the gen. 402, I.

Philo, *Philo* or *Philon, onis,* m.

Principal, *princeps, ipis,* m. and f.

Readily, easily, *facile,* adv.

Recover, restore, *recreo, are, avi, atum.*

So — as, with adjectives and adverbs, *tam — quam,* adv.

Such, *talis, e.*

These lines, these things, *haec,* n. pl.

Thought, *sententia, ae,* f.

Voice, a feeble voice, *vocula, ae,* f.

Walk, *ambulo, are, avi, atum.*

632. Exercise.

1. I have *no one* to whom I owe more than to you. 2. You have forgotten what I said in the beginning, that I could say more readily, especially in regard to such subjects, what I do not think, than what I think. 3. What can be so manifest and so clear, when we have looked upon the heavens, and have contemplated the celestial bodies, as that there is a God by whom these are governed? 4. This oration of Demosthenes, which I know you have often read, abounds in the most weighty words and thoughts. 5. When the principal of the Academy, Philo, fled from Athens and came to Rome, I committed myself entirely to him, impelled by a certain wonderful zeal for

philosophy. 6. He who fears that which cannot be avoided, can in no way live happily. 7. The Stoics say that it is not the part of a wise man to flee. 8. We do not doubt that the citizens are in flight; only let them escape. 9. I think that you have *never before* read a letter from me, unless written with my own hand: from this you will be able to infer how very busy I am; for, as I had no leisure time, and as it was necessary for me to walk for the purpose of recovering my voice, I dictated these lines while walking.

Lesson CX.

LATIN PERIODS.

633. The favorite type of the Latin sentence is that of the period. The writer groups his thoughts in such a manner, as not only to show their logical connections, but also to give to each group unity and completeness. The thoughts, when thus arranged, are readily embodied in the periodic form; but a flowing and well-rounded period is a work of great skill, and requires the hand of a master. In this lesson, therefore, we must be content to illustrate the general form of the Latin period, without attempting the higher qualities of style. See Models I. and II.

634. Models.

I. If you will carefully consider what power Mithridates had, what he accomplished, and what a hero he was, you will

I. *Si diligenter, quid Mithridātes potuĕrit, et quid effecĕrit, et qui vir fuĕrit, considerā-ris, omnĭbus regĭbus*

surely place this king before all the other kings with whom the Roman people waged war.

II. Cyrus in the conversation which he held at the time of his death, when he was very old, said that he had never perceived that his old age had become weaker than his youth had been.

quibuscum popŭlus Romānus bellum gessit, hunc regem nimīrum antepōnes.

II. *Cyrus eo sermōne quem moriens habuit, quum admŏdum senex esset, negat se unquam sensisse senectūtem suam imbecilliōrem factam, quam adolescĕntia fuisset.*

635. REMARKS.

1. MODEL I. — Observe, in studying this model (1), the compact structure of the whole, and (2) the unity of the sentence, especially as illustrated in the indirect questions, *quid — potuĕrit*, etc. IF YOU WILL CONSIDER, Latin idiom, *will have considered.* ALL THE OTHER; here other may be either expressed or omitted in rendering into Latin. In this passage the corresponding Latin word is omitted in Cicero.

2. MODEL II. — AT THE TIME OF HIS DEATH, *moriens*, lit. *dying.* SAID THAT HE NEVER, *negat se unquam*, lit. *denies that he ever.* Negat is in the Historical Present. See G. 467, III.

636. SYNONYMES.

To destroy, tear asunder, overthrow; *deleo, diruo, everto.*

1. *Deleo, ēre, ēvi, ētum ;* TO DESTROY, — the generic word for this meaning.

2. *Diruo, ĕre, dirui, dirŭtum ;* TO DESTROY, TO RUIN, — especially with the accessory idea of tearing asunder.

3. *Everto, ĕre, everti, eversum ;* TO OVERTHROW, TO SUBVERT.

637. VOCABULARY.

Agency, through my, &c., agency, *per me*, etc.; lit. *through me.*

Aid, *adjŭvo, āre, jūvi, jūtum.*

Appoint, *constituo, ĕre, ui, ūtum.*

At times, *interdum*, adv.

Chief, highest, *summus, a, um*, superlat. of *supĕrus.* G. 163, 3.

Commit, do, *facio, ĕre, feci, factum.*

Connect, *conjungo, ĕre, junxi, junctum.*

Connection, no connection, *nihil conjunctum*, n.; lit. *nothing connected.*

Consistent, be consistent with one's self, *sibi consentīre*, with *ipse, a, um*, in agreement with subject; *consentio, īre, sensi, sensum.*

Define, *defīnio, īre, īvi, ītum.*

Deserted, waste, *desertus, a, um.*

Devote one's self to, *se conferre ad* with acc.; *confĕro, ferre, tŭli, collātum.*

Dissension, *dissidium, ii*, n.

Excellence, goodness, *bonĭtas, ātis,* f.

Firmly established, firm, *firmus, a, um.*

For = against, *in*, prep. with acc.

He, she, it = this one, *hic, haec, hoc.*

Hostility, enmity, *odium, ii,* n.

Illustrious, most illustrious, highest, *summus, a, um.*

Kill, *enĕco, āre, enecui, enectum.*

Know, comprehend, *percĭpio, ĕre, cēpi, ceptum.*

Measure, *metior, īri, mensus sum,* dep.

Oppose one's self, *se opponĕre ;* *oppōno, ĕre, posui, posĭtum.*

Overcome, *vinco, ĕre, vici, victum.*

Right, the right, integrity, *honestas, ātis,* f.

Ruin, demolish, *diruo, ĕre, ui, ūtum.*

Several, *complūres, a* or *ia*, pl.

So — as, with verbs, *sic — ut.*

Such, so great, *tantus, a, um.*

Utterly, *fundĭtus*, adv.

638. EXERCISE.

1. Solon, when he was asked why he had appointed no punishment for him who should kill a father, replied that

he had thought that no one would commit so great a crime. 2. Leonidas, the king of the Lacedaemonians, opposed himself to the *enemy* at Thermopylae, when either a disgraceful flight or a glorious death was set before him. 3. He who so defines the chief good, that it has no connection with virtue, and who measures it by his own advantages, and not by the right, would not be able, if he should be consistent with himself, and should not at times be overcome by the excellence of his nature, to cultivate either friendship or justice. 4. There is no doubt that large forces of the enemy were destroyed in many battles. 5. I see that it is admitted among all that several cities, ruined and almost deserted, have, through your agency, been restored. 6. No state is so firmly established that it may not be utterly *overthrown* by hostilities and dissensions. 7. Those most illustrious men, Scipio Africanus, Caius Laelius, and Marcus Cato, would never have devoted themselves to the study of letters, if they were not at all aided by them in the knowledge and practice of virtue.

NOTES.

15. — 1. **Is useful,** *utilis est,* or *est utilis.* In this exercise, the 7
learner will adopt the former order. — 11. **Cicero;** for the position
of the object in Latin, see 13, I. 4. — **Cicero,** the most celebrated
of the Roman orators.

20. — 4. **Hannibal,** a celebrated Carthaginian general. — **Sa-** 9
guntum, a town in Spain. — 16. **Their,** *suum.* Remember that the
Number, as well as the *Gender* and *Case,* of the possessive, is deter-
mined, not by the noun to which it refers, but by that to which it
belongs. Here *suum,* their, refers to *puĕri,* boys, which is in the
plural, while it belongs to *patrem,* father, which is in the singular.

25. — 2. **Consul.** Under the Roman commonwealth, two *con-* 11
suls were annually chosen as joint presidents. — 8. **Socrates,** a
celebrated Athenian philosopher. — 10. **Herodotus,** a Greek historian.

30. — 9. **Catiline,** the notorious conspirator against the Roman 12
government. — 12. **Our pupils;** omit the possessive *our* in rendering into Latin: so also *your,* in the next sentence. See G. 447.

35. — 1. **Numa.** The emphatic subject should be placed at the 14
end of the sentence. See G. 594, II. — **Numa,** the second king of
Rome. — 12. **Athens,** the capital of Attica, in Greece.

40. — 3. **Is an honor to,** Lat. idiom, *is for an honor to.* See 16
G. 390. — 7. **As a present** = *for a present.* — 8. **I have** = *there
are to me.*

44. — 2. **The orator,** *oratŏris.* See G. 42, 4; 363. — 3. **De-** 17
mosthenes, the greatest of Athenian orators.

49. — 1. **Is a characteristic of,** Lat. idiom, *is of.* See G. 402, 19
I. — 8. **Our friends;** omit *our* in rendering. — 13. **Us,** *nostra.*
See G. 408, 1, 2).

54. — 8. **Talent,** *talentum,* a sum of money somewhat more than 21
$1000. It consisted of sixty *minae.* — 10. **Proud of** = *proud be-
cause of.* — 11. **Scipio,** a celebrated Roman general.

23   **59.** — 1. **Cato,** the name of several distinguished Romans. The most celebrated was Marcus Porcius Cato, the Censor. — 6. **Five years older** = *older by five years.*

24   **64.** — 1. **There were,** *fuērunt,* or *erant.* — **There** — omitted in rendering into Latin. The Perf. *fuērunt* simply states the historical fact, that *there were cities;* while the Impf. *erant* gives prominence to the continued existence of these cities. — 2. **Were you?** *fuistine ?* a question for information. See G. 346, II. 1. — **Corinth,** a beautiful city in Greece.

26   **69.** — 6. **Tarquin.** Tarquinius Priscus, the fifth king of Rome, is meant. He came from Tarquinii, a city of Etruria. — **In the reign of Ancus,** Lat. idiom, *Ancus reigning.* See G. 431, 2. Ancus Marcius was the fourth king of Rome. 7. **When Cicero was consul** = *in the consulship of Cicero.* See G. 431, 2.

29   **79.** — 1. **Saguntum.** Place the emphatic subject at the end of the sentence. See G. 594, II. — 3. **How many books have you** = *how many books are there to you ?* — 5. **Was a man of,** Lat. idiom, *was of.* See G. 402, III. — 6. **In your happiness** = *because of,* etc. — 8. **Servius.** Servius Tullius, the sixth king of Rome, is meant. — 14. **Pydna,** a town in Macedonia. — **At Pydna,** *ad Pydnam.*

35   **94.** — 7. **He had received,** *accepisset,* Subj. by Attraction. See G. 527. — 8. **Because they are diligent,** *quod diligentes sunt,* — a positive reason on the authority of the narrator. Hence the Indic. *sunt.* See G. 520, I. But in 9, where the Indirect Discourse is used, *sunt* becomes *sint.* See G. 531.

37   **99.** — 1. **Boys,** *puĕri.* Place the Vocative after the first clause. See G. 602, VI. — **The good.** See G. 441, 1. — 3. **Of the Roman people.** For the position of the Genitive, see G. 598, 3. — 4. **Is the part of,** Lat. idiom, *is of.* See G. 402, I.

39   **104.** — 5. **Inclined to play,** Lat. idiom, *inclined to playing.* — 8. **To ask for** = *to seek,* Supine in *um.* See G. 569.

41   **111.** — 2. **Another,** *alter;* as only two persons are mentioned. See G. 459, 3. — 4. **Xenophon,** a celebrated Greek historian. — 8. **Ennius,** a Roman poet. — 11. **Let us be content.** See G. 487.

42   **116.** — 1. **Saturnia,** an ancient citadel on the Capitoline Hill, the fabled beginning of Rome. — 2. **Ascanius,** the son of Aeneas, and founder of the city of Alba Longa in Italy.

43   **118.** — 2. **What ought?** etc. See G. 229; 525. — 5. **Camillus,** a distinguished Roman general. — 7. **Porsena,** a king of Etruria in Italy.

44   **120.** — 1. **New Carthage,** a town in Spain. — 5. **Cannae,** a

village in Apulia, famous for the victory of Hannibal over the Romans.—6. **Many states of Italy.** See G. 598, 3.—8. **Carthaginians**, the citizens of ancient Carthage in Northern Africa.

122.—1. **Your country,** *patriae tuae,* or *patriae.* See G.   45
447; 385.—2. **To come.** See G. 492, 2.—4. **Mithridates**, a celebrated king of Pontus.—5. **Sulla,** a distinguished Roman general.—7. **Capua,** the chief city of Campania in Italy.—10. **Caesar.** Julius Caesar, a distinguished Roman general and statesman, is meant.—11. **Nile,** a river in Egypt.

127.—1. **Gauls,** the inhabitants of ancient Gaul, embracing   47
modern France.—4. **Lacedaemonians,** the inhabitants of Lacedaemon, or Sparta, a celebrated city in Greece.—5. **Their king Leonidas,** *regem Leonidam.* Place these words after the verb, directly before the Relative.—**To occupy,** *qui occuparet.* See G. 500.—**Thermopylae,** the celebrated pass in Greece where Leonidas fell.

129.—8. **As a present.** See G. 390, II.—10. **Many years.**   48
See G. 378.—11. **Leuctra,** a town in Boeotia.

131.—1. **Pericles,** a celebrated Athenian statesman.—3.   49
Philip, a king of Macedonia.—5. **Chaeronea,** a town in Boeotia.

136.—3. **Their own valor,** *suam virtutem.* A possessive   51
with *own,* if not particularly emphatic, may be rendered by the Latin possessive standing before its noun. The Genitive of *ipse* is added when special emphasis requires it. See G. 452, 4.—6. **Belgians,** a warlike people in the north of Gaul.—7. **Must be accomplished.** See G. 229.—**By us.** See G. 388.

141.—1. **Helvetians,** a people in Gaul.—.**Their.** See G.   53
597, I.—3. **To encounter,** Infinitive, or *ad* with the Gerundive. —6. **Did see;** for Person, see G. 463, 1.—10. **For me to speak,** *ut dicam,* lit. *that I should (may) speak.*

147.—1. **Of the Romans.** Great freedom, it will be remem-   55
bered, is allowed in the arrangement of Latin words. A genitive or an adjective may often precede its noun, even when no emphasis is indicated; especially if perspicuity or euphony can be thus promoted. Indeed, the arrangement may often be left to the option of the writer.—3. **In their language** = *by means of their language.* See G. 414; 414, 4.—4. **Very brave.** See G. 444, 1.—10. **Them.** See 457; also G. 451, 1.

152.—1. **Greatly.** Place *valde* directly before the verb. See   57
G. 600, 3.—4. **To be burned.** See G. 551, II. 1.—5. **Orgetorix,** a Helvetian chieftain.—6. **To wage.** See G. 492, 2.—7. **Would be** = *was about to be.*—10. **His forces,** *copias;* the

possessive is unnecessary. See G. 447. — **Labienus**, a distinguished officer under Caesar in Gaul. — **Arar**, a river in Gaul, the Saône.

59   **158.** — 3. **How large a force**, *quantas copias*. In the sense of — force, forces, *copiae* (plur.), and not *copia*, is generally used. — 10. **Was Orgetorix?** etc. See G. 346, II. 2, 1). — 13. **Orgetorix**. Either like the English or with the addition of the simple predicate — *Orgetorix was the bravest*. See G. 346, II. 3. — 14. **Not**, *ne*, or *noli* with the Infinitive. See G. 538. — 15. **Let us encounter**. See G. 487.

61   **163.** — 1. **Had**. See G. 525; 481, I. 2. — 4. **Lemannus**, the Lake of Geneva in Switzerland. — 5. **The Rhone**, *Rhodănus*, a river in Gaul. — 6. **Their cities** = *the cities of them*. See 468, 2. — 7. **Aeduans**, a powerful tribe in Gaul. — 9. **Of the Romans**. See G. 598, 3.

63   **169.** — 1. **Caria**, a province in Asia Minor. — 4. **Was**, *fuisse*, referring not to the time of *dixisti*, but to the age of Caesar. — 5. **Carthage**, an ancient city in Northern Africa. — **Numantia**, an ancient city in Spain.

65   **174.** — 4. For the order of words, see G. 595. — 5. **That Geneva is**. See G. 551, I. — **Allobroges**, a powerful tribe in ancient Gaul. — 6. **Brutus, Collatinus**, the first consuls in Rome. — 9. In combining these names, connect *Marcus* and *Quintus* by a conjunction, and let the other parts of the names follow in the plural, *Tullii Cicerōnes*. See G. 439, 4.

68   **180.** — 6. **At this place**. See G. 422, 1, 1). — **Rhine**, a celebrated river in Europe. — 10. **That boast**. See G. 371, 1, 3), (2). — 13. **The same as**, *idem quod*. See G. 451, 5.

70   **186.** — 1. **Ariovistus**, a German chieftain in the time of Caesar. — 2. **By his own name**, *suo nomĭne*. *Ipsius* is unnecessary. — 4. **From his own name**, *e suo nomĭne*. — 5. **Whom**. See G. 385. — **Blind**. See G. 594, II. — 9. **Our opinion**, *sententiam*. The possessive should be omitted. — 12. **My opinion**. Here it is better to use the possessive to avoid all ambiguity.

72   **191.** — 6. **His**. The possessive before *commander* and *home* should be omitted in rendering into Latin. — **To be permitted**, *ut liceat*. See G. 492, 2. — 7. **Of what**. See G. 374, 5. — 8. **Of Ariovistus** = *from Ariovistus*.

74   **196.** — 3. **Tiberius Gracchus**, a statesman famous in the political history of Rome. — 4. **Publius Scipio Nasica**, a Roman citizen distinguished for his integrity. — 6. **Spoke Latin**, *Latĭne locūtum esse*. The Latin idiom uses the adverb *Latĭne* where

the English uses the noun Latin. — 9. **To take.** See G. 491. —
The city of Geneva, Lat. idiom, *the city Geneva.* See G. 363.
— 10. **To encounter.** Use the Infinitive in this sentence, but see
note on 141, 3.

202. — 3. **Sent,** *misisse,* referring to the historical fact that Ario-   77
vistus sent, etc. *Mittĕre* would mean *was sending* at the time of the
statement. See G. 541, 1. — 4. **I said so** = *I said it;* but *it* in
such cases should be omitted in rendering into Latin. See 457. — 5.
To the city of, etc. See G. 379, 2. — 6. **To their camp,** etc.,
Lat. idiom, *to Geneva to their camp.* — 9. **When a boy.** See G.
363, 3. — 11. **Your letter** = *your communication,* with no special
reference to its form.

207. — 2. **The good.** See 441, 1. — 3. **Are envied.** See G.   79
301, 3. — 7. **Of Ephesus,** *Ephĕsus,* in apposition with *nomen.* — 9.
By all. See G. 388. — 10. **What business,** Lat. idiom, *what of
business.* See G. 396, III. 2, 3). — 11. **Is a glory,** Lat. idiom, *is
for a glory.* See G. 390.

212. — 8. **For whom** = for whose interests, *cui ?* See G. 385,   81
3. — 11. **Was a detriment.** See G. 390.

218. — 3. **Acceptable,** — because of its value. — 6. **Peculiar**   84
to Athens, *proprium Athenārum.* See G. 391, 2, 4). — 8. **Borders,** *finĭbus.* See G. 384, 386. — 9. **Very near the camp.** See
G. 392, II.

224. — 2. **To make.** See G. 489. — 3. **In military affairs,**   86
rei militāris. See G. 399, 2, 2). — 5. **They had more zeal,**
Lat. idiom, *more of zeal was to them.* — 6. **Very desirous,** *avĭdi;*
the force of *very* being involved in *avĭdus.*

229. — 3. **Of great valor.** See G. 402, III. — 4. **Is character-**   89
istic of, Lat. idiom, *is of.* See G. 402, I. — 7. **Not;** for the position of *non,* see G. 602, IV.

235. — 2. **With . . . forces,** *omnĭbus copiis.* See G. 414, 7.   91
— **As aid,** *auxĭlio.* See G. 390. — 4. **More than five,** etc. See
G. 417, 3. — 6. **Antioch,** *Antiochĭa,* an ancient city of Syria. — 7.
Than that of. See G. 397, 1. — **Themistocles,** a celebrated
Athenian general. — **Solon,** the famous lawgiver of Athens.

241. — 5. **And your.** Repeat *et,* but use the possessive only   94
once. See 469; also G. 587, I. 6. — 6. **There was no need,**
nihil opus fuit. — 7. **Make the best use of** = *use best,* i. e. in
the best manner.

247. — 7. **Must be waged.** See G. 229. — 10. Here the   96
thought requires that prominent places should be given to the Latin
words for *man* and *capable.*

99   **252.** — 1. **Pythagoras,** a celebrated Grecian philosopher. —
Brutus, the deliverer of Rome from the oppression of Tarquin the
Proud. — **In which,** *quo.* See G. 426. — 3. **On the first day
of May,** *calendis Maiis,* lit. *on the May calends.* — 5. In this
sentence, omit *his* in rendering into Latin. — 6. **Two years afterwards.** See G. 418; 427. — 11. **Is a man of such eloquence,**
Lat. idiom, *is of,* or *with, such eloquence.* See G. 428. — **That he
delights.** See G. 494.

102   **258.** — 1. **In the consulship,** etc., Lat. idiom, *Cassius being
consul.* See G. 431. — **Under the yoke,** *sub jugum.* The yoke
was used as the symbol of submission and servitude. — 3. **Having
routed the army,** Lat. idiom, *the army having been routed.* —
Aquitanians, the inhabitants of ancient Aquitania in Gaul. — 4.
To fight = to or for fighting, *ad pugnandum.* — 9. **In the time,**
etc., Lat. idiom, *Cicero being alive.*

104   **263.** — 4. **Frequently.** See G. 443. — 5. **Assembled in the
temple,** Lat. idiom, *came together into the temple.* — **Jupiter
Stator.** *Stator,* the stayer, he who arrests the flight of soldiers and
causes them to stand fast, is one of the epithets of Jupiter, the king
of the gods. — 6. **Was the first,** etc., Lat. idiom, *the first accused.*
See G. 442, 1.

107   **268.** — 6. **Who oppose.** See G. 445, 3, 2); 463, 1. — 7.
There are some. See Model VII. — **Who fear.** See G. 501, I.
— 8. **As we ought,** Lat. idiom, *that which we ought.* See G.
445, 7. — 9. **To ascertain,** Lat. idiom, *who may ascertain.* See
G. 500; 445, 5. — **Are.** See G. 525. — 10. **Devoted himself
to** = *studied.* — **Which,** *quod.* See G. 445, 4.

110   **274.** — 2. **On the 8th of Nov.,** Lat. idiom, *on the sixth day
before the ides of November.* See G. 708; 708, 3; 709. — 4. **Such
was . . . madness.** See G. 453, 4. — 5. **The best books
which.** See Model V.; also G. 453, 5. — 7. **Their money.** See
G. 447.

112   **279.** — 1. **It would be better,** See Model V.; also G. 475,
4, 1). — 3. **Should have been.** See 475, 1. — 5. **Could he
not,** etc., Lat. idiom, *was he not able to order.* — 7. **Did judge.**
See G. 494. — **The best thing to do.** See G. 570, 1. — 10.
From the founding, etc., Lat. idiom, *from the city founded.* See
410; also G. 580.

114   **285.** — 1. **Like Catiline.** See G. 399, 3, 2). — **That they
dared.** See G. 494; 481, II. 1. — 6. **When consul.** See G.
363, 3. — **For the safety,** *ad salutem,* lit. *to the safety,* i. e. to
that end. See 380, III. — **Has been called.** See G. 482, 2. —

9. **Rest,** — in itself considered. — 10. **Rest,** i. e. as a means of invigorating its powers.

290. — 4. **Care must be taken,** *cavendum est.* — 6. **That =** but that, *quin.* — 8. **I fear that.** See G. 492, 4, 1). — 9. **To watch,** *vigilēmus,* lit. *that we should (may) watch.* See G. 496, 1. — 10. **From defending,** Lat. idiom, *by which he should less defend.* See G. 499. 117

296. — 1. **Ambassadors,** *legātos.* This word may stand after the verb, directly before the Relative clause. — **To establish,** *qui confirmārent,* lit. *who should establish.* See G. 500. — 2. **Faesulae,** a town in Etruria. — 4. **Will lose,** *amittas.* See G. 492, 4; 479. — 8. **To be read.** See G. 501, III. 119

301. — 4. **Unless you suppress =** *unless you shall suppress.* See G. 470, 2. — **Conscript Fathers.** The Roman senators were often thus addressed. — **For inaction.** See G. 410, II. — 8 **This conspiracy,** etc. See 419. 122

307. — 4. **That which,** *id quod.* But it is often better to begin the sentence with the Relative clause, and let the antecedent follow; as, *quod est,* etc., *id,* etc. — 5. **With your aid.** See G. 414. — 6. **Let not fear deter,** *ne timor deterreat.* See G. 488, 3. — **From watching.** See G. 499. — 8. **What is right.** See G. 527. 125

312. — 1. **Came,** *venit.* See G. 518, 3. — 2. **When they were.** See Model III.; also G. 518, II. — 3. **Because he has driven,** — the reason assigned by those who hate, not by the narrator. See G. 520, II. — 4. **Because he has driven,** — the reason assigned by the narrator himself. See G. 520, I. — 6. **These things,** *quae,* lit. *which things.* See G. 453. — 8. **Is recorded.** See G. 522, II. 127

317. — 2. **At the command,** etc., Lat. idiom, *the consul commanding.* See G. 431. — 3. **Upon =** *concerning.* — 4. **Difficult to say.** See G. 570. — 5. **Would preserve,** i. e. in the future. See G. 543. 129

323. — 1. **When he received.** See G. 531. — What mood would be used in the direct discourse? See G. 518, 3. — 6. **That,** *quin.* See G. 498, 3. — 7. **Who does not desire,** *qui non cupiat,* or *quin cupiat.* See also Syn. 618. 131

329. — 5. **Would have gone.** See G. 532, 2, 2). — 6. **When he comes.** See G. 532, 4. In the direct discourse this would be, *when I come = when I shall have come.* — 9. **Is the part of fortitude,** Lat. idiom, *is of fortitude.* See G. 402, I. 133

334. — 3. **Do not think.** See Model V.; also G. 535, 1, 3). — 6. **Let me know,** Lat. idiom, *make* (or *cause*) *that I may know.* 135

— **Are doing.** See G. 525. — 8. **At his own personal peril,** *suo solius periculo.* See G. 397, 3. — 9. **These books on philosophy,** Lat. idiom, *these concerning philosophy books.* See 419.

138 **340.** — 6. **To be happy.** See Model II. — 8. **In vain,** i. e. without success, without accomplishing his object. — 10. **To no purpose,** i. e. not only without accomplishing the desired object, but absolutely without any good result. — **Brought us,** Lat. idiom, *brought for us.* See G. 385. — 12. **To be wise.** See G. 547, II.

140 **346.** — 1. **Profess to be wise,** Lat. idiom, *profess themselves to be (that they are) wise.* — 2. **Who is unwilling.** See G. 501, I. — 5. **Upon the state.** See G. 386.

142 **351.** — 4. **He also says,** *idem dicit.* See G. 451, 3. — 5. **It is my duty,** *meum est.* See G. 404, 1. — 6. **What I think,** an indirect question. — **What you have done** = *that which you have done,* a Relative clause. See G. 525, 5, 1). — 7. **Whether — or.** See G. 526, II. 1. — **Of greater value,** *pluris.* See G. 402, III. 1. — 8. **That he had conquered.** See Model VIII.; also G. 554, IV.; 558, V. 2; 520, II. — 9. **That men are delighted.** See G. 556, II.

145 **357.** — 2. **That you are.** See G. 558, V. 1. — **Of securing.** See G. 563. — 4. **Upon the . . . saving,** etc., Lat. idiom, *upon the republic to be saved.* — 5. **For perceiving,** *ad* with the Gerundive. — 6. **To be plundered.** See G. 565, 3.

147 **362.** — 3. **Reading, writing.** Place the Latin word for the former at the end of the first clause, and that for the latter at the beginning of the second. See G. 595. — **For writing,** *scribendi,* lit. *of writing.* See G. 393, 1. — 6. **Of his hearers,** *audientium,* or *eorum qui audiunt.* See 438; also G. 575, 1; 577. — 7. **More necessary.** See G. 169, 2; 170. — **Than that of requiting,** Lat. idiom, *than requiting.* — 8. **To salute.** See G. 569.

149 **367.** — 3. In this sentence the relation of the different parts will be best shown by placing the verb before the object. — 4. **When they speak,** Lat. idiom, *speaking.* See G. 578, I. — 5. **From me,** *meam,* lit. *my.* See 462. — 7. **Having accomplished.** See G. 431, 2, (3).

152 **373.** — 1. **That.** See G. 498, 3. — 6. **And;** omit in rendering into Latin. See G. 587, I. 6. — **Pompey,** a celebrated Roman general. — 7. **In the temple,** — regarded simply as an edifice. — 8. **In this temple;** use the most general word.

154 **379.** — 2. **More,** *plura,* lit. *more things.* — **Have,** *habuero,* lit. *shall have had.* — 5. **Have to fear.** See G. 388, 1, 1).

384. — 1. **To see.** See G. 492, 3. — 4. **To be an honor,** 157
Lat. idiom, *to be for an honor.* See G. 390. — 5. **To say,** *qui dicĕrent,* lit. *who should say.* See G. 500. — 6. **To achieve,** *ad* with Gerundive. See G. 565, 3.

389. — 2. **To set forth**; place the Latin Infinitive in this 159
instance at the end of the sentence. See 595, VI. — 4. **If any one should free.** See Model II. — 6. **If the fear,** etc. See G. 431, 2, (1).

395. — 3. **Though he is.** See G. 515, II. — 5. **Caius Mucius.** 161
While Porsena was besieging Rome, Caius Mucius, afterwards surnamed Scaevola, attempted to deliver the city by slaying the king.

401. — 1. **When virtue governs.** See G. 431. — 2. **Hav-** 164
ing come, Lat. idiom, *when I had come.* See G. 518, II. — 3.
Arganthonius, a king of Tartessus in Spain. — 5. **At the age of eighty-five,** Lat. idiom, *having been born eighty-five years.* —
6. **Isocrates,** a celebrated Athenian orator. — **In his**; omit the possessive in rendering. See G. 447. — 8. **Plato,** a celebrated Greek philosopher. — 9. **While consul.** See G. 363, 3. — **Mari-**
us, a celebrated Roman general.

407. — 1. **Which we,** etc. See G. 604, I. — 7. **Clodius,** an un- 166
principled Roman, and a bitter enemy of Cicero. — 10. **Servilius Ahala,** Master of Horse under the Roman Dictator Cincinnatus. —
Spurius Maelius, a wealthy Roman knight. — **Because he was seeking.** See G. 578, II.

416. — 1. **Tarentum,** a town in Southern Italy. — 2. **Plautus,** 169
a celebrated Roman poet. — 3. **Just eighty-three.** See G. 452, 3. — **Before the consulship,** etc., Lat. idiom, *before Cicero consul.* See 409. — 4. **With the attendance,** etc., Lat. idiom, *fortune being the attendant.* — 5. **Of,** *de.* — 9. **From boyhood,**
Lat. idiom, *from a boy.* See 408. — 10. **The desire.** See 411.

425. — 3. **All . . . before Socrates.** See 419. — 6. **In an** 172
enemy, *in hoste posita.* — 7. **Temples around the forum.**
See 420. — 10. **Epicurus,** the famous Greek philosopher from whom the Epicureans have derived their name.

433. — 4. **Antiochus,** a king of Syria. — 5. **Achilles,** the 175
most famous Grecian hero in the Trojan war. — 7. **Wishes.** See G. 525. — 11. **Of Antony,** *Antonii.* Place this word at the beginning of the sentence. — **His**; omit in rendering into Latin.

445. — 1. Begin with *intĕrest, ut.* — 2. **Gorgias,** a celebrated 178
Greek rhetorician. — **Leontini,** an ancient town in Sicily. — 3.
Prodicus, a Greek rhetorician. — **Ceus,** or **Cea,** an island in the Aegean Sea. — 4. **Pharsalia,** a plain in Thessaly, famous for

Caesar's victory over Pompey. — **Atticus**, an intimate friend of Cicero. — 5. **Leuctra**, a town in Boeotia, famous for the victory of the Theban general Epaminondas over the Lacedaemonians. — 6. **One of the Seven**, Lat. idiom, *one from the Seven*, i. e. the Seven Wise Men of Greece. — 7. **Are no less useful**, Lat. idiom, *bring (impart) no less utility (advantage)*, or like the English. — **Warriors**, Lat. idiom, *those who wage war*. See 438. — 8. **Crotona,** a town in Southern Italy. — **In the fourth year**, etc., Lat. idiom, *Tarquinius Superbus reigning the fourth year*. See G. 431; 378. — **Tarquinius Superbus**, the seventh king of Rome. — 10. **While in exile**, Lat. idiom, *while they were in exile*. See G. 518, II. — 11. **So virtuous**, *ea virtūte*. See 441, and Model III. — **No other aim**, Lat. idiom, *nothing else if not (unless)*.

181   **455.** — 3. **Armenians**, a people in Asia. — 7. **Many weighty,** Lat. idiom, *many and weighty*. — 10. **As possible**. See 449. — 14. **Many of the best,** *multi optĭmi*, lit. *many best*.

185   **466.** — 5. **When I heard**. This is intended to designate *time* simply. — 6. **Have to learn**. See G. 388, 1, 1). — 7. **As much time**. See G. 396, III. 2, 3); 594, III. — 8. **As certain**, Lat. idiom, *for certain.*

187   **475.** — 2. **Cimbrians**, a people of Northern Europe, who invaded the Roman empire and were defeated by Caius Marius. — 3. **Miletus**, a city in Asia Minor. — 6. **His**, *ejus*, referring to Socrates. See 468, 2. — 10. **The town of Antioch**. See G. 379, 2.

190   **481.** — 2. **For the safety of**. See G. 602, II. 3. — 4. Place the Relative clause at the beginning of the sentence. See G. 604, II. — 7. **He**, i. e. Thales. — **Astyages**, king of Media in the sixth century B. C. — 10. **That of Cicero**. See 476, 4.

194   **491.** — 2. **You or I?** See G. 346, II. 2, 1). — 4. **The conversation**. See 484. — 11. **All the good**. See 485. — 12. **Sextus Roscius**, a citizen of Ameria in Italy, defended by Cicero in an oration still extant. — **Was constantly**. See G. 443.

197   **499.** — 1. **All the greatest**. See 485. — 2. **Now that . . . old**. See G. 363, 3. — 5. **It seems . . . that Crassus**, Lat. idiom, *Crassus seems*. See 494. — 6. **So far . . . from admiring**. See G. 496, 8. — 9. **Valor of Scipio**. See 492.

199   **505.** — 4. **It is said that**. See 494. — **Xerxes**, a celebrated king of Persia. — 6. **Men may live**. Use the impersonal construction. See 500, III. — 7. **One should contend**. See 495, 1.

203   **515.** — 4. **When I obtain**, Lat. idiom, *when I shall have obtained.* — 6. **Indeed while I**, *qui dum*, lit. *who while*. See G.

453. — 9. **One can live.** Use the Impersonal Passive Construction. See 495; 500, III.

521. — 1. **What counsel,** Lat. idiom, *what of counsel.* — 2. 206 **Each day** = every day, *quoque die.* — 3. **When boys.** See G. 363, 3. — **We had the opinion** = *the opinion was to us.* — 4. **That one cannot live.** Use the Pass. Impers. construction, *non posse vivi.* — 5. **Says that no one** = *denies that any one.*

528. — 1. **In the whole of Asia.** See G. 422, 1, 1). — 3. 209 **Would be ... to impel** = *would be able to impel.* — **You think,** *putāres,* not *putas,* as this clause is treated as a part of the conclusion, — *which you would in that event think best.* — 4. **I wish,** *velim,* lit. *I would wish,* — a modest, respectful form of expressing a wish. — **Would write.** See G. 493, 2. — **On what day.** Place this clause, on account of its importance, at the beginning of the sentence. — 6. **Should have been.** See G. 475, 1.

535. — 1. **That there were.** See G. 498, 3. — 2. **The study** 211 **in which,** *id studium in quo.* See 484. — **Be an honor to,** Lat. idiom, *be for an honor to.* See G. 390. — 3. **Have attained.** See G. 501, I. — 5. **As we wish** = *as we may wish.* — 6. **I desire,** *opto,* — involving no purpose. See Syn. 618. — 8. **Plans.** *Consilia* should begin the sentence to show its relation to both clauses. — 10. **Who ... statesmen.** See 438.

541. — 1. **We must give.** See 557, III. — 2. **Archytas,** a 214 Pythagorean philosopher of Tarentum in Italy. — **To remember** = *that he should remember,* — indirect discourse. See G. 530, II. — 3. **To hear.** Use the Infinitive, or *ad* with the Gerund. — 5. **For the safety,** *ad* with the Acc. See 380, III. — 7. **Dion,** a brother-in-law of the tyrant Dionysius of Syracuse. — **Of Syracuse.** See 435. — **To liberate,** *ut* with the Subjunctive, or *ad* with the Gerundive. Use the latter. — 9. **Suitable to command,** Lat. idiom, *suitable who may command.* See G. 501, III. — 10. **To pay his respects.** Use Supine. — 12. **To be presented,** Lat. idiom, *that he should be presented.* See G. 495.

550. — 2. **Cicero.** The subject may be placed either before or 217 after the participial clause. — 5. **Having achieved ... deeds.** Use the Abl. Abs. — **The ancient ... Olympus,** *Olympum urbem antiquam.* — 6. **Having conquered.** Use *quum* with the Subjunctive. — **Mantinea,** a city in Arcadia. — 9. **Requite your favor** = *requite,* or *return to you, the favor.* — **Be grateful** = *have gratitude.* Here *gratiam* may be omitted, as it can be so readily supplied from the preceding clause.

556. — 1. **On ... despising glory;** *de* with the Gerundive. 220

— 2. **Hippias**, a celebrated Greek rhetorician. — **Olympia, a** district in Elis, where the Olympic games were held. — 3. **Held with Cato.** This identifies the conversation. See 551, I. — 5. **At the age of nineteen**, Lat. idiom, *having been born nineteen years.* — 6. **What advice you gave** = *what you advised.* — 7. **Except injuries**, Lat. idiom, *if not (unless) injuries.* — 9. **And;** omit in rendering. See G. 587, I. 6.

223　　　**561.** — 1. **By means of money**, Abl. — 2. **One.** *One* should be omitted in rendering. — 3. **It must be admitted.** In the several sentences in this exercise, *must* is best rendered by the Periphrastic Conj. — **That . . . is.** With *concēdo*, either the Infinitive, or *ut* with the Subjunctive, may be used. — 7. **Ought to do,** i. e. in view of the circumstances of the case. See 557, III. — 8. **Should be.** Use the Impers. construction. — **Be arranged with reference to** = *be referred to.* — 10. **By a . . . admiration**, *admiratiōne.*

227　　　**569.** — 2. **That which one thinks**, *id quod sentit.* The Subjunctive would not be incorrect, but would be less definite. — 3. **Not . . . either . . . or** = *neither . . . nor.* See 581. — 5. **For administering**, *ad* with the Gerundive. See 380, III.; 545. — 6. **To be negligent.** See G. 547, II. — 7. **As I think you are aware** = *which I think you know.* — **Think.** See Syn. 576. — **I have acquaintance** = *there is to me an acquaintance.* — 8. **Whatever**, *quae — ea*, those things which.

230　　　**578.** — 2. **Consult for the interests of a part**, Lat. idiom, *consult for a part.* — 3. **I supposed.** See G. 501, I. — 4. **Ought to have reference** = *ought to be referred.* — 5. **To sacrifice.** Use the Infinitive. — 7. **Without giving some precepts**, etc., Lat. idiom, *no precepts of duty being* (in the mean time) *given.* This sense — *being given*, not *having been given* — is best expressed by the Fut. Pass. Part. *tradendis.* — 11. **Attain, suppose.** Subjunctive. See G. 518, II.; 527.

234　　　**587.** — 1. **Learned studies.** See 440, 2. — 4. **And.** See G. 587, I. 6. — **Are perishable.** For gender of adjective, see G. 439, 2, 3). — 10. **Perhaps the greatest hero**, *haud scio an summum.* See G. 526, II. 2, 2). — **Lysis**, a celebrated Pythagorean philosopher of Tarentum.

237　　　**594.** — 3. **Have been taught** = *educated, trained.* See 585. — **To arrange.** Use Subj. of Purpose. — 5. **Would speak.** Use Pres. Infin. — 6. **Deserve to be seen.** See G. 231. — 7. **Nothing new** = *nothing of new.* — 8. **Lost in thought**, *cogitatiōne impedīti*, engaged, occupied with thought. — 10. **I have**

been desiring. See G. 467, 2. — 12. **Though the tyrant was removed.** See G. 431, 2. — 13. **Also**; render by the proper form of *idem*. See G. 451, 3.

599. — 1. **And**; omit in rendering. See G. 587, I. 6. — 2. 240 **Which we**, etc. Insert this in the principal clause. See G. 604, I. — 3. **Dionysius**, the tyrant of Syracuse. — 5. **He who obeys**, *eum qui paret*, or *pareat*. The former is more definite, and, perhaps, preferable in this sentence. — 7. **Having retained**, *quum* with Subj. See 543, 3. — 9. **Caius Duillius**, a celebrated Roman commander, who gained a naval victory over the Carthaginians in the first Punic war. — 11. **To another**, *altĕri*, a second one, in contrast with *himself*. This contrast gives *altĕri* an emphatic position at the end of the sentence.

607. — 1. **Was expected to speak**, *dictŭrus esset*, was about 243 to speak. — **For the purpose of hearing him**; *causa* with the Gerund. See 380, IV. — 4. **To be better**, *quo meliōres essent*. See G. 497. In this sentence the Latin verb for *have taught* is treated as a Historical tense. Hence *essent*, not *sint*. See G. 482, 1. — **As Lysis taught Epaminondas of Thebes**, *ut Lysis Epaminondam Thebānum*, or, inverting the order, as is often done in illustrations, *ut Thebānum Epaminondam Lysis*. The verb *taught* should be omitted in rendering, because it can be readily supplied. — 5. **And not only** = nor only, *neque solum*. See 581. — **Literary works**, *monumenta litterārum*. See 440, 2. — 7. **To disguise the fact that those things**, Lat. idiom, *to disguise that those things*. — 8. **Solon.** The Athenians had made it a capital offence to propose the recovery of Salamis from the Megarians. Accordingly Solon pretended to be mad, that, in his supposed frenzy, he might with impunity urge the unpopular measure.

614. — 1. **It is related of . . . that . . . first who** 247 **reigned**, Lat. idiom, *Servius Tullius is related first to have reigned*. See 610, III.; also G. 542. — 2. **Having been unable**, *quum* with the Subj. — **To Tarquinii, a city of Etruria**, *Tarquinios*, *in urbem Etruriae*. *Urbem* is not treated simply as an Appositive to Tarquinios, but with the preposition *in* it becomes a modifier of the verb. See G. 379, 2; 423, 3, 3). — **Cypselus**, a celebrated tyrant of Corinth. — 5. **Lycurgus**, the celebrated Spartan lawgiver. — **The authority of the Delphic Apollo**, i. e. of the Oracle at Delphi. — 6. **Milo**, a famous athlete. — **Bearing** = *supporting*, or *sustaining the weight of*. Use *sustineo* in the Imperf. Subj. with *quum*. — 8. **As is admitted**, *id quod constat*. See G.

445, 7. — **To bring it**; omit the pronoun *it* in rendering. See 457. — 9. **They say,** *ferunt.* Place this verb after the Subject Acc. See 601. — 10. **Having been banished,** *quum,* with Subj.

250   **620.** — 2. **Themselves,** *se.* Place this at the beginning of the sentence to show its common relation to the several clauses. — **And**; omit. — 3. **The blessings which are past** = *past bless-ings.* — 4. **It seemed to me that.** See 610, I.; also G. 549, 4, 1). — **One of,** *unus ex,* one from. See G. 398, 4. — 5. **After the overthrow of the republic.** Use the Abl. Abs. — 10. **If we promise** = *if we shall promise.* See 627, III.; also G. 470, 2. — 11. **If we show** = *if we shall show.* — **Are about to state** = *shall be* (at that future time) *about to state.*

254   **626.** — 1. **I shall willingly communicate.** See 621, III. 1. — 3. **Will offend.** Use Pres. Subj. See G. 479. — 4. **My-self,** referring especially to native talents, *ingenium.* See 621, I. **Aid.** Use Plur. in Latin, *helps, aids.* See 411, 2. — 5. **This event** = *this thing.* — 6. **Treasures, possessions,** *res,* things. — 8. **Could have happened,** Lat. idiom, *was able to happen.* See G. 541, 3. — 10. **For empire,** *de imperio,* lit. *concerning empire.* — 11. **Letters,** *littĕrae,* written communications without special reference to epistolary form. See Syn. 200.

257   **632.** — 2. **Could say.** Use Present Infin. See G. 541, 1. — 4. **Weighty**; for the position of the Adj. in Latin, see G. 597, I. — 5. **Philo,** a celebrated Grecian philosopher. The Academy at Athens was a famous school of philosophy. — 7. **Say** — not = *deny.* — 9. **A letter from me.** See 462. — **For the purpose of recovering my voice.** Use *causa* with the Gerundive.

260   **638.** — 1. **For him,** *in eum,* against him. — **Should kill**; Plup. Subjunctive, to denote a completed action with reference to the time of punishment. — **Would commit,** Fut. Infin. — 6. **That it may not.** Use the Relative. See G. 501, I. — 7. **If they were not.** Insert the condition after the proper names, and observe that the words *by them* in the condition must be rendered by the noun *littĕris,* and the words *of letters* in the conclusion, by the pronoun *eārum,* referring back to that noun. — **In the knowledge and practice,** *ad* with Gerundive, lit. *to perceiving and prac-tising virtue.*

ENGLISH-LATIN VOCABULARY.

For Explanation of References and Abbreviations, see page xi.

A.

Abandon. *Relinquo, ĕre, lĭqui, lictum.*

Able, be able. *Possum, posse, potui.* G. 289.

Abound in. *Abundo, āre, āvi, ātum.*

About. To be about to, rendered by the Act. Periphras. Conj. G. 228.

Above. *Supra,* adv.

Absurd. *Absurdus, a, um.*

Abundance. *Copia, ae,* f.

Academy. *Academĭa, ae,* f.

Acceptable. *Acceptus, a, um; gratus, a, um.* See 216. Make acceptable, *probo, āre, āvi, ātum.*

Accommodate one's self to. *Obsĕquor, i, secūtus sum,* dep.

Accomplish. *Confĭcio, effĭcio, ĕre, fĕci, fectum; assĕquor, i, secūtus sum,* dep. Achievements are accomplished, *res geruntur.*

Accordance, in accordance with. *Ex, e,* prep. with abl. G. 434, 3.

According to one's desire. *Ex sententia.* See 339.

Account, on account of. *Propter,* prep. with acc.

Accumulate (trans.). *Augeo, ĕre, auxi, auctum.*

Accusation. *Crimen, ĭnis,* n.

Accuse. *Accūso, āre, āvi, ātum.*

Achieve. *Ago, ĕre, egi, actum.*

Achievement. *Res gesta.* See 474. Achievements are accomplished, *res geruntur.*

Achilles. *Achilles, is,* m.

Acquaintance, experience. *Usus, us,* m. A very intimate acquaintance, *summus usus.*

Acquainted, be, become, acquainted with. *Cognosco, ĕre, nōvi, nĭtum.*

Acquire. *Paro, āre, āvi, ātum.*

Acquit. *Absolvo, ĕre, solvi, solū-tum.*

Across. *Trans,* prep. with acc.

Act. *Ago, ĕre, egi, actum; facio, ĕre, feci, factum.*

Action, deed. *Factum, i,* n.

Adjacent, nearest. *Proxĭmus, a, um.*

Administer. *Gero, ĕre, gessi, gestum.*

Admiration, a feeling of admiration. *Admiratio, ōnis,* f.

Admire. *Miror, admĭror, āri, ātus sum,* dep.

Admit, confess. *Confiteor, ēri, fessus sum,* dep. Admit, concede, *concēdo, ĕre, cessi, cessum.*

Admitted, it is admitted. *Constat, constĭtit.*

Admonish. *Moneo, admŏneo, ĕre, ui, ĭtum.*

Admonition. *Admonitio, ōnis,* f.

13

Adorn. *Exorno, āre, āvi, ātum.* Adorn, clothe, *vestio, īre, īvi* and *ii, ītum.*

Advantage. *Emolumentum, i,* n.; *commŏdum, i,* n.; *utilĭtas, ātis,* f.

Adversary. *Adversarius, ii,* m. See 504.

Adversity. *Res adversae,* f. pl. G. 441, 4.

Advice. *Consĭlium, ii,* n. To give advice, *suadeo, ēre, suasi, suasum.* G. 385.

Advise. *Moneo, ēre, ui, ĭtum ; suadeo, ēre, suasi, suasum.*

Adviser. *Auctor, ōris,* m.

Aeduans. *Aedui, ōrum,* m. pl.

Affair, thing. *Res, rei,* f. Military affairs, *res militāris,* sing.

Affect. *Afficio, ēre, fēci, fectum.* Affect, prompt, *commŏveo, ēre, mōvi, mōtum.*

Affection. *Amor, ōris,* m. Dutiful affection, *piĕtas, ātis,* f.

Affluent, rich, copious. *Uber, ĕris.*

Africa. *Africa, ae,* f.

Africanus. *Africānus, i,* m.

After. *Post,* prep. with acc.

Afterwards. *Post,* adv.

Again and again. *Etiam atque etiam.*

Against. *Contra ; in ;* prep. with acc.

Age, period of life. *Aetas, ātis,* f. Old age, *senectus, ūtis,* f. At the age of, *natus, a, um,* with acc. of time. See 400.

Aged, old. *Senex, senis.*

Agency — through one's agency. *Per,* prep. with acc. See 232, 5.

Agis. *Agis, ĭdis,* m.

Ago. *Abhinc,* adv.

Agreeable. *Jucundus, a, um.* See 216.

Ahala. *Ahāla, ae,* m.

Aid. *Auxĭlium, ii,* n.; *adjumentum, i,* n. Means, *opes, opum,* f. pl. G. 133, 1.

Aid, to aid. *Adjŭvo, āre, jūvi, jūtum.*

Aim — propose to one's self no other aim. *Sibi nihil aliud nisi*

proponĕre (*propōno, ĕre, posui, posĭtum*). See 444.

Alba Longa. *Alba Longa, Albae Longae,* f.

Alexander. *Alexander, dri,* m.

Alive. *Vivus, a, um.*

All. *Omnis, e.* Each, every, *quisque, quaeque, quodque* and *quicque* or *quidque.* All together, *cunctus, a, um.* At all, *omnīno,* adv. Not at all, *nihil.* G. 380, 2.

Allobroges. *Allobrŏges, um,* m. pl.

Allow. *Concĕdo, ĕre, cessi, cessum.* Allow to pass, *intermitto, ĕre, mīsi, missum.*

Ally. *Socius, ii,* m.

Alone. *Solus, a, um.* G. 149. Without exception, *unus, a, um.* G. 149.

Already. *Jam,* adv.

Also. *Etiam,* adv. I, you, he, &c., also, *idem, eădem, idem.* See 350.

Although. *Etsi ; licet ; etiamsi ; quamquam ; quamvis.* G. 515, 516.

Always. *Semper,* adv.

Ambassador. *Legātus, i,* m.

Among. *Inter,* prep. with acc. Among, with, near to, *apud,* prep. with acc.

Amount, quantity. *Vis, vis,* f.

Ample. *Amplus, a, um.*

Ancient. *Antiquus, a, um ; pristĭnus, a, um.* See 162.

Ancus. *Ancus, i,* m.

And. *Et ; que ; atque* or *ac,* conj. G. 587, I. 2, 3. And yet = and, *et.* And not, *neque,* conj. And that too, *et is ; et is quidem (is ea, id).*

Anger. *Iracundia, ae,* f.

Annoyance. *Molestia, ae,* f.

Another. *Alius, a, ud.* G. 149; 149, 3. Another (of two), a fellow-creature, *alter, ēra, ĕrum.* G. 149; 149, 2. Another's, *aliēnus, a, um.*

Antioch. *Antiochīa, ae,* f.

Antiochus. *Antiŏchus, i,* m.

Antipater. *Antipăter, tri,* m.

Antony. *Antonius, ii,* m.

Any. *Ullus, a, um ;* G. 149 ; *ali-qui, qua, quod.* Any one, *quis.* Any thing, *quid.* G. 189. If any, *si quis.* G. 190, 2.

Apollo. *Apollo, inis,* m.

Apparel. *Vestitus, us,* m.

Appear, seem. *Videor, eri, visus sum.* See 577.

Appius. *Appius, ii,* m.

Apply to. *Confero, ferre, tuli, collatum, in* with acc. Apply one's self to, *se conferre ad* with acc. (*confero, ferre, tu-li, collatum*); *se applicare ad* with acc. (*applico, are, avi, atum*).

Appoint. *Constituo, ere, ui, utum.*

Approach. *Appropinquo, are, avi, atum ; accedo, ere, cessi, cessum.*

Appropriate, take. *Sumo, ere, sumpsi, sumptum.* Appropriate to, apply to, *confero, ferre, tuli, collatum, in* with acc.

Approve. *Probo, are, avi, atum.*

Aquitanians. *Aquitani, orum,*m.pl.

Arar. *Arar, aris,* m.; acc. *Ar-rim.*

Archytas. *Archytas, ae,* m.

Arganthonius. *Arganthonius,ii,*m.

Ariovistus. *Ariovistus, i,* m.

Arise, become. *Exsisto, ere, stiti, stitum.*

Aristotle. *Aristoteles, is,* m.

Armenian. *Armenius, ii,* m.

Arms. *Arma, orum,* n. pl. G. 131, 1, 4).

Army. *Exercitus, us,* m.; *agmen, inis,* n.; *acies, ei,* f. See 178. Army on the march, *agmen, inis,* n.

Around. *Circum,* adv., and prep. with acc.

Arouse. *Erigo, ere, rexi, rectum.*

Arrange (a line of battle). *Instruo, ere, struxi, structum.* Arrange with reference to, *refero, ferre, tuli, latum, ad* with acc. See 534.

Arrive. *Pervenio, ire, veni, ventum.* Arrive, come, *venio, ire, veni, ventum.*

Arrogance. *Arrogantia, ae,* f.

Art. *Ars, artis,* f.

As. *Ut,* adv. As = since, *quum,* conj. As, after *tam, quam,* adv. As = for, *pro,* prep. with abl. As to, after *ita, ut,* conj. with subjunct. As — as possible, *quam,* adv. with superlat. See 449. As much, *quantus, a, um.* As much — as, *tantus, a, um — quantus, a, um.* See 527. As soon as, *quum primum.* As, relative, especially after *idem,* etc., *qui, quae, quod.* As = that which, a thing which, *id quod.* See 267 ; also G. 445, 7.

Ascanius. *Ascanius, ii,* m.

Ascertain. *Cognosco, ere, novi, nitum.*

Ashamed, be ashamed. *Pudet, puduit* and *puditum est.* See 228 ; also G. 299 ; 410, III.

Asia. *Asia, ae,* f.

Ask. *Rogo, are, avi, atum.* Ask (a question), *interrogo, are, avi, atum.* Ask, inquire, *quaero, ere, quaesivi* and *ii, quaesitum.* Ask for, *peto, ere, ivi* and *ii, itum.* It is asked, *quaeritur, quaesitum est.*

Assemble. *Convenio, ire, veni, ventum.* Multitudes assemble, *concursus fit.* See 606.

Assembly. *Concio, onis,* f.

Assiduously. *Studiose,* adv.

Assign. *Tribuo, ere, ui, utum.*

Associate. *Socius, ii,* m.

Astyages. *Astyages, is,* m.

At. *Apud, ad,* prep. with acc. At the age of, *natus, a, um,* with acc. of time. See 400. At the suggestion of, *auctor,* in abl. abs. At all, *omnino,* adv. Not at all, *nihil.* G. 380, 2. At length, *tandem,* adv. At once, *jam,* adv. At times, *interdum,* adv.

Athenian. *Atheniensis, is,* m. and f.

Athens. *Athenae, arum,* f. pl.

Attack. *Adorior, iri, ortus sum,* dep.

Attain. *Consĕquor, assĕquor, i, secūtus sum,* dep.; *adipiscor, i, adeptus sum,* dep.

Attempt. *Conor, āri, ātus sum,* dep.; *tento, āre, āvi, ātum.*

Attend to, serve. *Servio, īre, īvi, ītum.* G. 385.

Attendance, with the attendance of. *Comes, ĭtis,* in abl. abs.

Attendant. *Comes, ĭtis,* m. and f.

Attention, study. *Studium, ii,* n.

Attention, exertion, work, *opĕra, ae,* f.

Attentive. *Attentus, a, um.*

Atticus. *Attĭcus, i,* m.

Attract. *Allĭcio, ĕre, lexi, lectum.*

Audacity. *Audacia, ae,* f.

Author. *Auctor, ōris,* m. and f.

Authority. *Auctorĭtas, ātis,* f.

Avail. *Valeo, ēre, ui, ĭtum.*

Avaricious. *Avārus, a, um.*

Avoid. *Vito, āre, āvi, ātum.*

Await. *Exspecto, āre, āvi, ātum.*

Award. *Tribuo, ĕre, ui, ūtum.*

Aware — be aware. *Scio, scire, scivi, scitum.*

B.

Banish, throw off. *Abjĭcio, ĕre, jĕci, jectum.* Banish, expel, *expello, ĕre, pŭli, pulsum.*

Base. *Turpis, e.*

Battle. *Proelium, ii, n.* A battle is fought, *pugnātur, ātum est,* impers.

Be. *Sum, esse, fui.* Be a characteristic of. See 426. Be a lawgiver, *leges scribo, ĕre, scripsi, scriptum.* See 438. Be a statesman, *rei publĭcae praesum, esse, fui.* See 438. Be a warrior, *bellum gero, ĕre, gessi, gestum.* See 444. Be able, *possum, posse, potui.* Be about to, Act. Periphrast. Conj. Be acquainted with, *cognosco, ĕre, nōvi, nĭtum.* Be ashamed, *pudet, puduit* and *pudĭtum est.* See 228; also G. 410, III. Be aware, *scio, scire, scivi, scitum.* Be born, *nascor,*

i, *natus sum.* Be busy, *occupatiōne distinĕri (distĭneo, ēre, ui, tentum).* See 631. How very busy one is, *quanta occupatiōne,* etc. Be conducive to, *condūco, ĕre, duxi, ductum.* See 289. Be consistent with one's self, *sibi consentĭre,* with *ipse, a, um,* in agreement with subject (*consentio, īre, sensi, sensum*). Be delighted with, *gaudeo, ēre, gavīsus sum.* Be destitute of, need, *egeo, indĭgeo, ēre, ui.* See 239, I. Be elated, *effĕror, ferri, elātus sum.* See 295. Be eminent, *unus, a, um, emĭneo, ēre, ui,* or *emineo* alone. Be engaged in, *sum, esse, fui, in* with abl. See 534. Be evident, *consto, āre, stĭti, stātum.* Be expected to, Act. Periphrast. Conj. Be free from, be without, *vaco, āre, āvi, ātum; careo, ēre, ui, ĭtum; egeo, ēre, ui.* See 239, I. Be grateful, *gratiam habeo, ēre, ui, ĭtum.* See 548. Be held = to be, *sum, esse, fui.* Be ignorant of, *ignōro, āre, āvi, ātum.* Be in command of, *praesum, esse, fui.* G. 386. Be in force, *vigeo, ēre, vigui.* Be intimate with, *familiarĭter utor, i, usus sum,* dep. G. 419, I. Be mad, *furo, ĕre, ui.* Be needful, there needs, is need of, *opus est, fuit.* G. 419, 3. Be on one's guard, *caveo, ēre, cavi, cautum.* Be one's intention, *in anĭmo sum, esse, fui.* See 206. Be subject to, obey, *pareo, ēre, ui, ĭtum.* G. 385. Be sufficient, be able, *possum, posse, potui.* Be the duty, mark, part, &c., of, often rendered by the Pred. Gen. See 426. Be the result, *evĕnio, īre, vēni, ventum.* Be the slave of, *servio, īre, ĭvi* and *ii, ĭtum.* G. 385. Be unable, *non possum, posse, potui.* Be unwilling, *nolo, nolle, nolui.* Be useful, *utĭlis, e, sum, esse, fui; utilĭtā-*

tem affĕro, ferre, attŭli, allātum.
See 444. Be willing, *volo, velle, volui.* Be without. See *Be free from.* Be wont, *soleo, ĕre, solĭtus sum.*

Bear. *Fero, ferre, tuli, latum.* Bear, suffer, *patior, pati, passus sum,* dep. Bear, support, *sustĭneo, ĕre, ui, tentum.*

Beautiful. *Pulcher, chra, chrum.*

Beauty. *Pulchritūdo, ĭnis,* f.

Because. *Quod, quia,* conj. See Lesson LXXX. Because of, *propter,* prep. with acc.

Become. *Fio, fiĕri, factus sum.* Become acquainted with, *cognosco, ĕre, nōvi, nĭtum.*

Befall. *Accĭdo, ĕre, i.*

Before. *Ante,* adv., and prep. with acc.

Begin. *Coepi, isse.* G. 297, I.

Beginning. *Initium, ii,* n.

Behalf, in behalf of. *Pro,* prep. with abl.

Behooves — it behooves. *Oportet, uit.*

Belgians. *Belgae, ārum,* m. pl.

Believe. *Credo, ĕre, dĭdi, dĭtum.* G. 385.

Beneficence. *Beneficentia, ae,* f.

Best. *Optĭmus, a, um.* G. 165. In the best manner, *optĭme,* adv.

Bestow. *Impertio, ĭre, ĭvi* and *ii, ĭtum.* Bestow upon, *confĕro, ferre, tŭli, collātum.*

Betake one's self. *Se conferre (confĕro, ferre, tŭli, collātum); se recipĕre (recĭpio, ĕre, cēpi, ceptum).*

Better. *Melior, ius.* G. 165. Better, preferable, *satius.* See 527.

Between. *Inter,* prep. with acc.

Bird. *Avis, avis,* f.

Bitterly. *Acerbe,* adv.

Blame. *Vitupĕro, āre, āvi, ātum.*

Blessing, good. *Bonum, i,* n.

Blind. *Caecus, a, um.*

Boast. *Glōrior, āri, ātus sum,* dep.

Book. *Liber, bri,* m.

Booty. *Praeda, ae,* f.

Borders, territory. *Fines, ium,* m.pl.

Born for. *Natus, a, um,* with dat., or *ad* with acc.

Both — and. *Et — et.*

Boy. *Puer, puĕri,* m.

Boyhood. See 408. From boyhood, *a puĕro.*

Branch of learning. *Doctrīna, ae,* f.

Brave. *Fortis, e.*

Bravely. *Fortĭter,* adv.

Break, offend against. *Viŏlo, āre, āvi, ātum.*

Bring. *Affĕro, ferre, attŭli, allātum.* Bring, bear, *fero, ferre, tuli, latum.* Bring to, *addūco, ĕre, duxi, ductum.* Bring to a close, *finio, ĭre, ĭvi* and *ii, ĭtum.*

Britain — of or from Great Britain, British. *Britannĭcus, a, um.*

Brother. *Frater, tris,* m.

Brutus. *Brutus, i,* m.

Build, make. *Facio, ĕre, feci, factum.*

Burn, burn up. *Exūro, ĕre, ussi, ustum.* Burn, set fire to, *incendo, ĕre, cendi, censum.*

Business. *Negotium, ii,* n. To have business, *negotium esse,* with dat. of possessor.

Busy, be busy. *Occupatiōne distinēri (distineo, ĕre, ui, tentum).* See 631. How very busy one is, *quanta occupatiōne,* etc.

But. *Sed; autem; vero.* G. 587, III. 2. But not, and not, *neque.*

By. *A, ab,* prep. with abl. By = from, in accordance with, *e, ex,* prep. with abl. By = through, *per,* prep. with acc. By letter, *per littĕras.* By myself, yourself, &c., *mecum,* etc. See 568. By no means, *minĭme,* adv. See 586.

C.

Caesar. *Caesar, ăris,* m.

Caius. *Cāius, ii,* m.

Calamity. *Calamĭtas, ātis,* f.

Call. *Nomĭno, voco, appello, āre, āvi, ātum.* See 184. Call to mind, *commemŏro, āre, āvi, ātum.*

Camillus. *Camillus, i,* m.

Camp. *Castra, ōrum,* n. pl.

Can, could. *Possum, posse, potui.*

Cannae. *Cannae, ārum,* f. pl.

Capable. *Capax, ācis.*

Capture. *Capio, ĕre, cepi, captum.*

Capua. *Capua, ae,* f.

Care — take care. *Caveo, ĕre, cavi, cautum.*

Care, care for. *Curo, āre, āvi, ātum.*

Carefully. *Diligenter,* adv.

Caria. *Caria, ae,* f.

Carry. *Porto, āre, āvi, ātum.*

Carthage. *Carthāgo, ĭnis,* f.

Carthaginian. *Poenus, i,* m.; *Carthaginiensis, is,* m. and f.

Cassius. *Cassius, ii,* m.

Catiline. *Catilīna, ae,* m.

Cato. *Cato, ōnis,* m.

Catulus. *Catŭlus, i,* m.

Cause. *Causa, ae,* f.

Cavalry. *Equitātus, us,* m.

Celebrated. *Clarus, a, um; celĕber, bris, bre.* See 233.

Celestial. *Coelestis, e.* Celestial bodies, *coelestia, ium,* n. pl.

Celts. *Celtae, ārum,* m. pl.

Censor. *Censor, ōris,* m.

Censorship. See 409.

Censure. *Reprehendo, ĕre, di, sum.*

Census — take the census of, *censeo, ĕre, ui, censum.* See 490.

Certain. *Certus, a, um.* A certain, *quidam, quaedam, quoddam* and *quiddam.*

Certainly. *Certe,* adv.

Ceus, of Ceus. *Ceus, a, um.*

Chaeronea. *Chaeronēa, ae,* f.

Change. *Muto, āre, āvi, ātum.*

Characteristic. See 426.

Chariot. *Currus, us,* m.

Cheerfulness. *Hilarĭtas, ātis,* f.

Chief. *Summus, a, um.* G. 163, 3.

Children. *Libĕri, ōrum,* m. pl.

Choice. *Conquisĭtus, a, um.*

Choose, select. *Elĭgo, ĕre, lēgi, lectum.*

Cicero. *Cicĕro, ōnis,* m.

Cimbrian. *Cimbrĭcus, a, um.* A victory over the Cimbrians, *Cimbrĭca victoria.*

Citadel. *Arx, arcis,* f.

Citizen. *Civis, civis,* m. and f.

City. *Urbs, urbis,* f. City walls, walls of the city, *moenia, ium,* n. pl. Founding of the city, *urbs condĭta.* G. 580.

Civil. *Civĭlis, e.* Civil, domestic, *domestĭcus, a, um.* Civil, belonging to the city, *urbānus, a, um.*

Claudius. *Claudius, ii,* m.

Clear. *Clarus, a, um; perspicuus, a, um.*

Cleopatra. *Cleopātra, ae,* f.

Clodius. *Clodius, ii,* m.

Close — bring to a close. *Finio, ĭre, ĭvi* and *ii, ĭtum.*

Coat of mail. *Lorĭca, ae,* f.

Collatinus. *Collatĭnus, i,* m.

Colleague. *Collēga, ae,* m.

Come. *Venio, ĭre, veni, ventum.* Come to the relief of, *subvĕnio, ĭre, vēni, ventum.* G. 386. To come, future, *futūrus, a, um.*

Command. *Impĕro, āre, āvi, ātum.* G. 385. Be in command of, *praesum, esse, fui.* G. 386. At the command of, Pres. Part. of *impĕro* in abl. abs.

Commander. *Imperātor, ōris,* m.

Commend, make acceptable. *Probo, āre, āvi, ātum.*

Commit, do. *Facio, ĕre, feci, factum.* Commit one's self, *se tradĕre; trado, ĕre, dĭdi, dĭtum.* Commit, commit to memory, *edisco, ĕre, didĭci.* Commit to writing, *littĕris mando, āre, āvi, ātum.*

Common. *Commūnis, e.*

Commonwealth. *Res publĭca, rei publĭcae,* f.

Communicate, relate. *Trado, ĕre, dĭdi, dĭtum.* Communicate, converse, *collŏquor, i, locūtus sum,* dep.

Companions — my, &c., companions. *Mei,* etc. G. 441, 1.

Compare. *Confĕro, ferre, tŭli, collātum.*

Compel. *Cogo, ĕre, coēgi, coactum.*

Complain. *Queror, i, questus sum,* dep.

Completely conquer. *Devinco, ĕre, vĭci, victum.*

Conceal. *Celo, āre, āvi, ātum; occulto, āre, āvi, ātum.*

Concede. *Concēdo, ĕre, cessi, cessum.*

Concerning. *De,* prep. with abl.

Concerns, it concerns. *Refert, tŭlit.* G. 408.

Condemn. *Damno, condemno, āre, āvi, ātum.*

Condition, state. *Status, us,* m.

Conducive — be conducive to. *Condūco, ĕre, duxi, ductum.* See 289.

Conduct. *Perdūco, ĕre, duxi, ductum.* Conduct one's self, *se gerĕre (gero, ĕre, gessi, gestum).*

Confess. *Confiteor, ēri, fessus sum,* dep.

Confidence. *Fides, ĕi,* f.

Confirm. *Confirmo, āre, āvi, ātum.*

Connected. *Contĭnens, entis.*

Connection — no connection. *Nihil conjunctum.* See 637.

Conquer. *Vinco, ĕre, vĭci, rictum.* Conquer completely, *devinco, ĕre, vĭci, victum.*

Conscript Fathers. *Patres Conscripti,* m. pl.

Consider. *Cogĭto, āre, āvi, ātum.* Consider as, *arbĭtror, āri, ātus sum,* dep. Consider, judge, *existĭmo, āre, āvi, ātum.*

Consistent—be consistent with one's self. *Sibi consentĭre,* with *ipse, a, um,* in agreement with subject *(consentio, īre, sensi, sensum).*

Consistently. *Convenienter,* adv.

Conspiracy. *Conjuratio, ōnis,* f.

Conspirators. *Conjurāti, ōrum,* m. pl.

Conspire. *Conjūro, āre, āvi, ātum.*

Constantly. *Assiduus, a, um.* G. 443.

Consternation. *Formīdo, ĭnis,* f. See 305.

Consul. *Consul, ŭlis,* m.

Consulship. See 409.

Consult, consult for, consult for the interest of. *Consŭlo, ĕre, ui, sultum.* G. 385, 3.

Contemplate. *Contemplor, āri, ātus sum,* dep.

Contend. *Decerto, āre, āvi, ātum; contendo, ĕre, di, tum.*

Content. *Contentus, a, um.* G. 419, IV.

Contract. *Contraho, ĕre, traxi, tractum.*

Contracted, small. *Angustus, a, um.*

Contrary to. *Contra, praeter,* prep. with acc.

Conversation. *Sermo, ōnis,* m.

Convict. *Convinco, ĕre, vĭci, victum.*

Corinth. *Corinthus, i,* f.

Correctly. *Recte,* adv.

Costly. *Pretiōsus, a, um.*

Could, can. *Possum, posse, potui.*

Counsel. *Consĭlium, ii,* n.

Country. *Patria, ae,* f.; *rus, ruris,* n.; *ager, agri,* m. See 245. From the country, in the country. G. 424, 2.

Courage. *Virtus, ūtis,* f.; *anĭmus, i,* m.

Course — to follow this course. *Hoc sequor, i, secūtus sum,* dep.

Cover, clothe. *Vestio, īre, īvi* and *ii, ītum.*

Crassus. *Crassus, i,* m.

Credit. *Fides, ĕi,* f.

Crime. *Scelus, ĕris,* n.

Cross. *Transeo, īre, ii, ĭtum.*

Crotona. *Croto, ōnis,* m. and f.

Crown. *Corōna, ae,* f.

Cruelty. *Crudelĭtas, ātis,* f.

Cultivate. *Colo, ĕre, colui, cultum.*

Culture. *Cultus, us,* m.

Curio. *Curio, ōnis,* m.

Curtius. *Curtius, ii,* m.

Custom, habit. *Consuetūdo, ĭnis,* f.; *mos, moris,* m. See 167.

Cypselus. *Cypsĕlus, i,* m.

D:

Daily. *In dies, in dies singŭlos; quotidie.* See 399.

Danger. *Pericŭlum, i,* n.

Dare. *Audeo, ĕre, ausus sum.*

Dated. *Datus, a, um.* See 366.

Day. *Dies, ĕi,* m. and f. G. 120. Day before, *pridie,* adv. First day of the month, *calendae, ārum,* f. pl. Fifth day of the month (generally), *nonae, ārum,* f. pl. G. 708, I. 2. Seventh day of the month in March, May, July, and October, *nonae, ārum,* f. pl. G. 708, I. 2. Three days, *triduum, ui,* n. From day to day, *in dies.*

Dear. *Carus, a, um.*

Death. *Mors, mortis,* f. Put to death, *occĭdo, ĕre, cĭdi,· cīsum; interfĭcio, ĕre, fēci, fectum.*

Debt. *Aes aliēnum,* n. See 454.

Decree. *Consultum, i,* n.

Deed. *Factum, i,* n. Deed, thing, *res, rei,* f. Good deed, *recte factum.* See 366.

Defence. *Praesidium, ii,* n.

Defend. *Defendo, ĕre, di, sum.* Defend, guard, *tueor, ĕri, ĭtus sum,* dep.

Defendant. *Reus, i,* m.

Define. *Defĭnio, ĭre, īvi, ĭtum.*

Delight. *Delecto, oblecto, āre, āvi, ātum.*

Delightful. *Dulcis, e.*

Deliver, give over. *Trado, ĕre, dĭdi, dĭtum.* Deliver (an oration), *habeo, ĕre, ui, ĭtum.*

Delphic. *Delphĭcus, a, um.*

Demand. *Postŭlo, āre, āvi, ātum.*

Demaratus. *Demarātus, i,* m.

Demosthenes. *Demosthĕnes, is,* m.

Deny. *Nego, āre, āvi, ātum.*

Depart, depart from. *Discēdo, ĕre, cessi, cessum.* Depart, go from, *exeo, ĭre, ii, ĭtum.* Depart, set out, *proficiscor, i, profectus sum.* Depart, go, *eo, ire, ivi, itum.*

Depend upon. *Posĭtus, a, um, esse, in* with abl. See 560.

Desert. *Desĕro, ĕre, sorui, sertum.*

Deserve. *Mereo, ĕre, ui, ĭtum; mereor, ēri, ĭtus sum,* dep. Deserve is often rendered by the Pass. Per. Conj. See G. 231.

Design. *Consilium, ii,* n.

Desirable. *Optabĭlis, e.*

Desire. *Cupidĭtas, ātis,* f.; *libĭdo, ĭnis,* f. According to one's desire, *ex sententia.* See 339.

Desire, to desire. *Cupio, ĕre, ĭvi, ĭtum; opto, āre, āvi, ātum; volo, velle, volui.* See 618.

Desirous of. *Cupĭdus, a, um; studiōsus, a, um.* Very desirous, greedy, *avĭdus, a, um.* See 222.

Despair of. *Despēro, āre, āvi, ātum,* with acc., or *de* with abl.

Despise. *Contemno, ĕre, tempsi, temptum.*

Destitute of. *Expers, tis.* To be destitute of, *egeo, indĭgeo, ĕre, ui.* See 239.

Destroy. *Deleo, ĕre, ēvi, ētum.*

Deter. *Deterreo, ĕre, ui, ĭtum.*

Detriment. *Detrimentum, i,* n.

Devise. *Invĕnio, ĭre, vēni, ventum.*

Devote one's self to. *Studeo, ĕre, ui; G. 385; incumbo, ĕre, cubui, cubĭtum, in* with acc. Devote one's self to, apply one's self to, *se conferre in* or *ad* with acc. (*confĕro, ferre, tŭli, collātum*).

Dictate. *Dicto, āre, āvi, ātum.*

Die. *Morior, i, mortuus sum,* dep.

Difference — there is a difference. *Intĕrest, fuit.*

Differently. *Alĭter,* adv.

Difficult. *Diffĭcĭlis, e.*

Dignity. *Dignĭtas, ātis,* f.

Diligence. *Diligentia, ae,* f.

Diligent. *Dilĭgens, entis.*

Diligently. *Diligenter,* adv.

Diminish. *Minuo, ĕre, ui, ūtum.*

Dine. *Coeno, āre, āvi, ātum.*

Dinner. *Coena, ae,* f.

Dion. *Dio* or *Dion, ōnis,* m.

Dionysius. *Dionysius, ii,* m.

Disagree. *Dissentio, ĭre, sensi, sensum.*

Discharge, fulfil. *Fungor, i, functus sum*, dep.

Discord. *Discordia, ae*, f.

Discourse. *Oratio, ōnis*, f.

Disgraceful. *Turpis, e.*

Disguise. *Dissimŭlo, āre, āvi, ātum.*

Displease. *Displĭceo, ēre, ui, ĭtum.* G. 385.

Dissension. *Dissidium, ii*, n.

Distinguished. *Clarus, a, um.* See 233.

Distrusting. *Diffĭsus, a, um.* See 625.

Divide. *Divĭdo, ĕre, vīsi, vīsum.*

Divine. *Divīnus, a, um.*

Do. *Facio, ĕre, feci, factum ; ago, ĕre, egi, actum.* Do, perform, *gero, ĕre, gessi, gestum.* Is doing, is done, *agĭtur, gerĭtur.*

Domestic. *Domestĭcus, a, um.*

Doubt — there is no doubt. *Non dubium est.* See 322.

Doubt, to doubt. *Dubĭto, āre, āvi, ātum.*

Doubtful. *Dubius, a, um.*

Dream. *Somnium, ii*, n.

Drive. *Pello, ĕre, pepŭli, pulsum.* Drive, cast out, *ejĭcio, ĕre, jēci, jectum.*

Due — one's due. *Suum, i*, n. G. 441.

Duillius. *Duillius, ii*, m.

Dumnorix. *Dumnŏrix, ĭgis*, m.

During, in. *In*, prep. with abl.

Dutiful affection. *Piĕtas, ātis*, f.

Duty. *Officium, ii*, n. To be the duty of, often rendered by the Pred. Gen. See 426; also G. 404, 1.

E.

Each, every. *Quisque, quaeque, quodque* and *quicque* or *quidque.* One each, *singŭli, ae, a.* Each topic, *quidque.*

Eager. *Alăcer, cris, cre ; studiōsus, a, um ; avĭdus, a, um.* See 222.

Eagerly. *Cupĭde ; vehementer*, adv.

Eagle. *Aquĭla, ae*, f.

Ear. *Auris, auris*, f.

Early, ancient. *Antĭquus, a, um.* Early in the morning, *mane*, adv.

Easily. *Facĭle*, adv.

Easy. *Facĭlis, e.*

Eclipse. *Defectio, ōnis*, f.

Edifice. *Aedes, is*, f. G. 132.

Egypt. *Aegyptus, i*, f.

Eighth of November. *Ante diem sextum idus Novembres (a. d. VI. id. Nov.).* G. 708.

Eighty. *Octoginta*, indecl.

Either — or. *Aut — aut ; vel — vel.* G. 587, II. 2.

Elated — be elated. *Effĕror, ferri, elātus sum*, pass. of *effĕro.*

Elegance. *Elegantia, ae*, f.

Elegantly. *Polīte*, adv.

Eloquence. *Eloquentia, ae*, f.

Eloquent. *Elŏquens, entis.*

Eminent, excelling. *Excellens, entis.* To be eminent, *unus, a, um, emĭneo, ĕre, ui ;* or *emineo* alone.

Emolument. *Emolumentum, i*, n.

Empire. *Imperium, ii*, n.

Enact. *Sancio, īre, sanxi, sanctum.* Enact, write, *scribo, ĕre, scripsi, scriptum.*

Encamp. *Castra pono, ĕre, posui, posĭtum.*

Encounter. *Subeo, obeo, īre, ii, ĭtum ; oppĕto, ĕre, petīvi* or *ii, ĭtum.*

Endeavor. *Conor, āri, ātus sum*, dep.

Endowed with. *Praedĭtus, a, um.* G. 419, III.

Endure. *Fero, ferre, tuli, latum.*

Enemy. *Hostis, is*, m. and f. ; *inimīcus, i*, m. See 344.

Engaged — be engaged in. *Sum, esse, fui, in* with abl. See 534.

Engagement, fight. *Proelium, ii*, n. ; *pugna, ae*, f. See 256. Naval engagement, *pugna navālis.*

Enjoy. *Fruor, i, fructus* and *fruĭtus sum*, dep. G. 419, I.

Enjoyment. *Delectatio, ōnis*, f.

Enlarge. *Amplio, āre, āvi, ātum.*

Ennius. *Ennius, ii*, m.

Entertain, hold. *Teneo, ēre, ui,*

tentum. Entertain gratitude, *gratiam habeo, ēre, ui, ĭtum.* See 548. Entertain the same sentiments, *eădem sentio, īre, sensi, sensum.*

Entertainment. *Convivium, ii,* n.

Entirely. *Omnīno,* adv.; *totus, a, um.* G. 149; 443.

Entitle. *Inscrĭbo, ēre, scripsi, scriptum.*

Envy, to look upon with envy. *Invĭdeo, ēre, vĭdi, vīsum.*

Epaminondas. *Epaminondas,ae,*m.

Ephesus. *Ephĕsus, i,* f.

Epicurus. *Epicūrus, i,* m.

Equal. *Par, paris.*

Equity. *Aequĭtas, ātis,* f.

Erudition. *Eruditio, ōnis,* f.

Escape. *Effŭgio, ēre, fŭgi.*

Especially. *Maxĭme, praesertim,* adv.

Establish. *Firmo, confirmo, āre, āvi, ātum.*

Established — firmly established. *Firmus, a, um.*

Esteem. *Aestĭmo, āre, āvi, ātum ; facio, ĕre, feci, factum.* Esteem lightly, despise, *contemno, ĕre, tempsi, temptum.*

Eternal. *Sempiternus, a, um.*

Etruria. *Etruria, ae,* f.

Even. *Etiam,* adv. Even if, *etiamsi,* conj. G. 516, III.

Evening. *Vesper, ĕris,* m. In the evening, *vespĕri.*

Event, issue. *Eventus, us,* m. Event, thing, *res, rei,* f.

Ever. *Unquam,* adv. Ever = always, *semper,* adv. For ever, *in perpetuum.*

Every. *Quisque, quaeque, quodque* and *quicque* or *quidque; omnis, e.*

Evident — be evident. *Consto, āre, stĭti, stătum.*

Evil. *Malum, i,* n.

Exalted, most exalted. *Summus, a, um.* G. 163, 3.

Example. *Exemplum, i,* n.

Exceedingly. *Vehementer, valde,* adv.

Excel. *Excello, ēre, cellui, celsum.*

Excellence, goodness. *Bonĭtas, ātis,* f.

Excellent. *Praeclārus, a, um.* Excellent, good, *bonus, a, um.*

Excellently. *Excellenter,* adv.

Excelling. *Excellens, entis.*

Except. *Praeter,* prep. with acc.

Exception — without exception. *Unus, a, um.* G. 176, 1.

Excessive. *Nimius, a, um.*

Excite. *Excĭto, āre, āvi, ātum.*

Exercise. *Exerceo, ēre, ui, ĭtum.*

Exertion, zeal. *Studium, ii,* n. Exertion, attention, *opĕra, ae,* f.

Exhort. *Hortor, cohortor, āri, ātus sum,* dep.

Exile. *Exsilium, ii,* n.

Exist. *Sum, esse, fui.*

Expect. *Exspecto, āre, āvi, ātum.* To be expected to; rendered by the Act. Periphrast. Conj. G. 228.

Expectation, opinion. *Opinio, ōnis,* f.

Expel. *Expello, ēre, pŭli, pulsum.*

Experience. *Usus, us,* m.

Expose one's self. *Se opponĕre* (*oppōno, ĕre, posui, posĭtum*).

Express, utter. *Elŏquor, i, locūtus sum,* dep. Express opinion, think, *censeo, ēre, ui, censum.* See 576. Express thanks, *gratias ago, ĕre, egi, actum.* See 548.

Extol. *Extollo, ēre,* with *laudĭbus* or *laudando.*

Eye. *Ocŭlus, i,* m.

F.

Fabius. *Fabius, ii,* m.

Fable. *Fabŭla, ae,* f.

Fabricius. *Fabricius, ii,* m.

Faesulae. *Faesŭlae, ārum,* f. pl.

Fail. *Defĭcio, ēre, fēci, fectum.*

Faith. *Fides, ĕi,* f.

False. *Falsus, a, um.*

Familiarly. *Familiarĭter,* adv.

Famous. *Clarus, a, um.* The

famous, sometimes rendered by *ille, a, ud.* G. 450, 4.

Far — so far. *Tantum*, adv. So far am I from, *tantum abest ut* with subj. See 498. Thus far, *adhuc*, adv.

Father. *Pater, tris,* m. Conscript Fathers, *Patres Conscripti,* m. pl.

Fault. *Culpa, ae,* f.

Favor. *Beneficium, ii,* n. To require a favor, *gratiam refĕro, ferre, tŭli, lātum.* See 548.

Favor, to favor. *Faveo, ĕre, favi, fautum.* G. 385.

Fear. *Metus, us,* m.; *timor, ōris,* m. See 305.

Fear, to fear. *Metuo, ĕre, ui; timeo, ĕre, ui; vereor, ĕri, verĭtus sum,* dep. Fear greatly, *pertimesco, ĕre, timui.*

Feast. *Epŭlae, ārum,* f. pl.

Feel the need of. *Indĭgeo, ĕre, ui.* See 239, I.; also G. 419, III.; 409, 1.

Feeling of admiration. *Admiratio, ōnis,* f.

Few. *Pauci, ae, a,* pl.

Fidelity. *Fidelĭtas, ātis,* f.; *fides, ĕi,* f.

Field. *Ager, agri,* m.

Fifth. *Quintus, a, um.* Fifth day of the month (generally), *Nonae, ārum,* f. pl. G. 708, I. 2.

Fiftieth. *Quinquagesĭmus, a, um.*

Fight, battle. *Pugna, ae,* f.

Fight, to fight. *Pugno, āre, āvi, ātum.* Fight (a battle), lit. *make, facio, ĕre, feci, factum.* See 257. A battle is fought, *pugnātur, ātum est.*

Fill. *Compleo, ĕre, ēvi, ētum.*

Find, by accident. *Invĕnio, ĭre, vēni, ventum.* Find, by search, *repĕrio, ĭre, pĕri, pertum.*

Finish, bring to a close. *Finio, ĭre, ĭvi* and *ii, ĭtum.*

Fire. *Ignis, is,* m. Set fire to, *inflammo, āre, āvi, ātum; incendo, ĕre, di, sum.* With fire and sword, *ferro ignĕque.* See 117.

Firmly established. *Firmus, a, um.*

First. *Primus, a, um.* First, for the first time, *primum,* adv. First day of the month, *Calendae, ārum,* f. pl.

Fitting — it is fitting. *Oportet, uit,* impers.

Five. *Quinque,* indecl.

Flaccus. *Flaccus, i,* m.

Flee. *Fugio, ĕre, fugi, fugĭtum; profŭgio, ĕre, fūgi.*

Flight. *Fuga, ae,* f.

Flourishing. *Florens, entis.*

Flow into. *Influo, ĕre, fluxi, fluxum.*

Foe. *Inimīcus, i,* m.

Follow. *Sequor, consĕquor, i, secūtus sum,* dep. Follow this course, *hoc sequor.*

Folly. *Stultitia, ae,* f. Surpass the folly of, *esse dementior.* See 480.

Fond of. *Amans, antis; cupĭdus, a, um; dilĭgens, entis.*

Foolish. *Demens, entis.*

For, prep. *Pro,* prep. with abl. For = about, concerning, *de,* prep. with abl. For = against, *in,* prep. with acc. For — because of, *propter,* prep. with acc. For = during, *per,* prep. with acc. For = to secure, *ad,* prep. with acc. For after *idoneus, parātus,* etc., *ad,* prep. with acc. For ever, *in perpetuum.* For his, &c., own sake, *propter sese (se).* For my, &c., sake, *mea causa,* etc. G. 414, 2, 3). For the purpose of, for the sake of, *causa* or *gratia* with gen. G. 414, 2, 3). For a long time, *jamdŭdum; jampridem.* G. 467, 2. For the first time, *primum,* adv. For the reason that, *propterea quod.*

For, conj. *Enim, nam,* conj.

Force. *Vis, vis,* f.; frequently used in pl. *vires, ium.* A force, forces, *copiae, ārum,* f. pl. To be in force, *vigeo, ĕre, vigui.*

Forced marches. *Magna itinĕra,* n. pl. See 246.

Ford. *Vadum, i,* n.

Forefathers. *Majōres, um,* pl.

Forget. *Obliviscor, i, oblitus sum,* dep. G. 406, II.

Form, make. *Facio, ĕre, feci, factum.*

Formerly. *Quondam, antea,* adv.

Forth — set forth. *Exprŏmo, ĕre, prompsi, promptum.* Set forth views, state, *praedico, āre, āvi, ātum.*

Fortify. *Munio, ire, ivi* and *ii, itum.*

Fortitude. *Fortitūdo, inis,* f.

Fortunate. *Fortunātus, a, um.*

Fortune. *Fortūna, ae,* f. To be one's good fortune, *contingo, ĕre, tigi, tactum.*

Forty. *Quadraginta,* indecl.

Forum. *Forum, i,* n.

Forward — look forward to. *Exspecto, āre, āvi, ātum.*

Found. *Condo, ĕre, didi, ditum.*

Founding of the city. *Urbs condita.* G. 580.

Four. *Quattuor,* indecl.

Fourth. *Quartus, a, um.*

Free. *Liber, ĕra, ĕrum.* To be free from, *vaco, āre, āvi, ātum; careo, ĕre, ui, itum; egeo, ĕre, ui.* See 239, I.

Free from. *Libĕro, āre, āvi, ātum.* G. 425, 3, 2).

Frequently. *Saepe, crebro,* adv.; *frequens, entis.* G. 443.

Friend. *Amicus, i,* m. My, &c., friends, *mei, ōrum,* etc., m. pl. G. 441, 1. Friend of the people, *populāris, is,* m. and f.

Friendly. *Amicus, a, um.*

Friendship. *Amicitia, ae,* f.

From. *A, ab; e, ex;* prep. with abl. G. 434, 3. From, after verbs of hindering, *quominus,* conj. G. 499. From boyhood, *a puĕro.* From day to day, *in dies.* From that place, thence, *inde,* adv.

Fulfil. *Fungor, i, functus sum,* dep. G. 419, I.

Full, in full numbers. *Frequens, entis.*

Fully — more fully. *Plurĭbus verbis.* See 514.

Furnish. *Orno, āre, āvi, ātum.*

G.

Gain. *Emolumentum, i,* n.

Game. *Ludus, i,* m.

Garden. *Hortus, i,* m.

Gate. *Porta, ae,* f.

Gaul. *Gallia, ae,* f.

Gaul, a Gaul. *Gallus, i,* m.

General. *Imperātor, ōris,* m.

Geneva. *Genĕva, ae,* f.

Genius. *Ingenium, ii,* n.

German. *Germānus, i,* m.

Gift. *Donum, i,* n.

Give. *Do, dare, dedi, datum.* Give, deliver, *trado, ĕre, didi, ditum.* Give, confer, *confĕro, ferre, tuli, collātum.* Give advice, *suadeo, ĕre, suasi, suasum.* G. 385. Give heed, *opĕram do, dare, dedi, datum.* Give precepts, *praecipio, ĕre, cĕpi, ceptum.*

Gladly. *Laete,* adv.

Glorious. *Gloriōsus, a, um.*

Glory. *Gloria, ae,* f.

Glory in. *Glorior, āri, ātus sum,* dep.

Go. *Eo, ire, ivi* and *ii, itum.* Go from, *exeo, ire, ii, itum.*

God. *Deus, i,* m. G. 45, 6.

Gold. *Aurum, i,* n.

Golden. *Aureus, a, um.*

Good. *Bonus, a, um.* Good deed, *recte factum,* n. See 366. Good will, *benevolentia, ae,* f. To be one's good fortune, *contingo, ĕre, tigi, tactum.*

Good, a good. *Bonum, i,* n.

Goodness. *Bonitas, ātis,* f.

Gorgias. *Gorgias, ae,* m.

Govern. *Guberno, āre, āvi, ātum; rego, ĕre, rexi, rectum.*

Government. *Regnum, i,* n.

Gracchus. *Gracchus, i,* m.

Grain. *Frumentum, i,* n.

Grandson. *Nepos, ōtis,* m.

Grateful — be grateful. *Gratiam habeo, ēre, ui, ĭtum.* See 548.

Gratitude. *Gratia, ae,* f. To entertain gratitude, *gratiam habeo, ēre, ui, ĭtum.*

Gravity. *Gravĭtas, ātis,* f.

Great. *Magnus, a, um.* Great, illustrious, *amplus, a, um.* Great, severe, *gravis, e.* How great, *quantus, a, um.* So great, *tantus, a, um.*

Great Britain — of or from Great Britain. *Britannĭcus, a, um.*

Greater. *Major, us.* G. 165. Of greater value, *pluris.* G. 402, III. 1. To render a greater service, *plus prosum, prodesse, profui.* G. 290.

Greatest. *Maxĭmus, a, um.* G. 165. Greatest (in rank), highest, *summus, a, um.* G. 163, 3.

Greatly. *Valde, magnopĕre,* adv. Greatly, with *intĕrest* and *refert, magni.* G. 408, 3.

Greece. *Graecia, ae,* f.

Greedy. *Avĭdus, a, um.*

Greek. *Graecus, a, um.*

Greek, a Greek. *Graecus, i,* m.

Greek, in Greek. *Graece,* adv.

Grieve. *Doleo, ēre, ui, ĭtum.*

Guard — be on one's guard. *Caveo, ēre, cavi, cautum.*

Guard, to guard. *Custōdio, īre, ivi* and *ii, ĭtum.* Guard, defend, *tueor, ēri, ĭtus sum,* dep.

Guidance — under the guidance of. *Dux, ducis,* in abl. abs.

Guide. *Dux, ducis,* m. and f.

H.

Habit. *Consuetūdo, ĭnis,* f. See 167.

Hand. *Manus, us,* f.

Hannibal. *Hannĭbal, ălis,* m.

Happen. *Fio, fiĕri, factus sum,* dep. Happen, of desirable occurrences, *contingo, ĕre, tĭgi, tactum.* Of undesirable, *accĭdo, ĕre, cĭdi.* See 624.

Happily. *Beāte, felicĭter,* adv.

Happiness, success. *Felicĭtas, ātis,* f.

Happy. *Beātus, a, um.*

Harm. *Injuria, ae,* f.

Harmony. *Concordia, ae,* f.

Hasten. *Contendo, ĕre, di, tum.*

Hate. *Odi, odisse.* G. 297, I.

Hatred. *Odium, ii,* n.

Have. *Habeo, ēre, ui, ĭtum ; sum, esse, fui,* with dat. of possessor. To have business, *negotium esse,* with dat. of possessor. To have confidence in, *fidem habeo, ēre, ui, ĭtum* with dat. To have a prosperous voyage, *ex sententia navĭgo, āre, āvi, ātum.* See 339. To have reference to, *refĕror, ferri, lātus sum, ad* with acc. See 577.

He, she, &c. *Is, ea, id.* He himself, &c., *ipse, a, um.* He, &c., he also = the same, *idem, eădem, idem.* He, &c. = this one, *hic, haec, hoc.*

Health. *Valetūdo, ĭnis,* f.

Hear. *Audio, īre, ĭvi, ĭtum.*

Hearer. *Audiens, entis,* m. and f. ; *audĭtor, ōris,* m. ; *is qui audit.* See 438.

Hearing, in the hearing of, pres. part. of *audio* in abl. absol. See 555.

Heaven, heavens. *Coelum, i,* n.

Heavy. *Gravis, e.*

Heed, give heed to. *Opĕram do, dare, dedi, datum.*

Held, to be held = to be. *Sum, esse, fui.*

Helvetian. *Helvetius, a, um.*

Helvetians. *Helvetii, ōrum,* m. pl.

Herald. *Praeco, ōnis,* m.

Here. *Hic,* adv.

Hero. *Vir, viri,* m.

Herodotus. *Herodōtus, i,* m.

Hesitate. *Dubĭto, āre, āvi, ātum.*

High. *Altus, a, um.* High, ample, *amplus, a, um.* High, great (price), *magnus, a, um.* At a high price, *magno.* G. 416.

Highest, of the highest degree. *Summus, a, um.* G. 163, 3.

Highest results, *summa, ŏrum,* n. pl. G. 441, 1. Highest welfare of the state, highest public welfare, *summa res publīca.*

Highly, with verbs of valuing. *Magni.* Very highly, *maxĭmi.* More highly, *pluris.* How highly, *quanti.* G. 402, III. 1.

Himself. *Sui, sibi.* Himself, intensive, *ipse, a, um.* By himself, *secum.*

Hippias. *Hippias, ae,* m.

His. *Suus, a, um;* not reflexive, *ejus.* See 468, 2. His own things, productions, *sua, ŏrum,* n. pl. G. 441, 1.

History. *Historia, ae,* f.

Hold. *Teneo, ĕre, ui, tentum.* Have, *habeo, ĕre, ui, ĭtum.*

Home. *Domus, i,* f. G. 117, 1.

Homer. *Homĕrus, i,* m.

Honestly. *Honeste,* adv.

Honor. *Honor, ŏris,* m.; *honestas, ātis,* f.

Honorable. *Honestus, a, um.*

Hope. *Spes, spei,* f.

Hope; to hope. *Spero, āre, āvi, ātum.*

Horse. *Equus, equi,* m.

Hortensius. *Hortensius, ii,* m.

Hostile. *Inimīcus, a, um.*

Hostility, enmity. *Odium, ii,* n.

Hour. *Hora, ae,* f.

House, one's house. *Domus, us* and *i,* f. G. 117, 1. Walls of my, &c., house, *mei parĭĕtes,* etc. See 378.

How. *Quam,* adv. How great, how large, *quantus, a, um.* How highly, with verbs of valuing, *quanti.* G. 402, III. 1. How long, *quousque,* adv. How many, *quot,* indecl. How very busy one is, *quanta occupatiŏne distĭnētur (distĭneo, ĕre, ui, tentum).* See 631.

However. *Quamvis,* adv. However much, *quantumvis,* adv.

Hundred. *Centum,* indecl.

I.

I. *Ego, mei.* I, emphatic, *egŏmet.* G. 184, 3. I myself, *ipse, a, um.* I would that, *utĭnam,* adv. G. 488, 1.

Ides. *Idus, uum,* f. pl. G. 708, I. 3.

If. *Si,* conj. See Lesson LXXVII. If only, *dummŏdo,* conj. If any, *si quis.* G. 190, 2.

Ignorance — keep in ignorance. *Celo, āre, āvi, ātum.* G. 374, 2, 1); 3, 1).

Ignorant — be ignorant of. *Ignōro, āre, āvi, ātum.* To keep ignorant of, in regard to, *celo, āre, āvi, ātum, de* with abl. G. 374, 3, 1).

Illustrious. *Illustris, e.* Most illustrious, highest, *summus, a, um.* G. 163, 3.

Imitate. *Imĭtor, āri, ātus sum,*dep.

Immediately. *Jam,* adv.

Immense. *Ingens, entis.*

Immortal. *Immortālis, e.*

Impel. *Impello, ĕre, pŭli, pulsum.* Impel, incite, *concĭto, āre, āvi, ātum.*

Impious. *Impius, a, um.*

Implore. *Oro, āre, āvi, ātum.*

Important, great. *Magnus, a, um.* It is important, *intĕrest, fuit.* G. 408.

Impose upon. *Impōno, ĕre, posui, 'posĭtum.*

Impudence. *Impudentia, ae,* f.

In. *In,* prep. with abl. In accordance with, *e, ex,* prep. with abl. In behalf of, *pro,* prep. with abl. In regard to, *de,* prep. with abl.; sometimes rendered by the gen. In = situated in, *posĭtus, a, um, in* with abl. In the censorship, consulship, life, reign, etc., of. See 409. In the presence of, *apud,* prep. with acc. In the vicinity of, *ad,* prep. with acc. In a spirited manner, *acrĭter,* adv. In full numbers, *frequens, entis.* In vain, *frustra; nequidquam,* adv. See 838.

Inaction, inactivity. *Inertia, ae,* f.

Incite. *Incito, āre, āvi, ātum.*

Inclined. *Propensus, a, um.*

Increase, intrans. *Cresco, ĕre, crevi, cretum;* trans., *augeo, ĕre, auxi, auctum.*

Incursion. *Incursio, ōnis,* f.

Indeed. *Quidem; enim; tandem;* adv. See 606. Indeed I, &c. See 514.

Individual, one. *Unus, a, um.* G. 176, 1.

Induce. *Indūco, ĕre, duxi, ductum.*

Industry. *Industria, ae,* f.

Infer. *Colligo, ĕre, lĕgi, lectum.*

Influence. *Indūco, addūco, ĕre, duxi, ductum.*

Inform. *Certiōrem facio, ĕre, feci, factum.* See 527. Inform, teach, *doceo, ĕre, ui, doctum.*

Inhabitant. *Incŏla, ae,* m. and f.

Injure. *Noceo, ĕre, ui, ĭtum.* G. 385.

Injury. *Injuria, ae,* f.

Inner. *Interior, ius.* G. 166.

Innocence. *Innocentia, ae,* f.

Innumerable. *Innumerabĭlis, e.*

Inquire. *Quaero, ĕre, quaesivi, ĭtum.*

Inscribe. *Inscrībo, ĕre, scripsi, scriptum.*

Insolence. *Insolentia, ae,* f.

Instance, thing. *Res, rei,* f.

Instruct. *Erūdio, īre, īvi* and *ii, ĭtum.* Instruct, teach, *doceo, ĕre, docui, doctum.*

Instructor. *Praeceptor, ōris,* m.

Integrity. *Integrĭtas, ātis,* f.

Intention — be one's intention. *In anĭmo sum, esse, fui,* with dat. of possessor. See 206.

Interest — object of interest. *Quod visendum est.* See 527.

Interests, advantage. *Utilĭtas, ātis,* f.

Interests, it interests. *Intĕrest, fuit.* G. 408.

Interrupt. *Interpello, āre, āvi, ātum.*

Intimate—a very intimate acquaint-

ance. *Summus usus.* To be intimate with, *familiarĭter utor, i, usus sum,* dep. G. 419, I.

Into. *In,* prep. with acc.

Introduce, bring in. *Indūco, ĕre, duxi, ductum.*

Invent, devise. *Fingo, ĕre, finxi, fictum.* See 605.

Invention. *Inventum, i,* n.

Invite. *Voco, āre, āvi, ātum;* see 184, 2; *invito, āre, āvi, ātum.*

Is doing, is done. *Agĭtur; gerĭtur.*

Island. *Insŭla, ae,* f.

Isocrates. *Isocrătes, is,* m.

It. *Is, ea, id; ille, a, ud.* It itself, *ipse, a, um.* It, the same thing, *idem, eădem, idem.* Its, *suus, a, um; ejus.* See 468, 2.

Italy. *Italia, ae,* f.

Itself. *Sui, sibi;* intensive, *ipse, a, um.*

J.

Journey. *Iter, itinĕris,* n.

Joy. *Gaudium, ii,* n.; *laetitia, ae,* f. See 294.

Joyful. *Laetus, a, um.*

Judge. *Judex, ĭcis,* m.

Judge, to judge. *Judĭco, āre, āvi, ātum.* Judge, consider, *existĭmo, āre, āvi, ātum.*

July — sixth of July. *Pridie Nonas Quintĭles.* G. 708; 437, 1.

July — of July. *Quintĭlis, e.*

June — of June. *Junius, a, um.*

Junius. *Junius, ii,* m.

Jupiter. *Jupĭter, Jovis,* m.

Just. *Justus, a, um.* Just, with numbers, *ipse, a, um.* G. 452, 3.

Justice. *Justitia, ae,* f.

Justly. *Juste,* adv.

K.

Keep. *Servo, āre, āvi, ātum.* Keep from, *prohibeo, ĕre, ui, ĭtum.* Keep from, keep off, *arceo, ĕre, ui, arctum.* G. 425, 2, 2). Keep in ignorance, *celo, āre, āvi, ātum.* G. 374, 2, 1); 3, 1). Keep ignorant of, in regard to, *celo, āre, āvi, ātum, de* with abl. G. 374, 3, 1).

Kill. *Enĕco, āre, ui, nectum.*

Kind. *Benignus, a, um.*

Kind, class. *Genus, ĕris,* n. Every kind, *omne genus,* n.

Kindness. *Benignĭtas, ātis,* f.

King. *Rex, regis,* m.

Know, know how. *Scio, scire, scivi, scitum.* Know, be acquainted with, *cognosco, ĕre, nōvi, nĭtum.* Know, comprehend, *percĭpio, ĕre, cĕpi, ceptum.* Know, understand, *intellĭgo, ĕre, lexi, lectum.* Not to know, *nescio, ĭre, ĭvi* and *ii, ĭtum.*

Knowledge. *Scientia, ae,* f. See also Note on 638, 7, page 276. Practical knowledge, *usus, us,* m.

Known — well known, sometimes rendered by *ille, a, ud.* G. 450, 4.

L.

Labienus. *Labiēnus, i,* m.

Labor. *Labor, ōris,* m.

Lacedaemonian. *Lacedaemonius, ii,* m.

Laelius. *Laelius, ii,* m.

Lake. *Lacus, us,* m.

Land. *Terra, ae,* f. On sea and land, *terra marĭque.*

Language, tongue. *Lingua, ae,* f.

Large. *Magnus, a, um.* How large, *quantus, a, um.*

Lasting. *Sempiternus, a, um.*

Latin, in Latin. *Latīne,* adv.

Law. *Lex, legis,* f.; *jus, juris,* n. See 405. Civil law, *jus civĭle.* The law of nations, *jus gentium.*

Lawful — it is lawful. *Licet, licuit* and *licĭtum est,* impers.

Lawgiver. *Is qui leges scribit* (*scribo, ĕre, scripsi, scriptum*). See 438.

Lay waste. *Vasto, āre, āvi, ātum.*

Lead. *Duco, ĕre, duxi, ductum.* Lead across, *tradūco, ĕre, duxi,*

ductum. Lead on, *addūco, ĕre, duxi, ductum.* Lead out, *edūco, ĕre, duxi, ductum.* Lead (a life), live, *vivo, ĕre, vixi, victum.*

Leader. *Dux, ducis,* m. and f.

Learn. *Disco, ĕre, didĭci.* Learn, receive, hear, *accĭpio, ĕre, cĕpi, ceptum.*

Learned. *Doctus, a, um.* Learned, of learning, *doctrĭnae.* See 440, 2.

Learning. *Doctrĭna, ae,* f.; *erudĭtio, ōnis,* f. Branch of learning, *doctrĭna, ae,* f.

Least. *Minĭmus, a, um;* G. 165; *minĭme,* adv.

Leisure. *Otium, ii,* n. At leisure, *otiōsus, a, um.*

Leisure, unoccupied. *Vacuus, a, um.*

Lemannus. *Lemannus, i,* m.

Length — at length. *Tandem,* adv.

Leonidas. *Leonĭdas, ae,* m.

Leontini — of Leontini, Leontine. *Leontīnus, a, um.*

Less. *Minor, us;* G. 165; *minus,* adv.

Let = cause that. *Facio, ĕre, feci, factum, ut* with subj.

Letter of the alphabet. *Littĕra, ae,* f. Letter, epistle, *epistŏla, ae,* f.; *littĕrae, ārum,* f. pl. See 200. By letter, *per littĕras.* Letter from me, &c., *mea epistŏla,* or *epistŏla a me,* etc. See 366. Letters, literature, *littĕrae, ārum,* f. pl.

Leuctra. *Leuctra, ōrum,* n. pl. Of Leuctra, Leuctrian, *Leuctrĭcus, a, um.*

Liberal. *Liberālis, e.*

Liberality. *Liberalĭtas, ātis,* f.

Liberate. *Libĕro, āre, āvi, ātum.* G. 425, 8, 2).

Liberty. *Libertas, ātis,* f.

Life. *Vita, ae,* f. Period of life, *aetas, ātis,* f.

Light. *Lux, lucis,* f.

Lighten. *Levo, āre, āvi, ātum.*

Lightly. *Levĭter,* adv. Esteem lightly, despise, *contemno, ĕre, tempsi, temptum.*

Like. *Simĭlis, e.*
Line of battle. *Acies, ĕi, f.*
Lines — these lines, these things. *Haec,* n. pl.
Literary = of letters. *Litterārum.* See 440, 2.
Literature, letters. *Littĕrae, ārum,* f. pl.
Little—think little of, despise. *Contemno, ĕre, tempsi, temptum.*
Live. *Vivo, ĕre, vixi, victum.* One lives, men live, *vivĭtur, victum est,* impers.
Live, living. *Vivus, a, um.*
Load, to pile up. *Exstruo, ĕre, struxi, structum.*
Long. *Longus, a, um.* Long continued, very long, *perdiuturnus, a, um.* For a long time, *jamdūdum, jamprĭdem.* G. 467, 2. How long, *quousque,* adv.
Long for. *Expĕto, ĕre, petīvi* and *ii, ītum.*
Look — look forward to. *Exspecto, āre, āvi, ātum.* Look upon, *suspĭcio, ĕre, spexi, spectum.* Look upon with envy, *invĭdeo, ĕre, vidi, vīsum.* G. 385.
Lose. *Amitto, ĕre, mīsi, missum.*
Loss. Rendered by the Perf. Pass. Part. of *amitto, ĕre, mīsi, missum.* G. 580.
Lost, engaged, busy. *Impedītus, a, um.*
Loud, great. *Magnus, a, um.* With a loud voice, *magna voce.*
Love. *Amor, ōris, m.*
Love, to love. *Amo, āre, āvi, ātum.*
Lucius. *Lucius, ii, m.*
Lucullus. *Lucullus, i, m.*
Lycurgus. *Lycurgus, i, m.*
Lysis. *Lysis, ĭdis, m.*

M.

Macedon — of Macedon, a Macedonian. *Macēdo, ŏnis, m.*
Macedonia. *Macedonia, ae, f.*
Mad — be mad. *Furo, ĕre, ui.*

Madness. *Furor, ōris, m.*
Maelius. *Maelius, ii, m.*
Magian, pl. the Magi. *Magus, i, m.*
Magistrate. *Magistrātus, us, m.*
Magnificent. *Magnifĭcus, a, um.*
Maiden. *Virgo, ĭnis, f.*
Mail, coat of mail. *Lorīca, ae, f.*
Make. *Facio, ĕre, feci, factum;* *effĭcio, ĕre, fēci, fectum.* Make acceptable, *probo, āre, āvi, ātum.* Make a boast, *glorior, āri, ātus sum,* dep. Make use of, *utor, i, usus sum,* dep. G. 419, 1.
Man. *Homo, ĭnis,* m. and f.; *vir, viri,* m. See 239, II.
Manifest. *Apertus, a, um.*
Manilius. *Manīlius, ii, m.*
Manius. *Manius, ii, m.*
Manner. *Modus, i,* m. In a spirited manner, *acrĭter,* adv. In the best manner, *optĭme,* adv.
Mantinea. *Mantinēa, ae, f.*
Many, many of the. *Multi, ae, a,* pl. How many, *quot,* indecl. So many, *tot,* indecl.
March. *Iter, itinĕris,* n. Forced marches, *magna itinĕra.* See 246. On the march, *in itinĕre.*
March—of March. *Martius, a, um.*
Marcius. *Marcius, ii, m.*
Marcus. *Marcus, i, m.*
Marius. *Marius, ii, m.*
Mark. See 426.
Mars. *Mars, Martis, m.*
Master. *Magister, tri, m.*
Mausolus. *Mausōlus, i, m.*
May, it may be that. *Fiĕri potest ut,* with subj.
May — of May. *Maius, a, um.*
Mean. *Volo, velle, volui,* with ethical dat. G. 389, 2.
Means, property. *Res, rei,* f. Means, resources, *opes, opum,* f. pl. By no means, *minĭme,* adv. See 586.
Measure. *Metior, īri, mensus sum,* dep.
Memory. *Memoria, ae, f.*
Mention. *Commemŏro, āre, āvi, ātum;* *dico, ĕre, dixi, dictum.*
Mercury. *Mercurius, ii, m.*
Messenger. *Nuntius, ii, m.*

Miletus — of Miletus, Milesian. *Milesius, a, um.*

Military. *Militāris, e.* Military, pertaining to war, *bellĭcus, a, um.* Military affairs, military science, *res militāris.*

Milo. *Milo* and *Milon, ōnis,* m.

Mina. *Mina, ae,* f.

Mind. *Anĭmus, i,* m. ; *mens, mentis,* f. See 355. To occupy the mind, *in anĭmo versor, āri, ātus sum,* dep. See 454. To call to mind, *commemŏro, āre, āvi, ātum.* To recall to mind, *recordor, āri, ātus sum,* dep. G. 406, II.

Minister. *Minister, tri,* m.; *ministra, ae,* f.

Minister to. *Minister, tra, sum, esse, fui,* with gen. See 560.

Mithridates. *Mithridātes, is,* m.

Modest. *Modestus, a, um.*

Modesty. *Verecundia, ae,* f.

Money, sum of money. *Pecunia, ae,* f. Money, copper, *aes, aeris,* n.

Month. *Mensis, is,* m.

Monument. *Monumentum, i,* n.

Moral worth. *Honestas, ātis,* f. ; *virtus, ūtis,* f.

More. *Plus, pluris ;* G. 165, 1 ; *magis,* adv. More highly, with verbs of valuing, of more value, *pluris.* G. 402, III. 1. More fully, *plurĭbus verbis.* See 514.

Morning, early in the morning. *Mane,* adv.

Most exalted. *Summus, a, um.* G. 163, 3.

Mother. *Mater, tris,* f.

Mountain. *Mons, montis,* m.

Mourn over. *Maereo, ēre.*

Move. *Moveo, commŏveo, ēre, mōvi, mōtum.* Move, affect, *affĭcio, ēre, fēci, fectum.*

Much. *Multum,* adv. Much, exceedingly, *valde,* adv. Much, with comparatives, *multo,* adv. Very much, *plurĭmum,* adv. However much, *quantumvis,* adv.

Mucius. *Mucius, ii,* m.

Multitude. *Multitūdo, ĭnis,* f. Mul-

titudes assemble, *concursus fit.* See 606.

Muse. *Musa, ae,* f.

Must. See 557.

My. *Meus, a, um.*

Myself, reflexive, not intensive. *Ego, mei ;* intensive, *ipse, a, um.* By myself, *mecum.*

N.

Name. *Nomen, ĭnis,* n.

Name, to name. *Nomĭno, appello, āre, āvi, ātum.* See 184.

Narrow. *Angustus, a, um.*

Nasica. *Nasĭca, ae,* m.

Nation. *Gens, gentis,* f.; *popŭlus, i,* m. The law of nations, *jus gentium.*

Native talent. *Ingenium, ii,* n.

Nature. *Natūra, ae,* f.

Naval. *Navālis, e.* A naval battle, naval engagement, *pugna navālis.*

Near. *Prope (propius, proxĭme),* adv. Near, near to, *ad, apud,* prep. with acc.

Nearest. *Proxĭmus, a, um.* G. 166.

Nearly. *Paene,* adv.

Necessary. *Necessarius, a, um.* It is necessary, *necesse est, fuit.*

Necessity. *Necessĭtas, ātis,* f.

Need—there is need of, there needs. *Opus est, fuit.* G. 419, 3. To need, *egeo, indĭgeo, ēre, ui.* See 239, I. To feel the need of, *indĭgeo, ēre, ui.*

Needful — to be needful (there needs, is need of). *Opus est, fuit.* G. 419, 3.

Neglect. *Neglĭgo, ēre, lexi, lectum.*

Negligent. *Neglĭgens, entis.*

Neither — nor. *Neque* or *nec — neque* or *nec.*

Never. *Nunquam,* adv.

New. *Novus, a, um.* New Carthage, *Carthāgo Nova,* f.

Night. *Nox, noctis,* f.

Nile. *Nilus, i,* m.

Nineteen. *Undevigĭnti,* indecl.

Ninetieth. *Nonagesĭmus, a, um.*

No. *Nullus, a, um ;* G. 149; *non,* adv. No one, *nemo, ĭnis,* m. and f. G. 457, 2. That no one, in clauses denoting purpose, *ne quis.* G. 190, 2. By no means, *minĭme,* adv. See 586. To no purpose, *nequidquam,* adv.

Noble. *Nobĭlis, e.* Noble-minded, honorable, *honestus, a, um.*

Nomination—without a nomination from the people. *Injussu popŭli.* G. 414, 2, 3).

Nones. *Nonae, ārum,* f. pl. G. 708, I. 2.

Nor. *Neque* or *nec,* conj.; with imperatives, *neve,* conj.

Not. *Non,* adv.; interrog., *nonne;* G. 346, II. 1; with imperatives, *ne,* adv. Not at all, not = not at all, *nihil.* G. 380, 2. Not, followed by either — or = neither — nor, *neque* or *nec — neque* or *nec.* Not even, *ne quidem.* See 577. Not only — but also, *non solum* or *non modo — sed etiam.* Not very, *non ita,* adv. Not yet, *nondum,* adv. And not, but not, *neque* or *nec.* Not to know, *nescio, ĭre, ĭvi* and *ii, ĭtum.* To say — not = to deny, *nego, āre, āvi, ātum.*

Nothing. *Nihil,* n. indecl.

Nourish. *Alo, ĕre, ui, altum* and *alĭtum.*

Novel. *Novus, a, um.*

Now. *Nunc,* adv. Now, already, *jam,* adv.

Numa. *Numa, ae,* m.

Numantia. *Numantia, ae,* f.

Number. *Numĕrus, i,* m. In full numbers, *frequens, entis.* G. 443.

Numitor. *Numĭtor, ōris,* m.

O.

O, oh that. *Utĭnam,* adv. G. 488, 1.

Obedience. *Obtemperatio, ōnis,* f.

Obey. *Pareo, ēre, ui, ĭtum.* G. 385.

Object, thing. *Res, rei,* f. Object of interest, *quod visendum est.* See 527.

Observe, keep. *Servo, āre, āvi, ātum.* Observe, retain, *teneo, ēre, ui, tentum.*

Obstinacy. *Pertinacia, ae,* f.

Obtain. *Potior, ĭri, ĭtus sum,* dep.; G. 419, I.; *nanciscor, i, nactus sum,* dep. Obtain, find, *invĕnio, ĭre, vēni, ventum.*

Occasion—there is occasion. *Opus est, fuit.* G. 419, 3.

Occult. *Occultus, a, um.*

Occupy. *Occŭpo, āre, āvi, ātum.* To occupy the mind, *in anĭmo versor, āri, ātus sum,* dep. See 454.

Of, concerning. *De,* prep. with abl. Of, from, *a, ab,* prep. with abl. Out of, *e, ex,* prep. with abl. Of, after superlatives=among, *inter,* prep. with acc. Of, before proper nouns. See 435, 436. Of greater value, *pluris.* G. 402, III. 1.

Offend. *Offendo, ĕre, di, sum.* G. 385, 1. Offend against, *viŏlo, āre, āvi, ātum.*

Offer. *Affĕro, ferre, attŭli, allātum.*

Often. *Saepe,* adv.

Oh that. *Utĭnam.* G. 488, 1.

Old. *Senex, senis ;* as substant., old man. Old age, *senectus, ūtis,* f.

Older. *Major, ōris,* or *major natu.*

Olive tree. *Olea, ae,* f.

Olympia. *Olympia, ae,* f.

Olympus. *Olympus, i,* m.

On = concerning, on the subject of. *De,* prep. with abl. On account of, *propter,* prep. with acc. On the part of, often rendered by the gen. On sea and land, *terra marĭque.* On the march, *in itinĕre.*

Once. *Semel,* adv. Once, formerly, *quondam,* adv. At once, *jam,* adv.

One. *Unus, a, um.* G. 176, 1. One, any one, any thing, *quis.*

See 500, III.; also G. 190. One's self, *sui, sibi.* One's, one's own, *suus, a, um.* No one, *nemo, ĭnis,* m. and f. G. 457, 2. That no one, in clauses denoting purpose, *ne quis.* G. 190, 2. One each, *singŭli, ae, a,* pl.

Only. *Modo,* adv.

Open, to open. *Apĕrio, ĭre, ui, pertum.*

Open. *Apertus, a, um.* Open adversary, *palam adversarius, ii,* m.

Openly. *Palam,* adv.

Opinion. *Sententia, ae,* f.; *opinio, ōnis,* f. To express opinion, *censeo, ēre, ui, censum.*

Opponent. *Adversarius, ii,* m.

Oppose. *Obsisto, ĕre, stĭti, stĭtum; obsto, āre, stĭti, stātum.* To oppose one's self, *se opponĕre (oppōno, ĕre, posui, posĭtum).*

Opulent. *Opulentus, a, um.*

Or. *Aut,* conj.; in questions, *an,* conj. Or not, usually *annon* in direct questions, *necne* in indirect.

Oration. *Oratio, ōnis,* f.

Orator. *Orātor, ōris,* m.

Oratory. *Dicendi, o,* gerund of *dico.*

Order. *Jubeo, ēre, jussi, jussum.*

Orgetorix. *Orgetŏrix, ĭgis,* m.

Other. *Alius, a, ud.* G. 149; 459. The other, the second of two, *alter, ĕra, ĕrum.* G. 149; 149, 2; 459. The others, the rest, *cetĕri, ae, a,* pl. Of others, another's, *aliĕnus, a, um.*

Ought. *Debeo, ēre, ui, ĭtum.* Also rendered by the Pass. Periphrast. Conj. G. 229.

Our. *Noster, tra, trum.* Our own things, productions, *nostra, -rum,* n. pl. G. 441, 1.

Out of. *E, ex,* prep. with abl. G. 434, 3. To set out, *proficiscor, i, profectus sum,* dep.

Overcome. *Vinco, ĕre, vici, victum.*

Overthrow of. Rendered by the perf. pass. part. of *everto, ĕre,* *verti, versum.* See 439; also G. 580.

Overthrow, to overthrow. *Everto, ĕre, verti, versum.*

Owe. *Debeo, ēre, ui, ĭtum.*

Own, often expressed by the possessive, or when more emphatic by the gen. of *ipse, a, um,* with the possessive. G. 452, 4.

Ox. *Bos, bovis,* m. G. 90, 2.

P.

Pain. *Dolor, ōris,* m.

Paint. *Pingo, ĕre, pinxi, pictum.*

Painting. *Tabŭla picta,* f. See 378.

Panathenaicus. *Panathenaĭcus, i,* m.

Parent. *Parens, entis,* m. and f.

Part. *Pars, partis,* f. On the part of, to be the part of, often rendered by the gen. See 426.

Pass — allow to pass. *Intermitto, ĕre, mĭsi, missum.*

Past. *Praeterĭtus, a, um.*

Path. *Semĭta, ae,* f.

Pay one's respects to. *Salūto, āre, āvi, ātum.*

Peace. *Pax, pacis,* f. To reduce to a state of peace, *paco, āre, āvi, ātum.*

Peculiar to. *Proprius, a, um.*

Penalty. *Poena, ae,* f.

People, a people. *Popŭlus, i,* m. Friend of the people, *populāris, is,* m. and f. Without a nomination from the people, *injussu popŭli.* G. 414, 2, 3).

Perceive. *Percĭpio, ĕre, cĕpi, ceptum; perspĭcio, ĕre, spexi, spectum; sentio, ĭre, sensi, sensum.* Perceive, discern, *cerno, ĕre.*

Perfect. *Perfectus, a, um.*

Perform. *Ago, ĕre, egi, actum; gero, ĕre, gessi, gestum.*

Perhaps. *Forsĭtan, fortasse,* adv.; sometimes rendered by *haud scio an* with subj. See 586.

Pericles. *Perĭcles, is,* m.

Peril. *Perĭcŭlum, i,* n.

Perishable. *Cadŭcus, a, um.*

Permitted — it is permitted. *Licet, licuit* and *licĭtum est,* impers.

Perpetual. *Perpetuus, a, um.*

Perseus. *Perseus, ei,* m.

Personal, of one's self alone, gen. of *solus, a, um.* G. 149; 397, 3.

Persuade. *Persuădeo, ĕre, si, sum.* G. 385.

Pertain to. *Pertĭneo, ĕre, ui, tentum.*

Pharsalian, of Pharsalus, or Pharsalia. *Pharsalius, a, um.*

Philip. *Philippus, i,* m.

Philo. *Philo* or *Philon, ŏnis,* m.

Philosopher. *Philosŏphus, i,* m.

Philosophy. *Philosophia, ae,* f.

Pity. *Misereor, ēri, ĭtus sum,* dep.; G. 406, 1; *misĕret, uit,* impers. G. 410, III. See 228.

Place. *Locus, i,* m. G. 141. From that place, *inde,* adv. To take place, *fio, fiĕri, factus sum.* G. 294.

Plan. *Consilium, ii,* n.

Plato. *Plato* and *Platon, ŏnis,* m.

Plautus. *Plautus, i,* m.

Play. *Ludo, ĕre, lusi, lusum.*

Please. *Placeo, ĕre, ui, ĭtum.* G. 385.

Pleased — be pleased, rejoice. *Laetor, āri, ātus sum,* dep.

Pleasure. *Voluptas, ātis,* f. Pleasure, enjoyment, *delectatio, ŏnis,*f.

Plunder. *Dirĭpio, ĕre, ui, reptum.*

Poem. *Poēma, ătis,* n.

Poet. *Poēta, ae,* m.

Point, thing. *Res, rei,* f.

Pompey. *Pompēius, eii,* m.

Poor. *Pauper, ĕris.* Poor, with limited means, *inops, ŏpis.*

Popilius. *Popilius, ii,* m.

Porsena. *Porsĕna, ae,* m.

Possess. *Possĭdeo, ēre, sēdi, sessum.* Possess, have, *habeo, ĕre, ui, ĭtum.*

Possessed of. *Praedĭtus, a, um.* G. 419, III.

Possession. *Possessio, ŏnis,* f. Possessions, things, *res, rerum,* f. pl.

Possible — as . . . as possible. *Quam,* adv. with superlat. See 449.

Power. *Potentia, ae,* f. Regal power, *regnum, i,* n.

Powerful. *Potens, entis.*

Practical knowledge. *Usus, us,* m.

Practice. See Note on 638, 7, page 276.

Practise. *Colo, ĕre, colui, cultum.*

Praetor. *Praetor, ōris,* m.

Praetorship. See 409.

Praise. *Laus, laudis,* f.

Praise, to praise. *Laudo, āre, āvi, ātum.*

Praiseworthy. *Laudabĭlis, e.*

Pray, I pray, parenthetical. *Quaeso.*

Precept. *Praeceptum, i,* n. To give precepts, *praecĭpio, ĕre, cēpi, ceptum.*

Preceptor. *Praeceptor, ōris,* m.

Preceptress. *Praeceptrix, ĭcis,* f.

Predict. *Praedĭco, ĕre, dixi, dictum.*

Prefer. *Praefĕro, ferre, tŭli, lātum; antepōno, ĕre, posui, posĭtum.* Prefer, would rather, *malo, malle, malui.* G. 293.

Preferable. *Satius.* See 527.

Prepared. *Parātus, a, um.*

Presence — in the presence of. *Apud,* prep. with acc.

Present. *Donum, i,* n.

Present, to present. *Dono, āre, āvi, ātum.* To present one's self, *se praebēre (praebeo, ĕre, ui, ĭtum).*

Present, at hand. *Praesens, entis.*

Preserve. *Servo, conservo, āre, āvi, ātum.*

Preside over. *Praesum, esse, fui.* G. 386.

Presume. *Credo, ĕre, dĭdi, dĭtum.*

Pretend. *Simŭlo, āre, āvi, ātum.*

Price. *Pretium, ii,* n.

Pride. *Superbia, ae,* f.

Prince. *Princeps, ĭpis,* m.

Princely. *Regālis, e.*

Principal. *Princeps, ĭpis,* m. and f.

Priscus. *Priscus, i,* m.

Prize. *Praemium, ii,* n.

Prize, to prize. *Aestĭmo, āre, āvi, ātum.*

Proceed. *Pergo, ĕre, perrexi, perrectum.*

Proclaim. *Proclāmo, āre, āvi, ātum.*

Prodicus. *Prodĭcus, i, m.*

Produce, bear. *Fero, ferre, tuli, latum.*

Profess. *Profĭteor, ēri, fessus sum, dep.*

Profit. *Utilĭtas, ātis, f.*

Profit, to profit. *Condūco, ĕre, duxi, ductum.* See 289.

Profitable. *Fructuōsus, a, um.*

Promise. *Promissum, i, n.*

Promise, to promise. *Pollĭceor, ēri, pollicĭtus sum, dep.*

Prompt, affect. *Commŏveo, ĕre, mōvi, mōtum.*

Pronounce, speak. *Dico, ĕre, dixi, dictum.*

Proof. *Testimonium, ii, n.*

Properly, worthily enough. *Satis digne, adv.*

Property, means. *Res, rei, f.*

Propose to one's self no other aim. *Nihil sibi aliud nisi proponĕre (propōno, ĕre, posui, posĭtum).* See 444.

Prosperity. *Res secundae, f. pl.* G. 441, 4.

Prosperous. *Felix, ĭcis; · beātus, a, um.* See 393. To have a prosperous voyage, *ex sententia navĭgo, āre, āvi, ātum.* See 339.

Protection — to receive under protection. *In deditiōnem accĭpio, ĕre, cēpi, ceptum.*

Proud. *Superbus, a, um.*

Prove. *Probo, āre, āvi, ātum.*

Provide for. *Provĭdeo, ĕre, vĭdi, vīsum.* G. 386.

Province. *Provincia, ae, f.*

Prudence. *Prudentia, ae, f.*

Ptolemy. *Ptolemaeus, i, m.*

Public. *Publĭcus, a, um.* Highest public welfare, *summa res publĭca, f.*

Publius. *Publius, ii, m.*

Punic. *Punĭcus, a, um.*

Punishment. *Supplicium, ii, n.*

Punishment, penalty, *poena, ae, f.*

Pupil. *Discipŭlus, i, m.*

Purchase. *Emo, ĕre, emi, emptum.*

Purpose, wish. *Sententia, ae, f.* For the purpose of, *causa* with gen. G. 414, 2, 3). To no purpose, *nequidquam,* adv.

Pursue. *Sequor, i, secūtus sum, dep.*

Pursuit, study, exertion. *Studium, ii, n.*

Put to death. *Occĭdo, ĕre, di, sum; interfĭcio, ĕre, feci, fectum.*

Pydna. *Pydna, ae, f.*

Pythagoras. *Pythagŏras, ae, m.*

Pythagorean. *Pythagorēus, a, um.*

Q.

Queen. *Regīna, ae, f.*

Question. *Quaestio, ōnis, f.*

Quickly. *Celerĭter,* adv.

Quiet. *Otium, ii, n.*

Quintus. *Quintus, i, m.*

R.

Raise, conduct. *Perdūco, ĕre, duxi, ductum.*

Ranks in line of battle. *Acies, ēi, f.*

Rare. *Rarus, a, um.*

Rather, more. *Magis,* adv. Would rather, *malo, malle, malui.* G. 293.

Read. *Lego, ĕre, legi, lectum.*

Readily. *Facĭle,* adv.

Reason. *Ratio, ōnis, f.* For the reason that, *propterea quod,* conj.

Recall, mention. *Commemŏro, āre, āvi, ātum.* Recall to mind, *recordor, āri, ātus sum,* dep. G. 406, II.

Receive. *Accĭpio, ĕre, cēpi, ceptum.*

Recollection. *Memoria, ae, f.*

Record. *Perscrĭbo, ĕre, scripsi, scriptum.*

Recover. *Recupĕro, āre, āvi, ātum.*

Recover, restore, *recreo, āre, āvi, ātum.*

Reduce to a state of peace. *Paco, āre, āvi, ātum.*

Reference — to arrange with reference to. *Refĕro, ferre, tŭli, lātum, ad* with acc. See 534. To have reference to, *refĕror, ferri, lātus sum, ad* with acc. See 577.

Refinement. *Humanĭtas, ātis,* f. Refinements, culture, *cultus, us,* m.

Refute. *Refūto, āre, āvi, ātum; refello, ĕre, felli.*

Regal power. *Regnum, i,* n.

Regard — in regard to. *De,* prep. with abl.; sometimes rendered by gen. See 577.

Regard, hold. *Habeo, ĕre, ui, ĭtum.* Think, regard as, *puto, āre, āvi, ātum; statuo, ĕre, ui, ūtum.*

Reign — in the reign of. Pres. Part. of *regno,* in abl. abs. (*regno, āre, āvi, ātum*).

Reign, to reign. *Regno, āre, āvi, ātum.*

Rejoice, rejoice in. *Gaudeo, ĕre, gavĭsus sum; laetor, āri, ātus sum,* dep.

Rejoicing, joy. *Laetitia, ae,* f.

Relate. *Narro, āre, āvi, ātum; fero, ferre, tuli, latum; trado, ĕre, dĭdi, dĭtum.*

Release. *Libĕro, āre, āvi, ātum.* G. 425, 3, 2).

Relief — to come to the relief of. *Subvĕnio, ĭre, vēni, ventum.* G. 386.

Relying upon. *Fretus, a, um.* G. 419, IV.

Remain. *Maneo, ĕre, mansi, mansum.* It remains, *relĭquum est, fuit, ut* with subj.

Remarkable. *Singulāris, e.*

Remember. *Memĭni, meminisse;* G. 297, I.; 406, II.; *reminiscor, i.* G. 406, II.

Remissness. *Nequitia, ae,* f.

Remove, take away. *Tollo, ĕre, sustŭli, sublātum.*

Render service. *Prosum, prodesse,* *profui.* See 606; also G. 290; 386.

Renew. *Instauro, āre, āvi, ātum.*

Repeat. *Reddo, ĕre, dĭdi, dĭtum.*

Repent. *Poenĭtet, uit,* impers. G. 410, III. See 228.

Reply. *Respondeo, ĕre, di, sum.*

Report. *Rumor, ōris,* m.

Repose. *Tranquillĭtas, ātis,* f.

Republic. *Res publĭca, rei publĭcae,* f.

Request. *Rogātus, us,* m.

Require, compel. *Cogo, ĕre, coēgi, coactum.*

Requite a favor. *Gratiam refĕro, ferre, tŭli, lātum.* See 548.

Rescue. *Erĭpio, ĕre, ripui, reptum.*

Reside. *Habĭto, āre, āvi, ātum.*

Resources, means. *Opes, opum,* f. pl.

Respects — pay one's respects to. *Salūto, āre, āvi, ātum.*

Rest. *Quies, ētis,* f.; *requies, ētis,* f. See 283.

Rest upon, be situated in. *Posĭtus, a, um, sum, esse, fui, in* with abl.

Rest, the rest. *Cetĕri, ae, a,* pl.

Restore. *Recreo, āre, āvi, ātum.*

Restrain. *Arceo, ĕre, ui, arctum.*

Result. *Exĭtus, us,* m. Highest results, *summa, ōrum,* n. pl. See 415. To be the result, *evĕnio, ĭre, vēni, ventum.*

Retain. *Teneo, ĕre, ui, tentum.*

Return. *Redeo, ĭre, ii, ĭtum.* Return, turn back, *revertor, i, versus sum,* dep. G. 273, III., *verto.*

Revolution. *Res novae,* f. pl. See 223.

Reward. *Praemium, ii,* n. Reward, wages, *merces, ēdis,* f.

Rhetorician. *Rhetor, ōris,* m.

Rhine. *Rhenus, i,* m.

Rhone. *Rhodānus, i,* m.

Rich. *Dives, ĭtis.* G. 165, 2.

Riches. *Divitiae, ārum,* f. pl.

Right. *Rectus, a, um.* Right, the right, *fas,* n. indecl. See 405, 1. The right, integrity, *honestas, ātis,* f.

Rightly. *Recte*, adv.

River. *Flumen, ĭnis*, n.

Road. *Via, viae*, f.

Robber. *Praedo, ŏnis*, m.

Roman. *Romānus, a, um.*

Roman, a Roman. *Romānus, i*, m.

Rome. *Roma, ae*, f.

Romulus. *Romŭlus, i*, m.

Roscius. *Roscius, ii*, m.

Rout. *Pello, ĕre, pepŭli, pulsum.*

Route. *Iter, itinĕris*, n.

Ruin, demolish. *Diruo, ĕre, ui, ūtum.*

Rule. *Dominatio, ŏnis*, f.

Rule, to rule. *Rego, ĕre, rexi, rectum ; impĕro, āre, āvi, ātum.* G. 385.

Rumor. *Rumor, ŏris*, m.

S.

Sabine. *Sabīnus, a, um.*

Sacred. *Sanctus, a, um ; sacer, cra, crum.*

Sacrifice, to spend. *Profundo, ĕre, fūdi, fūsum.*

Sad. *Tristis, e.*

Safe. *Salvus, a, um.* Safe, secure, *tutus, a, um.* See 321.

Safety. *Salus, ūtis*, f.

Saguntum. *Saguntum, i*, n.

Sail. *Navĭgo, āre, āvi, ātum.*

Sake — for the sake of. *Causa* or *gratia* with gen. G. 414, 2, 3). For my, &c., sake, *mea causa*, etc.

Salute. *Salūto, āre, āvi, ātum.*

Same. *Idem, eădem, idem.* To entertain the same sentiments, *eădem sentio, īre, sensi, sensum.*

Satisfy. *Satisfacio, ĕre, fēci, factum.* G. 26, 2, 3), (b); 385.

Saturnia. *Saturnia, ae*, f.

Save. *Servo, conservo, āre, āvi, ātum.*

Say. *Dico, ĕre, dixi, dictum.* Say, relate, *fero, ferre, tuli, latum.* They say, *ferunt.* Say — not, deny, *nego, āre, āvi, ātum.*

Scaevola. *Scaevŏla, ae*, m.

Scarcely, scarcely yet. *Vixdum*, adv.

School. *Ludus, i*, m.; *schola, ae*, f.

Science, learning. *Doctrīna, ae*, f. Military science, *res militāris*, f.

Scipio. *Scipio, ŏnis*, m.

Sea. *Mare, maris*, n. On sea and land, *terra marĭque.*

Second, another. *Alter, ĕra, ĕrum.* G. 149; 149, 2. A second time, *itĕrum*, adv.

Secure, safe. *Tutus, a, um.* See 321.

Secure, to secure, conciliate. *Concĭlio, āre, āvi, ātum.*

Sedition. *Seditio, ŏnis*, f.

See. *Video, ĕre, vidi, visum.* See that, take care that, *curo, āre, āvi, ātum.*

Seek. *Quaero, ĕre, quaesīvi, quaesītum ; peto, appĕto, expĕto, ĕre, petīvi* and *ii, ītum.* Seek, pursue, *sequor, i, secūtus sum*, dep.

Seem. *Videor, ĕri, visus sum.* See 577.

Seize. *Rapio, ĕre, ui, raptum.*

Select. *Elĭgo, ĕre, lēgi, lectum.*

Select, selected. *Exquisītus, a, um.*

Self, one's self, reflexive. *Sui, sibi ;* intensive, *ipse, a, um.*

Sell. *Vendo, ĕre, dĭdi, dĭtum.*

Senate. *Senātus, us*, m.

Senator. *Senātor, ŏris*, m.

Send. *Mitto, ĕre, misi, missum.*

Sense. *Sensus, us*, m.

Sentiments — entertain the same sentiments. *Eădem sentio, īre, sensi, sensum.*

Serve. *Servio, īre, īvi* and *ii, ītum.* G. 385.

Service — render service. *Prosum, prodesse, profui.* See 606; also G. 290; 386.

Servilius. *Servilius, ii*, m.

Servitude. *Servĭtus, ūtis*, f.

Servius. *Servius, ii*, m.

Set, set before. *Propōno, ĕre, posui, posĭtum.* Set fire to, *inflammo, āre, āvi, ātum ; incendo, ĕre, cendi, censum.* Set forth, *exprŏmo, ĕre, prompsi, promp-*

tum. Set forth views, state, *prae-dico, āre, āvi, ātum.* Set out, *proficiscor, i, profectus sum,* dep.
Seven. *Septem,* indecl.
Seventh time. *Septĭmum,* adv.
Seventh day of the month, — in March, May, July, and October. *Nonae, ārum,* f. pl. G. 708, I. 2.
Several. *Complūres, a* or *ia,* pl.
Severe. *Sevērus, a, um.* Severe, grievous, *gravis, e.*
Sextus. *Sextus, i,* m.
Share. *Communĭco, āre, āvi, ātum.*
Sharply. *Acrĭter,* adv.
Short, brief. *Brevis, e.*
Shoulder. *Humĕrus, i,* m.
Show. *Ostendo, ĕre, di, sum* and *tum; monstro, demonstro, āre, āvi, ātum.*
Sicily. *Sicilia, ae,* f.
Silent. *Mutus, a, um.*
Silver. *Argentum, i,* n.
Since, as. *Quum, quoniam,* conj. Since, ago, *abhinc,* adv.
Six. *Sex,* indecl.
Six hundredth. *Sexcentesĭmus, a, um.*
Sixth. *Sextŭs, a, um.* Sixth of July, *pridie Nonas Quintĭles.* G. 708, III.; 437, 1.
Sixtieth. *Sexagesĭmus, a, um.*
Skilled in, skilful in. *Perītus, a, um.*
Slave — be the slave of. *Servio, ῑre, ῑvi* and *ii, ῑtum.* G. 385.
Slay. *Interfĭcio, ĕre, fēci, fectum; occīdo, ĕre, cīdi, cīsum.*
Sleep. *Dormio, ῑre, ῑvi, ῑtum.*
Small. *Parvus, a, um.* Small, contracted, *angustus, a, um.*
So. *Tam, ita,* adv.; sometimes rendered by *is, ea, id.* See 444. In such a manner, *sic,* adv. So greatly, to such an extent, *adeo,* adv. So — as, with adjectives, *tam — quam,* adv.; with verbs, *sic — ut,* adv. So far, *tantum,* adv. So far am I from, *tantum abest, ut* with subj. See 498. So great, *tantus, a, um.* So many, *tot,* indecl. So much, *tantus, a, um; tantopĕre,* adv. So that,

ut, conj. Not so much, *non tam,* adv.
Socrates. *Socrătes, is,* m.
Soldier. *Miles, ῑtis,* m. and f.
Solon. *Solo* and *Solon, ōnis,* m.
Some. *Nonnulli, ae, a,* pl. Some, any, *alĭqui, qua, quod.* Some one, a certain one, *quidam, quaedam, quoddam.* Somebody, something, *alĭquis.* G. 191. At some time, *aliquando,* adv.; *alĭquo tempŏre.* G. 426. Some — others, *alii — alii.* G. 459.
Sometime. *Aliquando,* adv.
Sometimes. *Interdum,* adv.
Son. *Filius, ii,* m.
Soul. *Anĭmus, i,* m.
Sovereignty. *Imperium, ii,* n.
Spain. *Hispania, ae,* f.
Sparta. *Sparta, ae,* f.
Speak. *Dico, ĕre, dixi, dictum; loquor, i, locūtus sum,* dep.
Spend. *Consūmo, ĕre, sumpsi, sumptum.* Of time, *ago, ĕre, egi, actum.*
Spirit, courage. *Anĭmus, i,* m.
Spirited, in a spirited manner. *Acrĭter,* adv.
Spurius. *Spurius, ii,* m.
Squander. *Profundo, ĕre, fūdi, fūsum.*
Stadium. *Stadium, ii,* n.
Start, set out. *Proficiscor, i, profectus sum,* dep.
State, condition. *Status, us,* m. To reduce to a state of peace, *paco, āre, āvi, ātum.* The state, *civĭtas, ātis,* f. State, commonwealth, *res publĭca, rei publĭcae,* f. The highest welfare of the state, *summa res publĭca.*
State, say. *Dico, ĕre, dixi, dictum.*
Statesman. *Is qui rei publĭcae praeest (praesum, esse, fui).* See 438.
Station, to place. *Collŏco, āre, āvi, ātum.*
Stator. *Stator, ōris,* m.
Statue. *Signum, i,* n.
Stoic. *Stoĭcus, i,* m.
Strengthen. *Alo, ĕre, alui, alĭtum* and *altum.*

14

Strife. *Pugna, ae,* f.

Strive. *Nitor, niti, nisus* and *nixus sum,* dep.

Strong, ample. *Amplus, a, um.* In the strongest terms, *amplissimis verbis.*

Strongly. *Valde,* adv.

Student of. *Studiōsus, a, um.*

Studiously. *Studiōse,* adv.

Study. *Studium, ii,* n.

Subject, thing. *Res, rei,* f. On the subject of, concerning, *de,* prep. with abl.

Subject — to be subject to. *Pareo, ēre, ui, ĭtum.* G. 385.

Succeed. *Succēdo, ēre, cessi, cessum.* G. 386.

Success. *Felicĭtas, ātis,* f.

Successful. *Secundus, a, um.*

Such. *Talis, e;* sometimes rendered by *qui, quae, quod.* Such, so great, *tantus, a, um.* Such — as, *talis, e* — *qualis, e; is, ea, id* — *qui, quae, quod; tantus, a, um* — *quantus, a, um.* See 534.

Sudden. *Subĭtus, a, um.*

Suffer. *Patior, i, passus sum,* dep.

Suffering, pain. *Dolor, ōris,* m.

Sufficient — to be sufficient, be able. *Possum, posse, potui.*

Sufficiently. *Satis,* adv.

Suggestion — at the suggestion of. *Auctor,* in abl. absol. See 504.

Suitable. *Idōneus, a, um.*

Suitably = worthily enough. *Satis digne,* adv.

Sulla. *Sulla, ae,* m.

Sum of money. *Pecunia, ae,* f.

Sumptuous. *Sumptuōsus, a, um.*

Sun. *Sol, solis,* m.

Sunset. *Solis occāsus, us,* m.

Superbus. *Superbus, i,* m.

Supplicate. *Supplĭco, āre, āvi, ātum.*

Suppose, think. *Arbĭtror, āri, ātus sum,* dep.; *puto, āre, āvi, ātum.*

Suppress. *Comprĭmo, ēre, pressi, pressum.*

Supreme. *Summus, a, um.* G. 163, 3

Sure. *Certus, a, um.*

Surely. *Certe,* adv.

Surpass. *Supĕro, āre, āvi, ātum.* To surpass the folly of = to be more foolish than, *sum, esse, fui, dementior, ius.*

Surround. *Circumdo, āre, dĕdi, dătum; cingo, ēre, cinxi, cinctum.*

Sword. *Ferrum, i,* n. See 117. With fire and sword, *ferro ignēque.*

Syllable. *Syllăba, ae,* f.

Syracuse. *Syracūsae, ārum,* f. pl. Of Syracuse, Syracusan, *Syracusius, a, um.*

T.

Table. *Mensa, ae,* f.

Tablet. *Tabŭla, ae,* f.

Take, take up. *Capio, ēre, cepi, captum.* Take, appropriate, *sumo, ēre, sumpsi, sumptum.* Take, carry, *porto, āre, āvi, ātum.* Take away, *tollo, ēre, sustŭli, sublātum.* Take care, *caveo, ēre, cavi, cautum.* Take place, *fio, fĭeri, factus sum.* Take the census of, *censeo, ēre, ui, censum.* See 490.

Talent, native talent. *Ingenium, ii,* n. Talent, mental ability, *mens, mentis,* f. Talent, a sum of money, *talentum, i,* n.

Tarentum. *Tarentum, i,* n.

Tarquin, Tarquinius. *Tarquinius, ii,* m.

Tarquinii. *Tarquinii, ōrum,* m. pl.

Tarry. *Commŏror, āri, ātus sum,* dep.

Teach. *Doceo, ēre, ui, doctum.* Teach, instruct, *erŭdio, ire, ivi* and *ii, ĭtum.* Teach, train up, *instituo, ēre, ui, ūtum.* See 585.

Teacher. *Doctor, ōris,* m.; *magister, tri,* m. See 423.

Tear. *Lacrĭma, ae,* f.

Tedious, long. *Longus, a, um.*

Tell. *Dico, ēre, dixi, dictum.*

Temperate. *Tempĕrans, antis.*

Temple. *Templum, i,* n.; *aedes, is,* f.; *fanum, i,* n. See 371.

Ten. *Decem,* indecl.

Terms — in the strongest terms. *Amplissimis verbis.*

Terrify. *Terreo, ěre, ui, ĭtum.*

Territory. *Fines, ium,* m. pl.

Thales. *Thales, is,* m.

Than. *Quam,* conj.

Thank. *Gratias ago, ěre, ěgi, actum.* See 548.

Thanks. *Gratiae, ārum,* f. pl. G. 132. To express thanks, *gratias ago, ěre, egi, actum.*

That. *Ille, a, ud ; is, ea, id,* less strongly demonstrative than *ille.* And that too, *et is ; et is quidem.* G. 451, 2.

That, in that. *Quod,* conj. That, expressing purpose or result, *ut,* conj. with subj. That, expressing purpose, when the dependent clause contains a comparative, *quo,* conj. with subj. That = but that, *quin,* conj. with subj. G. 498.

The = that, emphatic. *Ille, a, ud ;* not emphatic, *is, ea, id.* The — the, with comparatives, *quo — eo.* See 454.

Theban, of Thebes. *Thebānus, a, um.*

Theft. *Furtum, i,* n.

Their, theirs. *Suus, a, um ;* not reflexive, *eōrum, eārum.* See 468, 2. Their own things, productions, *sua, ōrum,* n. pl. G. 441, 1.

Themistocles. *Themistŏcles, is,* m.

Then. *Tum,* adv.

There. *Illic,* adv.

Thermopylae. *Thermopȳlae, ārum.* f. pl.

Thing. *Res, rei,* f.

Think. *Sentio, īre, sensi, sensum ; puto, āre, āvi, ātum ; arbĭtror, āri, ātus sum,* dep. Think, be of opinion, *censeo, ēre, ui, censum.* See 576. Think, ponder, *cogĭto, āre, āvi, ātum.* Think out, *commentor, āri, ātus sum,* dep.

Think little of, despise, *contemno, ěre, tempsi, temptum.*

Third. *Tertius, a, um.*

Thirty. *Triginta,* indecl.

Thirty-eight. *Duodequadraginta,* indecl.

This. *Hic, haec, hoc.* This = that, not strongly demonstrative, *is, ea, id.*

Thou, you. *Tu, tui.* Thou thyself, you yourself, intensive, *ipse, a, um.*

Though. See Lesson LXXVIII.

Thought, opinion. *Sententia, ae,* f. Thought, reflection, *cogitatio, ōnis,* f.

Thousand. *Mille.* G. 178.

Three. *Tres, tria.* Three days, *triduum, ui,* n.

Three hundred. *Trecenti, ae, a,* pl.

Through. *Per,* prep. with acc.

Thus. *Sic,* adv. Thus far, *adhuc,* adv.

Thy, your. *Tuus, a, um.*

Thyself, yourself, emphatic or reflexive, not intensive. *Tu, tui.* By thyself, by yourself, *tecum.*

Tiberius. *Tiberius, ii,* m.

Tigranes. *Tigrānes, is,* m.

Till. *Colo, ěre, colui, cultum.*

Time. *Tempus, ŏris,* n. At some time, *aliquando,* adv.; *aliquo tempŏre.* G. 426. At times, *interdum,* adv. For the first time, *primum,* adv. The second time, *itěrum,* adv. The seventh time, *septĭmum,* adv. For a long time, *jamdūdum ; jampridem,* adv. G. 467, 2. In the time of. See 255, 2.

Timid. *Timĭdus, a, um.*

To. *Ad,* prep. with acc. To, towards, of friendly feelings and conduct towards a person, *erga,* prep. with acc. To no purpose, *nequidquam,* adv.

Toil, labor. *Labor, ŏris,* m.

To-morrow. *Cras,* adv.

Tongue. *Lingua, ae,* f.

Too. *Nimis,* adv.; often expressed by the comparative. See 448.

And that too, *et is; et is quidem (is, ea, id).* G. 451, 2.

Topic — each topic, each thing. *Quidque.*

Torture. *Crucio, āre, āvi, ātum.*

Touch. *Tango, ĕre, tetĭgi, tactum.*

Towards. *Adversus, versus,* prep. with acc.; *versus,* adv. G. 433, 2. Towards, of friendly feelings and conduct towards a person, *erga,* prep. with acc.

Town. *Oppĭdum, i,* n.

Treachery, treason. *Prodĭtio, ōnis,* f.

Treasures, things. *Res, rerum,* f. pl.

Tried. *Spectātus, a, um.*

Troublesome. *Molestus, a, um.*

True. *Verus, a, um.*

Trumpeter. *Tubĭcen, ĭnis,* m.

Trust, to hope. *Spero, āre, āvi, ātum.* Trust in, *confīdo, ĕre, fīsus sum.* G. 419, II.; 4, 2).

Truth. *Verĭtas, ātis,* f.; *verum, i,* n. G. 441, 2.

Try. *Tento, āre, āvi, ātum.*

Tullius. *Tullius, ii,* m.

Twenty. *Vigintĭ,* indecl.

Twice. *Bis,* adv.

Two. *Duo, duae, duo.* G. 176, 2.

Tyranny. *Tyrannis, ĭdis,* f.

Tyrant. *Tyrannus, i,* m.

U.

Unable, be unable. *Non possum, posse, potui.*

Unbridled. *Effrenātus, a, um.*

Uncertain. *Incertus, a, um.*

Under. *Sub,* prep. with acc. and abl. G. 435. Under the guidance of, *dux, ducis,* in abl. abs.

Understand. *Cognosco, ĕre, nōvi, nĭtum.*

Understanding. *Mens, mentis,* f.

Undertake. *Suscĭpio, ĕre, cēpi, ceptum.*

Unfriendly. *Inimĭcus, a, um.*

Unhappy. *Infēlix, ĭcis.*

Unharmed. *Incolŭmis, e; sine injuria.* See 504.

Unimpaired. *Intĕger, gra, grum.*

Unless. *Nisi,* conj. G. 507.

Unmindful. *Immĕmor, ŏris.*

Unnecessary. *Non necessarius, a, um.*

Unpopularity. *Invidia, ae,* f.

Until. *Dum, dŏnec,* conj. G. 522.

Unusual. *Inusitātus, a, um.*

Unwilling — to be unwilling. *Nolo, nolle, nolui.* G. 293.

Unwillingly. *Invītus, a, um.* G. 443.

Upon. *In,* prep. with acc. and abl. G. 435. Upon, concerning, *de,* prep. with abl.

Upright. *Probus, a, um.*

Urge. *Impello, ĕre, pŭli, pulsum.*

Use, make use of. *Utor, i, usus sum,* dep. G. 419, I.

Useful. *Utĭlis, e.* To be useful, *utĭlis, e, sum, esse, fui; utilitātem affĕro, ferre, attŭli, allātum.* See 444.

Usefulness. *Utilĭtas, ātis,* f.

Useless. *Inutĭlis, e.*

Utter. *Elŏquor, i, locūtus sum,* dep.

Utterly. *Fundĭtus,* adv.

V.

Vain — in vain. *Frustra, nequidquam,* adv. See 838.

Valor. *Virtus, ūtis,* f.

Value, price. *Pretium, ii,* n. Of greater value, of more value, *pluris.* G. 402, III. 1.

Vender. *Vendĭtor, ōris,* m.

Verres. *Verres, is,* m.

Verse. *Versus, us,* m.

Very. *Valde;* often rendered by the superlative. See 448. Very, with nouns, *ipse, a, um.* G. 452, 2. Very much, *plurĭmum,* adv. Very highly, with verbs of valuing, *maxĭmi.* G. 402, III. 1). Not very, *non ita,* adv. How very busy one is, *quanta occupatĭōne distinētur.* See 631.

Viands. *Epŭlae, ārum,* f. pl.

Vice. *Vitium, ii,* n.
Vicinity — in the vicinity of, near. *Ad,* prep. with acc.
Victor. *Victor, ōris,* m.
Victory. *Victoria, ae,* f. Victory over the Cimbrians, *Cimbrica victoria.*
Views — set forth views, state. *Praedico, āre, āvi, ātum.*
Vigilant. *Vigilans, antis.* •
Vigilantly, sharply. *Acriter,* adv.
Village. *Vicus, i,* m.
Violate. *Vĭŏlo, āre, āvi, ātum.*
Virtue. *Virtus, ūtis,* f.
Visit. *Viso, ĕre, visi, visum.*
Voice. *Vox, vocis,* f. A feeble voice, *vocŭla, ae,* f.
Voyage — have a prosperous voyage. *Ex sententia navĭgo, āre, āvi, ātum.* See 339.

W.

Wage. *Gero, ĕre, gessi, gestum.* Wage against, *infĕro, ferre, tŭli, illātum.* G. 386.
Wait. *Exspecto, āre, āvi, ātum.*
Walk. *Ambŭlo, āre, āvi, ātum.* Walk, go along, *ingrĕdior, i, ingressus sum,* dep.
Wall. *Murus, i,* m.; *moenia, ium,* n. pl.; *paries, ĕtis,* m. See 377. Walls of the city, city walls, *moenia, ium,* n. pl. Walls of my, &c., own house, *mei,* etc., *parĭĕtes.* See 378.
War. *Bellum, i,* n.
Warrior. *Is qui bellum gerit (gero, ĕre, gessi, gestum).* See 444.
Watch. *Vigĭlo, āre, āvi, ātum.*
Way, manner. *Modus, i,* m. In no way, *nullo modo;* in no thing, *nulla re.*
Wealth. *Divitiae, ārum,* f. pl.
Wealthy. *Dives, ĭtis.*
Weary. *Defatĭgo, āre, āvi, ātum.*
Weep at. *Illacrĭmor, āri, ātus sum,* dep. G. 386.
Weighty. *Gravis, e.*
Welfare, advantage. *Commŏdum,*

i, n. Highest welfare of the state, highest public welfare, *summa res publĭca.*
Well. *Bene,* adv. Well known, sometimes rendered by *ille, a, ud.* G. 450, 4.
What, interrog. *Qui, quae, quod,* adj.; *quis, quae, quid,* substant.
Whatever. *Quisquis, quaequae, quodquod* and *quicquid* or *quidquid.* Whatever = that which, *is, ea, id — qui, quae, quod.*
When. *Quum,* adv. *When* and *while* are sometimes rendered by the abl. abs., by a participle, by an adjective, or by an appositive. See Lesson LXXIX.; also G. 431, 1 and 2, (1); 578, I.; 442; 363, 3. When, interrog., *quando,* adv.
Where. *Ubi,* adv.
Whether. *Num,* conj.; in double questions, *utrum; num; ne,* enclit. conj. Whether — not, *nonne.* Whether — or, *utrum — an.* G. 346, II. 2.
Which, relat. *Qui, quae, quod;* interrog., *qui, quae, quod,* adj.; *quis, quae, quid,* substant. Which one, of two, *uter, utra, utrum.* G. 149.
While. *Dum,* conj. G. 522. When, *quum,* conj. See also "When."
Who, which, what, relat. *Qui, quae, quod;* interrog., *qui, quae, quod,* adj., *quis, quae, quid,* substant.
Whoever. *Quisquis, quaequae, quodquod* and *quicquid* or *quidquid.* Whoever = he, etc. — who, *is, ea, id — qui, quae, quod.*
Whole, the whole of. *Totus, a, um;* G. 149; *cunctus, a, um; omnis, e; universus, a, um.*
Wholly, whole. *Totus, a, um.* G. 149; 443.
Why. *Quare; cur;* adv.; *quid.* G. 454, 2.
Wicked. *Scelerātus, a, um; imprŏbus, a, um.*
Wickedness. *Scelus, ĕris,* n.

Will — good will. *Benevolentia, ae*, f.

Willing — be willing. *Volo, velle, volui*. G. 293.

Willingly. *Libenter*, adv.

Winter. *Hiems, ĕmis*, f. Winter quarters, *hiberna, ōrum*, n. pl.

Wisdom. *Sapientia, ae*, f.

Wise. *Sapiens, entis*.

Wisely. *Sapienter*, adv.

Wish. *Volo, velle, volui*. G. 293.

With. *Cum*, prep. with abl. With, among, near to, at the house of, *apud*, prep. with acc. With is sometimes rendered by the abl. abs. With the attendance of, *comes, ĭtis*, in abl. abs. With each other, *inter se*. G. 448, 1. With fire and sword, *ferro ignĕque*. See 117.

Withdraw, call off. *Avŏco, āre, āvi, ātum*. Withdraw, retire, *se removēre (remŏveo, ēre, mōvi, mōtum); decēdo, ēre, cessi, cessum*.

Within. *Intra*, prep. with acc.

Without. *Sine*, prep. with abl.; sometimes rendered by *nullus, a, um*, G. 149, in agreement with noun; sometimes by *quin*, conj. with subj. See 571; also G. 498, 3. Without exception, alone, *unus, a, um*. G. 176, 1. Without a nomination from the people, *injussu popŭli*. G. 414, 2, 3). To be without, *vaco, āre, āvi, ātum; careo, ēre, ui, ĭtum; egeo, ēre, ui*. See 239, I.

Witness. *Testis, is*, m. and f.

Witness, to witness. *Specto, āre, āvi, ātum*.

Wonder, wonder at. *Miror, āri, ātus sum*, dep.

Wonderful. *Mirabĭlis, e; admirabĭlis, e; mirus, a, um*.

Wont, be wont. *Soleo, ēre, solĭtus sum*.

Word. *Verbum, i*, n. Word for word, *ad verbum*. See 361.

Work, monument. *Monumentum, i*, n.

World. *Mundus, i*, m.

Worship. *Venĕror, āri, ātus sum*, dep.

Worth, moral worth. *Honestas, ātis*, f.; *virtus, ūtis*, f.

Worthily. *Digne*, adv.

Worthy. *Dignus, a, um*.

Would rather. *Malo, malle, malui*. G. 293.

Would that. *Utĭnam*, adv. G. 488, 1.

Write. *Scribo, ĕre, scripsi, scriptum*.

Writing. *Scriptum, i*, n. To commit to writing, *littĕris mando, āre, āvi, ātum*.

Wrong. *Pravus, a, um*.

Wrong, crime. *Nefas*, n. indecl.

X.

Xenophon. *Xenŏphon, ontis*, m.

Xerxes. *Xerxes, is*, m.

Y.

Year. *Annus, i*, m.

Yesterday. *Heri*, adv.; *hesterno die*. G. 426. Yesterday's, of yesterday, *hesternus, a, um*.

Yet. *Tamen*, adv.

Yoke. *Jugum, i*, n.

You, thou. *Tu, tui*. You yourself, *ipse, a, um*.

Young man. *Adolescens, entis*, m.; *juvĕnis, is*, m.

Your. *Vester, tra, trum*. Your, thy, *tuus, a, um*. Your companions, &c., *vestri, ōrum; tui, ōrum*; m. pl. G. 441, 1.

Yourself, emphatic, not intensive. *Tu, tui*; intensive, *ipse, a, um*. By yourself, *tecum*.

Youth. *Juvĕnis, is*, m. and f.

Z.

Zeal. *Studium, ii*, n.